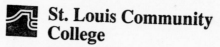

Star Trek: Parallel Narratives

Also by Chris Gregory

BE SEEING YOU
Decoding *The Prisoner*

Star Trek

Parallel Narratives

Chris Gregory

St. Martin's Press
New York

STAR TREK

St. Martin's Press, Scholarly and Reference Division, 175 Fifth Avenue, New York, N.Y. 10010

First published in the United States of America in 2000

This book is printed on paper suitable for recycling and made from fully managed and sustained forest sources.

Printed in Great Britain

ISBN 0–312–22583–0

Library of Congress Cataloging-in-Publication Data
Gregory, Chris, 1955–
Star trek : parallel narratives / Chris Gregory.
p. cm.
Includes bibliographical references and index.
ISBN 0–312–22583–0 (cloth)
1. Star Trek films—History and criticism.   2. Star Trek television programs—History and criticism.   I. Title.
PN1995.5.S694G73   1999
791.45'75—dc21   99–28964
                                                         CIP

To Di, for all her patience and love

from the pen of Chris Gregory is a website showcasing Chris Gregory's work in both non-fiction and fiction fields. It can be found at: www.digital-generation.co.uk

Contents

Introduction: 'to boldly go ...' – approaching the texts of *Star Trek*

Today, images abound everywhere. Never has so much been depicted and watched. We have glimpses at any moment of what things look like on the other side of the planet, or the other side of the moon. Appearances registered and transmitted with lightning speed.

Yet ... something has innocently changed ... Now appearances are volatile. Technological innovation has made it easy to separate the apparent from the existent. And this is precisely what the present system's mythology continually needs to exploit. It turns appearances into refractions, like mirages, refractions not of light but of appetite. In fact, a single appetite, the appetite for more ...

(John Berger, *Tate*, Spring 1977)

TV functions as a social ritual ... in which our culture engages in order to communicate with its collective self ...

(John Fiske and John Hartley, 1978, p. 23)

Space, the final frontier. These are the voyages of the Starship Enterprise. Its five-year mission – to explore strange new worlds, to seek out new life and new civilisations – to boldly go where no man has gone before.

(Captain Kirk's voiceover, original *Star Trek* credit sequence, written by Gene Roddenberry)

Over the course of more than three decades *Star Trek* has evolved into an unparalleled multimedia phenomenon, comprising five television series, eight major Hollywood movies and numerous novelisations, not to mention a highly lucrative 'spin-off' merchandising industry. Its characters, locations and familiar catchphrases such as 'Beam me up, Scotty', 'To boldly go', 'Make it so' and 'Engage!' are recognised across the globe and its highly visible and organised fan base has created an international network of conventions, publications and artefacts. Its prominence in American culture was underlined as early as 1976 when NASA, in response to a concerted letter-writing campaign by fans, named the first space shuttle *Enterprise*. Today it can be considered to be one of the most valuable 'cultural properties' in the world.

Although the original series was cancelled in 1969 after only three seasons, creator Gene Roddenberry's insistence on maintaining its thematic depth and consistency (despite much network pressure to tone down its more 'controversial' aspects) eventually paid off. *Star Trek*'s use of the medium of popular TV to explore such themes as racism, sexism, economic and political colonialism, the duality of personality, propaganda and media manipulation had created a passionate interest among its fans which ensured that through continual reruns throughout the 1970s, its audience steadily increased. By the late 1970s, demands for its return in some form were intense. The motion pictures that followed developed into a movie cycle paralleled in popularity in recent times only by the James Bond films. The 'new *Trek*' TV series, *The Next Generation* (1987–94), *Deep Space Nine* (began 1993) and *Voyager* (began 1995), have all achieved major commercial success and have brought up to date, elaborated on and – lately – challenged Roddenberry's original concepts. Far more sophisticated in terms of dramatic interplay and visual settings than their original model, the new series have expanded the 'texts' of *Star Trek* into a 'parallel universe' with its own highly developed cosmology and 'future history', which has many of the qualities of a modern mythological system.

In recent decades there has been a considerable body of theoretical work on television by writers in the field of cultural studies and a number of studies of the TV audience have focused on TV science fiction. John Tulloch and Manuel Alvarado's *Doctor Who: The Unfolding Text* (1983) was a study of the long-running series' changing conditions of production, ideological influences and perceived effect on various audience groups over a 20-year span. Henry Jenkins' *Textual Poachers* (1992) examines the phenomenon of fan culture, concentrating particularly on *Star Trek* fans, and evaluating ways in which fans have 'reappropriated' elements of the *Star Trek* universe, particularly through the creation of their own fiction. Tulloch and Jenkins have also collaborated on *Science Fiction Audiences: Watching Doctor Who and Star Trek* (1995), which examines how the audiences of these series are constituted and the role they have played in the development of the series themselves. There is also some discussion and evaluation of the institutional factors regarding the production processes, and of the importance of genre and authorship in the series. Camille Bacon-Smith's *Enterprising Women* is another study of the *Star Trek* audience, concentrating particularly on female fan fiction. Although I have been to some extent influenced by these works (and have referred to them at various points in this book), it must be stressed that *Star Trek: Parallel Narratives* is not primarily conceived of as a work of cultural studies. The cultural studies approach seeks to explain television as a semiological system by concentrating on its effect on audiences, whereas my principal purpose is to explore and evaluate *Star Trek* as both a series of texts and an evolving modern mythological system. In attempting to open up debates about the aesthetics of popular culture in general, and of the TV series in particular, I have drawn upon a range of approaches including that of mythological studies and related work in the field of anthropology.

It is perhaps surprising that, despite the deluge of memoirs from actors and producers, assorted 'guides' to the various series, *Star Trek* 'technical manuals', encyclopaedias, interactive CDs, Klingon dictionaries and numerous other publications, very few volumes of critical writing on the 'texts' of *Star Trek* have seen the light of day. The same could be said, however, for the vast majority of the products of television. Over the last four decades critics of other forms of popular culture have developed appropriate discourses through which those forms can be assessed and analysed. Film Studies has refined critical perspectives which, particularly through concentration on issues of authorship, genre and narrative and formal visual elements, have made it into an established academic subject with its own methodology and critical reasoning. Even popular music, while it may not have been institutionalised within the education system in the same way, has a thriving critical culture within many magazines, journals and books. Yet it appears that television is still largely perceived by critics and audiences alike to be an 'inferior' medium.

It is worth reflecting here on the perceptual differences between the audience's experience of these two apparently very similar media. In a cinema, viewers are in darkness in front of a huge screen, and everything about this 'total environment' encourages them to concentrate fully on the film. A cinema film is likely to be watched in the presence of many other people, giving it the status of public 'performance'. In contrast, the same movie may be watched on TV or video at home with a much less intense degree of absorption. Friends may call, babies may cry, the telephone may ring, meals or drinks may be being prepared. The use of remote TV controls also encourages 'channel surfing' – rapidly flicking from one channel to another. TV as a medium seems to manifest what Stephen Heath refers to as its 'seamless equivalence with social life …' (in Mellencamp, 1990, p. 267). The existence of regular viewing slots for particular programmes structures both patterns of TV viewing and individual lifestyles, and TV's programming schedules become ritualised as part of everyday routines. It may well be that TV's qualities of domestic and social intimacy make detached or serious analysis more difficult. As Robert C. Allen points out: 'it is the very ubiquity of television and the intricate ways it is woven into the everyday lives of so many people that make it so difficult to analyse …' (Allen, 1992, p. 3).

Much of the approach of this book is derived from my belief that the products of TV are often undervalued because (perhaps as a result of this apparent 'ubiquity') there seems to be little consensus on the nature of the specific aesthetic qualities of the medium. Although *Star Trek* also exists in the form of films, it is primarily a product of the dramatic and institutional conditions that govern TV production. I have placed particular focus on how the changing nature of these conditions has governed the development and evolution of *Star Trek* as a whole. In doing so I have also concentrated on three aspects of the series that reflect on its 'televisual' nature: its status as a multi-authored text; its use of 'postmodern' self-reflexive ironic devices; and its qualities as a mythological system.

One reason that TV series are often seen as an 'inferior' form of popular art may be the difficulty of ascribing their 'authorship'. In Film Studies the 'auteur theory' (first developed in the 1950s by the *Cahiers du Cinéma* critics like Truffaut and Godard) promoted the idea that a film director can be likened to the author of a book or an artist who creates a painting. This was a key factor leading to film coming to be taken more seriously as an art form. Yet the 'auteur theory' has proved to be problematical, in that it is really only applicable to films in which the director is the main creative agent. Even then – with the contributions of writers, producers, cinematographers and other creative artists involved – it is difficult to ascribe credit for *all* the effects in a film to its director. In fact the relative creative input of directors, writers and producers varies from film to film. In television the production process is even more complex and variable. TV directors generally have to conform to a 'house style' and as such are limited in their creative role. Writers of individual episodes obviously have a strong creative input, although a set of series like *Star Trek* has used stories by literally hundreds of authors. The most powerful creative figures in the making of a TV series are invariably its executive producers and their immediate subordinates, who are responsible for guiding and maintaining its overall 'shape'. Although Gene Roddenberry and his successor as executive producer, Rick Berman, can certainly be identified as perhaps the most prominent influences on *Star Trek* storylines, the notion that *Star Trek* – or almost any long-running series – can be said to have one 'author' may be an example of what Marshall McLuhan called 'rearviewmirrorism' – the application of outdated critical concepts based on the misguided application of the values of a print-based culture to the products of the electronic age. In any product of modern popular culture, be it a record, a movie, a book or a video game, there is inevitably some degree of shared authorship.

In this book I have attempted to approach the issue of authorship in a way which is appropriate to the medium of the TV series by recognising that the influence of creative individuals varies, depending on their (often shifting) positions in the creative hierarchy that controls TV series production and that, in dealing with a TV series, it is necessary to focus on a series of different *levels* of authorship. In my analyses of each series in Chapters 2 to 6, I have focused on the contributions of producers to the overall shape of the series, while commenting more on the work of individual writers in terms of specific episodes. I have also identified growing thematic 'trends' (such as the tendency for later *TNG* stories to have 'family' themes) that have had an effect on the overall direction of *Star Trek*. At the same time I have traced the way in which *Star Trek* has gradually evolved from its original, often 'naïve' 'Roddenberryesque' approach to its latter-day 'self-aware' status under the tenure of Rick Berman; and examined how the 'promotion' of successful writers such as Ronald D. Moore and Ira Steven Behr to 'producer' status has indicated their growing influence on *Star Trek*.

A commercially successful series will generally (unless deliberately conceived as having a limited life) continue for as long as it is popular. Some series – such as the western *Gunsmoke*, which ran from 1955 to 1975 – lasted in this way for decades. As series develop and change, their original format may shift in a way that invariably leads to them becoming less naturalistic and more stylised. A good example is the British series *The Avengers* (1960–9), which began as a fairly gritty and 'realistic' spy drama but which soon gravitated towards a form of highly stylised and mannered 'tongue-in-cheek' fantasy. This tendency is most exaggerated in television's most characteristically 'televisual' form, the soap opera, where the need to keep familiar characters involved in ongoing storylines can over the years inevitably strain credibility. This is particularly ironic in the case of the leading British soap operas, *Coronation Street* (began 1960) and *EastEnders* (began 1985), where the 'life stories' of leading characters build up into catalogues of divorce and disaster which ultimately tend to conflict with the series' essentially 'everyday' realist ethos. American 'soaps' such as *Dynasty* and *Dallas*, without such realist constraints, built in plot lines to explain the departure of major actors which have even stretched as far as having their characters abducted by aliens (merely as a very contrived plot device, rather than as any serious attempt at science fiction). TV series may often begin with realist principles, but their prolongation tends to require increasing 'suspension of disbelief' among audiences. As Fiske and Hartley point out: 'Television, a highly conventional medium, constantly uses signs that teeter on the brink of becoming clichés ...' (1978, p. 63). While this tendency towards overstylisation is one of the main reasons that TV series have rarely been regarded as 'serious' drama, it is crucial to realise that much of what has been criticised about TV – its continual repetition and formulaic nature – is actually an intrinsic part of its distinctive aesthetic, which great numbers of viewers implicitly understand. A great deal of the pleasure audiences derive from TV series rests on a 'knowingly' ironic comprehension of the way television conventions are juxtaposed and manipulated. In the case of *Star Trek*, the audience is perfectly aware that the main characters will survive at the end of each week's episode, and that there must be some kind of 'adventure' to motivate the drama. Audiences implicitly understand that this framework is merely a conventional structure and take much pleasure in their own ironic recognition of this fact. In this way *Star Trek*'s audience has learned to 'read' the psychological, social or political themes which are coded into its fictional scenario.

In the new *Trek* series, the use of ironic references to the original series is one particular source of audience pleasure. A good example is the unnamed holographic Doctor of *Voyager*, who frequently uses the phrase 'I'm a doctor, not a ...', a famously overused prelude to the familiar complaints of the original series' Dr McCoy. In fact, the

Doctor's entire characterisation can be read as a 'postmodern' or 'knowing' update of the grumbling, ascerbic McCoy. The *Star Trek* films of the 1980s featuring the original cast draw much ironic humour from the juxtapositioning of familiar *Star Trek* characters – fixed forever in the minds of viewers in terms of their visual appearance in the garishly coloured original series – against modern filmic textures, surfaces and locations. Thus in *Star Trek: The Motion Picture* Kirk (now a Starfleet admiral) bemoans being tied to a 'desk job' in a way that casts him as a middle-aged 'rebel' who has had to 'settle down' to the 'harsh realities of life'. His fate parallels that of so many 1960s social rebels in a period of growing conservatism. In *Star Trek IV: The Voyage Home*, where the crew of the *Enterprise* have between transported to present-day San Francisco, Kirk (whose knowledge of twentieth-century cultural mores seems to be a little limited) hilariously explains away Spock's strange demeanour and speech patterns by claiming that 'he had too much LDS in the 60's'. Earlier in the same film Spock silences an arrogant punk on a city bus – who insists on blasting out his music at full volume – by means of the 'Vulcan neck pinch', to the cheers of his fellow passengers. The humour of both scenes works because they dramatically place *Star Trek* in the realm of what Jean Baudrillard calls the 'hyperreal' – a space within which 'fiction' and 'reality' may cross each other's boundaries – to produce effectively defamiliarising moments such as these. Although these examples are taken from films, they rely for their effectiveness on the audience having been made familiar with the characters over previous repeated viewings of the TV series.

The intimate 'rapport' built up between viewers and characters over repeated viewings of long-running series, serials or soap operas positions TV viewers in a similar mode to that of listeners to traditional oral tales. For many thousands of years storytellers or 'bards' were key figures in cultural development, often acting for the majority of people (who lived in isolated communities) as their main source of news about the rest of the world as well as being an important focus of each community's social and religious life. Since the early 1950s television has established itself as the source of a constant flow of stories which has continued to reflect (or, as some would argue, dictate) the changing morality of society. It has returned the oral mode of communication to the prominence it once had in the days when traditional storytellers held sway. Fiske and Hartley state that, in this capacity as social ritual, it is television which now takes on the 'bardic' role:

the classically conceived bard functions as a mediator of language, one who composes out of the available linguistic resources of the culture a series of consciously structured messages which serve to communicate to members of that culture a confirming, reinforcing version of themselves. The traditional bard rendered the central concerns of his day into verse. We must remember that television renders our everyday perceptions into an equally specialised, but less formal, language system ... (1978, p. 85)

The prophetic 1960s writings of Marshall McLuhan traced the decline of the print-orientated culture which had dominated human civilisation for 500 years – what he called the 'Gutenberg Galaxy' – and argued that it was being superseded by a 'Global Village' of instant world-wide communication, dominated by oral and visual modes of transmission:

After three thousand years of specialist expansion and increasing specialism and alienation in the technological extensions of our bodies our world has become compressed by dramatic reversal. As electronically contracted, the globe is no more than a village ... (McLuhan, 1964, p. 6)

In the context of the resurgence of the oral mode of communication, television series (with their ever-developing and expanding storylines) have the capability of effectively 'mimicking' or reproducing the ancient mythological process. Like the 'fireside' listeners of traditional storytellers, television's audiences delight in continual repetition, in fantastic heroics and dream-like imaginary scenarios, and in melodramatic high tragedy and comedy. In general, they also expect the stories to have moral qualities which resonate with their own values. As McLuhan states: 'Electric circuitry confers a mythic dimension on our ordinary individual and group actions. Our technology forces us to live mythically ... (1967, p. 114).

Television programming is structured around the winning of audience loyalty and the continuing existence of any series depends on its popularity with the public, as indicated by its 'ratings'. The most popular stories on TV, like the most popular mythological sagas, are inevitably those which cast the most reflection on modern life and are thus of most relevance to the viewers. As with traditional tales, only the most popular and thus the most resonant of such stories survive. The storytellers of today's 'Global Village' thus tend to work in a number of well-established popular genres. In this context, it is no surprise that science fiction – a *mythos* of the future – has supplanted the western – a *mythos* of the past – as the most popular film and TV genre and that the biggest Hollywood blockbusters of the last 20 years have almost all been SF movies, from *Star Wars* (1977) to *ET* (1982) to *Jurassic Park* (1992) and *Independence Day* (1996). Clearly, the concern with 'future-myth' is now a central one, as evidenced by the current popularity of 'alien encounter' magazines and the growth of UFO-watching societies, as well as the recent plethora of 'cult' SF TV series such as *The X-Files, Dark Skies, Sliders* and the heavily *Star Trek*-influenced *Babylon 5*. Each 'cult' series might be said to have acquired its own 'tribal' following. As McLuhan argues, the direct, oral way that the technologies of television and recorded sound communicate has reasserted powerful tribal instincts in the mass audience: 'we are back in an acoustic space. We have begun again to structure the primordial feeling, the tribal emotions from which a few centuries of literacy have divorced us ...' (1967, p. 63).

As I have outlined in more detail in Chapter 7, over the years *Star Trek* has attained many of the qualities of a mythological system. It has evolved into an interconnected 'web' of stories in a way that parallels the development of traditional sagas, odysseys or mythic story cycles. Its characters tend to be representative figures of various aspects of the human condition and they are invariably presented with 'heroic' challenges that emphasise those symbolic roles. Like many traditional mythological systems it has created its own 'world', in which 'fantastical' events such as physical transformations or 'time shifts' may frequently occur. *Star Trek* stories, like mythical tales, are presented within the form of a highly conventionalised dramatic structure, into which is characteristically built an overriding moral imperative. Its audience is perfectly prepared to accept that the characters will undergo frequent last-minute escapes from apparently impossible life-threatening situations. Indeed, the eventual outcome of a *Star Trek* story (in terms of the survival of its heroes) is generally predictable. In the original series Kirk and Spock are frequently captured and imprisoned by various alien races, but they invariably find a means to escape. On several occasions they manage to defuse a threat to the entire universe. In *TNG* Captain Picard is at various times taken over by an alien race, implanted with memories of an entire lifetime and confronted with an 'after-death' experience. His life is always under threat but we have little doubt of his eventual survival. What matters, though, is not the outcome of the stories but the degree of ingenuity with which these 'mythic' figures achieve their ends.

There is every reason to believe that the makers of the new *Trek* series are perfectly aware of the mythological/ritual way their programmes communicate. Evidence of this may be found in *DS9*'s *The Storyteller*, wherein the space station's engineer Miles O'Brien is forced to take on the 'bardic' role of storyteller for a small 'peasant' village which is perpetually threatened by a hideous sky-bound 'energy monster', the Dal'Rok. By village tradition, only the telling of stories – which are essentially endless versions of the same story – can repulse the monster. Yet eventually O'Brien discovers that his predecessor, the 'Sirrah', had created the Dal'Rok by technological means as a way of keeping the village (which had previously been plagued by bloody feuds) united. Here the Sirrah's stories can be seen as a provocative parallel with those of television itself, which – through technological means not understood by most of its audience – creates a 'docile' and 'united' public in its 'global village'.

Throughout this book I have placed much emphasis on the ways in which the new *Trek* series have both developed and questioned the ethics and approach of Gene Roddenberry's original conception of *Star Trek*. In focusing particularly on the ways in which the new series have referred to, 'played with' and incorporated elements of 'classic *Trek*', I have also examined the development of *Star Trek* as a reflection of the differences within popular culture – and in the medium of TV in particular – that distinguish the 1990s from the 1960s. Part I: '*Star Trek*, television and cinema', outlines the specific narrative forms and conventions of the TV series and examines how the differences between the media environments of the 1960s and the 1980s and 1990s are reflected in the contrasting approaches of the original series and the new *Trek* series. The bulk of this section consists of an evaluation of the overall narrative development of *Star Trek* in both televised and filmed versions, which also traces the impact of changes in the writing staff on the storylines. (The material in this section only covers *DS9* up to the end of its fifth season and *Voyager* up to the end of its third season, as both series are still in production as I write.)

In later sections of the book I have examined a number of *Star Trek*'s key episodes in greater depth and have investigated its significance in a wider cultural context. Part II, '*Star Trek*, myth and ritual' considers the ritualistic role of 'cult' television in our culture, indicates various ways in which *Star Trek* can be considered a modern 'mythic text' and examines the influence of science fiction and other generic forms on

Star Trek. Part III, 'Psychological, political and social themes in *Star Trek*', investigates the nature of various aspects of *Star Trek*'s liberal-humanist approach to storytelling. In both sections I have again discussed the differences between 1960s and 1980s/1990s *Star Trek* and have focused on the way in which the 'new *Trek*' has built on the foundations laid by the original series in highlighting and reflecting both contemporary ethical issues and fundamental universal human dilemmas.

Part I

Star Trek, television and cinema

Just as history begins with writing, so it ends with TV. Just as there was no history when there was no linear time sense, so there is post-history now when everything that ever was in the world becomes simultaneously present to our consciousness ...

(Marshall McLuhan, 1968, p. 35)

DATA: I believe he means 'television', sir. That particular form of entertainment did not last much beyond the year 2040 ...
(From *The Neutral Zone, Star Trek: The Next Generation*, 1988)

Chapter 1

Classicism, televisuality and post-modernity: *Star Trek* and the narrative structures of television

From the late 1940s until the early 1980s the TV industry in the USA was dominated by a small number of monolithic organisations. The three major networks – ABC, NBC and CBS – had complete control over programming, and there was little differentiation between demographic segments of the audience. Like Hollywood in the heyday of its 'studio system' in the 1930s and 1940s, 1960s TV series production was led by a 'mass family audience' strategy that resulted in many bland or 'wholesome' dramas hidebound by the perceived necessity of avoiding 'offence'. Just as the Hollywood studios had done in earlier years, the TV networks operated a system of self-censorship which not only excluded sexual and overtly violent incidents but also made producers very wary of any material that might cause any kind of controversy. As a result the majority of TV series concentrated on action rather than ideas and tended to avoid any overt or even covert social or political comment. A great many were formulaic westerns (such as *Gunsmoke*, *Bonanza* or *The Rifleman*), cop shows (such as *Dragnet* or *The Untouchables*), fast-paced comedies (such as *I Love Lucy* or *The Dick Van Dyke Show*) or sentimentalised soap operas (such as *The Waltons* or *Peyton Place*). The central characters of such series were generally 'lovable' and invariably morally unimpeachable and the outcome of the stories was generally highly predictable. In a courtroom drama such as *Perry Mason* the hero would inevitably win all his cases on a weekly basis.

The dramatic action of each series also had to be fitted into standardised timeslots imposed by advertisers, which increased the tendency towards formulaic and predictable plots. A series like *Star Trek* must fit roughly 45 minutes of footage into an hour-long slot. Each episode follows TV's 'classical' format of four 'acts', preceded by a short pre-credits 'teaser', interspersed with lengthy commercial breaks. The structure itself becomes a kind of 'musical' code sequenced around what TV scriptwriters themselves refer to as a series of 'beats'. With its prominent and highly stylised use of incidental music to focus on particular moments of emotion and heightened drama, the TV series naturally becomes inclined towards an 'operatic' mode, which emphasises the representative rather than the realistic qualities of the characters. The early *Star Trek* itself has frequently (if often somewhat disparagingly) been called a 'space opera'. Yet its 'operatic' features – where the central characters are (either passionately or dispassionately) given the chance to emote – are what often made it particularly distinctive.

There is no doubt that the rigid structuring of episodes that advertising demands has the potential to impose considerable dramatic limitations, as does the equally advertising-led notion that each 'act' must culminate in a dramatic 'moment' that will not only keep the viewer 'hanging on' for the next segment but also leave their emotions heightened so as to be more responsive to the commercials. Yet, as Richards (1997, p. 4) points out, this standard 'five-act' structure mimics that of Greek, Shakespearean and much traditional drama. It can be argued that such a structure forces a positive 'narrative discipline' upon scriptwriters and presents its audience with a stock of 'universal' symbols. Certainly the structure itself becomes a recognisable sign-system, a ritualised 'procession' of narrative events which eventually becomes implicitly understood and recognised by its media-literate audience. Thus in *Star Trek*, 'action' sequences such as fight scenes are frequently implicitly understood by the audience to be a necessary adjunct to the plot, part of the visual and narrative world of the programme. *Star Trek* heroes are put through an unbelievable number of testing situations and survive countless dangers. But the modern viewer generally recognises this as a dramatic convention of the medium.

The original series of *Star Trek* presents largely unchanging characters who must inevitably solve whatever crisis they encounter within a 45-minute show. This narrative format, which is designed to pick up any 'casual viewers' and allow them entry into the 'world' of the programme at any point in a series, demands that each episode is a self-contained drama. In the original series it is rare for the characters to refer to incidents in previous episodes, and there is little sense of the passage of time. Thus there is no introductory segment to the 'five-year mission' and no conclusion. The dramatic high points tend to be key moments when the conventions of the 'classical' form are in some way challenged by various disruptions of the basic repetitive 'rhythm' of the stories. As Christopher Anderson states:

> these stories develop through formulaic repetition and the invoca-
> tion of references, stereotypes and clichés ... this is necessarily the
> way in which popular culture works. Meaning develops according
> to a delicate operation of similarity and difference. In this process
> a single story gains significance both through its identification
> with stories that preceded it and through its disruption of those
> stories ... (in Newcomb, 1994, pp. 191–2)

The workings of this 'delicate operation of similarity and difference' (or as Fiske and Hartley (1978, p. 63) call it, the juxtapositioning of seemingly contradictory signs) can be seen in the nature of audience reaction to the early *Star Trek* episodes. The first episode to attract large amounts of fan mail was *The Naked Time*, in which a psychological disease affects the crew of the *Enterprise*, making them act out extremely emotional sides of their personalities. What had clearly caught viewers' attention most was the internal struggle they saw Spock going through to contain his feelings. Later episodes like *This Side of Paradise* (where Spock is affected by 'hallucinatory' plants which cause him to embrace fully his buried emotional side) and *Amok Time* (where he experiences the psychologically disturbing effects of the Vulcan mating cycle) were amongst the most popular segments of the original series. Viewers, of course, knew that Spock would inevitably return to his usual 'logical' self, but drew great pleasure from seeing him temporarily reveal his 'inner core'. But, as Anderson emphasises, the 'play of similarity and difference' that characterises TV aesthetics is a 'delicate' one. Too much 'difference' can destroy a character's integrity. By the time of the original series' third and final season Spock's 'emotional side' becomes overexploited. In *The Way to Eden* he 'jams' with a group of 'space hippies' and in *All Our Yesterdays* the time travel he undergoes turns him into a more 'primitive' version of himself who eats meat and takes pleasure in killing. By this time audiences had seen Spock's emotional side so many times that such displays were losing their effectiveness and becoming merely exploitative.

Much of the early *Star Trek* is certainly conventional TV drama, but its adoption of a number of moral and philosophical positions that identified it clearly with the liberal-humanist tradition provided it with the unique qualities which were to ensure that its fascination for its fans would extend well past its cancellation date. In Roddenberry's future Utopia-Earth, war, poverty, disease and the nation-state have been eliminated. Individuals do not appear to be obsessed with material possessions. It is even intimated that money as we know it now does not exist. The Federation itself is an ideal of liberal democracy – a voluntary organisation of like-minded worlds – in contrast to the 'evil empires' of Klingon and Romulus. Its adherence to the philosophy of the 'Prime Directive' also seemed to point (if not always consistently) towards direct criticism of Earth's imperialist and racist past. We are constantly reminded that 'man' has 'risen above' such tendencies. By introducing the 'Vulcan' concept of 'Infinite Diversity in Infinite Combinations', Roddenberry also made clear that in Federation society racial and sexual differences and all forms of biological diversity were seen as positive elements to be celebrated. In the Federation's 'ideal future', both racism and sexism are 'things of the past'.

Despite the existence of this scenario, Roddenberry's attempts to cast blacks and women in prominent roles were often opposed by the network. But he succeeded in doing so to an extent that in the context of 1960s mainstream US TV was unprecedented. Merely placing a black woman (Nichelle Nichols as Uhura) on the bridge of the *Enterprise*, even if her character was rarely developed in any meaningful way, was a radical step at this time. In her autobiography Nichols (1995, pp. 164–5) reveals that, disillusioned with the many episodes in which her role was restricted to telling the captain that 'hailing frequencies were open' she was considering leaving the programme but was dissuaded from doing so by none other than Dr Martin Luther King. The third season episode *Plato's Stepchildren* featured an onscreen kiss between Kirk and Uhura, which was the first time a white man had been seen kissing a black woman in an American TV series. Network officials feared that the scene might lead to a boycott of *Star Trek* in the southern states, despite the fact that the script clearly indicated that Kirk was being forced to kiss her by an alien being. There is little doubt that such 'controversies' contributed to the imminent cancellation of the series.

By the time *Star Trek* returned to television in 1987, the entire broadcasting environment had changed. Following the rise of cable and satellite TV and the spread of the VCR, the supremacy of the networks had been severely weakened. The expansion of programming had led to a greater diversification of the types of programmes produced. In addition to this, the techniques of the advertising culture had become vastly more sophisticated, as had the demographic analyses of audiences on which it based its projections. As a result the obsessional quest for the 'family' audience that had dominated network thinking in its 'classical' hegemonic era had been replaced by a desire among TV programme makers to serve a variety of perceived audiences. One of the key 'target audiences' was that of males aged 18–50, within which *Star Trek* generally scored very highly, as it did among high-income earners. But despite these changes, advertising schedules continue to dominate US TV and the basic 'classical' structure of individual episodes (as described above) remained in place.

When *The Next Generation (TNG)* was turned down by the networks, Paramount decided to launch the series straight into syndication. This was considered a somewhat risky step at the time, and would certainly have been impossible in the network-dominated 1960s, but *TNG* was a ratings triumph, quickly becoming the top-ranking first-run syndication show. Its writers and producers now had freedom from network interference and were able to proceed without the kind of restrictions Roddenberry had faced in the 1960s. They were also helped by the fact that the institutional changes in the TV industry had created a space for 'quality' programming that was not previously perceived to exist. A TV series was now much more likely to include implicit comment on serious social issues or to express a political viewpoint. Censorship rules on the presentation of sexual material had also greatly relaxed, and multi-racial casting had become generally acceptable. Many of the restrictive codes prevalent in 1960s' TV (such as the emphasis on 'action-melodrama' and the demand that TV heroes be of unimpeachable character) had loosened, so that a TV series could more easily absorb the influence of serious drama and film. There was also a definite sense in which the products of popular media like TV had become more culturally valued. As Steven Connor asserts:

In the early 1980s ... the sense of what constituted culture began to broaden and distort. It was not just that the sheer flood of contemporary writing and cultural production began to lap at the doors of literature and art-historical courses that tended not to recognise the significance of the contemporary, but also that a worrying fluidity began to affect the boundaries between high culture which had traditionally been the preserve of universities and mass culture. Popular forms like television, film and rock music began to lay claim to some of the seriousness of high cultural forms ... high culture responded with an additional adoption of pop forms and characteristics ... (Connor, 1989, p. 6)

John Thornton Caldwell describes how in the 1980s a certain section of mainstream TV began to create a new aesthetic style which he identifies as a direct reaction to the economic crisis caused by the success of cable and the VCR. Caldwell labels this new style 'televisuality' because it incorporates certain aesthetic strategies that are unique to the medium of TV. He argues that:

starting in the 1980s ... television moved from a framework that approached broadcasting primarily as a form of word-based rhetoric and transmission ... to a visually based mythology, a framework and aesthetic based on an extreme self-consciousness of style ... (Caldwell, 1995, p. 4)

Caldwell points out that 1980s 'televisual' shows such as such as *Moonlighting* and *Beauty and the Beast* deliberately used visual approaches that paid homage to cinematic genres in a way that allowed the audience to take part in the pleasure of their recognition (1995, p. 4). At the same time the values of 'authorship' came to the fore as renowned cinema auteurs such as Steven Spielberg (*Amazing Stories*), David Lynch (*Twin Peaks*) and George Lucas (*Young Indiana Jones*) launched their own TV shows. Meanwhile (as was the case with *Star Trek*) much of series TV was in itself being made by the same studios that were producing movies, thus further blurring the aesthetic differences between the products of TV and cinema. The widespread use of VCRs now made it possible for fans of particular shows to record and keep programmes, a factor which contributed to TV being seen as a less 'disposable' medium. To be 'worth' recording, a show had to contain enough narrative depth to justify further viewings. Also, the viewing of a programme was no longer tied to a particular timeslot, which separated its consumption from the ubiquitous 'flow' of television. The use of VCRs may also create a 'time shift' effect, whereby viewers may find themselves accidentally watching 'yesterday's programmes'. As Richard Dienst observes:

What the VCR makes possible, in fact, is the further ramification of televisual time by altering its speed, and in this sense it retools the televisual apparatus for a new economic cycle ... we are currently witnessing the development of relative modes of socialising time, based on the absolute socialisation already posited by the apparatus itself ... (1994, p. 35)

All these factors contributed to the evolution of 'cult series' that created discrete 'worlds' into which viewers, through continual watching and (importantly) 're-watching' (with the help of the VCR), could immerse themselves. As Caldwell states:

> *Beauty and The Beast, The X-Files, Quantum Leap, Star Trek* and *Max Headroom* all initiated fan activity not simply because they were visual, but because they also utilised self-contained and volatile narrative and fantasy worlds, imaginary constructs more typical of science fiction. Their preoccupation with alternate worlds – a defining focus of virtual reality – justified and allowed for extreme narrative and visual gambits and acute narrative variations ... like sci-fi, televisuality developed a system/genre of alternate worlds that tolerated and expected both visual flourishes – special effects, graphics, acute cinematography and editing – and narrative embellishments – time travel, diegetic masquerades and out-of-body experiences ... such forms, simultaneously embellished and open, invite viewer conjecture ... (1995, p. 261)

Star Trek now presents an entire 'parallel universe' with its own political, economic and social system, a symbolic landscape in which a great many contemporary concerns, ranging from euthanasia to disability to abortion to genetic engineering, can be explored. While building on the structures and concepts of the original series, in its recreated form it has shed many of the narrative limitations that previously characterised it and has evolved its own sophisticated ways of juxtaposing character, generic conventions, ideologies and scientific prediction, as well as absorbing a considerable number of cinematic influences. The gradual transition from the 'series' to the 'serial' mode has encouraged the development of many interwoven 'story arcs' and character 'backstories'. The complex history of alliances and conflicts between the major players in galactic politics – the Federation, the Klingons, the Cardassians, the Romulans, the Borg and the Dominion – now forms a constantly shifting political backdrop to the action, and often provides motivation for the stories.

The evolution of *Star Trek* in the 1980s and 1990s into such a multilayered and self-referential 'web' of narratives is a measure of the differences in popular culture between recent decades and what now appears to be the comparatively 'primitive' or 'innocent' era of the 1960s. Since its inception TV has been a characteristically postmodern medium, whose everyday intimacy with the viewer naturally inclines it towards decidedly ironic or self-referential positions. Contemporary *Star Trek* episodes (and the movies featuring the *Next Generation* crew) tend to assume that the audience already possesses considerable knowledge of the *Star Trek* 'universe'. Both character and setting, though repeated on a weekly basis, are mutable. Many storylines involve the 'possession' of familiar characters by alien entities or other external forces, so providing 'parallel' versions of the characters. Others suggest the existence of an infinite number of entire 'parallel universes', some of which are extremely similar to our own. Space and time in *Star Trek* stretch in infinite directions and 'reality' can be reconfigured in any number of ways. This mirrors the way in which the present media environment has broken up the immediacy of the TV medium. With all the *Star Trek* series being constantly rerun, many viewers will tune in to an episode without necessarily knowing when it was made or how it relates in terms of 'story time' to other episodes they may have watched recently.

This 'time shift' effect is reflected in *Star Trek*'s 'time paradox' episodes which are among its most distinctive creations. The notion that by travelling into the past an individual could affect and change the future, so that what we now think of as the past might have 'never existed' sets up the notion of an infinite number of possible 'time lines' (each of which is itself an 'alternative universe'). In this narrative environment even death is not necessarily the end of a character's story. In *TNG*'s *Yesterday's Enterprise* the past history of the Federation, as depicted in the previous two seasons of episodes, is changed, so that some of the events of those episodes now 'never happened'. Tasha Yar, who had been 'killed' two seasons before in *Skin Of Evil*, now returns from another time line to die a more fitting death. There are numerous other instances (outlined in more detail later) where the 'present time line' in which contemporary episodes take place is threatened with annihilation. Thus *Star Trek*'s storytelling universe exists in a condition where there are no 'absolutes', only an infinite number of different possibilities.

Much of the pleasure of audiences of the new *Trek* series comes from recognition of allusive references within individual episodes to various aspects of its own history, so fulfilling Jean Baudrillard's assertion that: 'Post-modern culture is a culture of the present made from fragments of the past, a toying with historical ruins ... (in Storey, 1988, p. 165). References to Kirk and his crew (whose adventures occur some 80 years or so earlier) in the new *Trek* series identify them as 'legendary' figures of a 'frontier era' when Starfleet's actions were not so hidebound by the diplomatic and political realities which dominate the later seasons of *The Next Generation* and the entire span of *DS9*. In comparison to the 'innocence' of the dramatic style of the original series, the greater narrative complexity and dramatic realism of the modern series positions them as the product of an 'age of experience', again mirroring the differences in sensibility between the 1990s and the 1960s. These differences are made explicit in *TNG's Relics*, which features a guest appearance by James Doohan as Scotty, who has been frozen in stasis for many years after an accident in space. The prevailing tone is one of pathos, as Scotty finds his engineering skills outmoded by the newer technology and thus feels 'useless' until given the chance – in a crisis where sudden improvisation is necessary – to prove his worth. In perhaps the episode's most poignant scene, Scotty revisits an empty replica of the original *Enterprise* on the holodeck and bemoans his lost heyday. Scotty truly is from a different 'era' and can never really fit into the world he has woken into. His dilemma symbolises the transformation of cultural sensibilities by the spread of new technology over the past three decades. The cultural and technological differences between the twenty-fourth century of new *Trek* and the twenty-third century of the original series are frequently emblematic of changes in the 'real world' in the last thirty years.

As Linda Hutcheon points out (1989, pp. 179–207), it is in the nature of postmodern re-creations of the past to have a rather ambivalent relationship to their antecedent texts and this frequently involves a recognition of those texts' ideological or stylistic limitations. In the new *Trek* series 'tributes' to 'classic *Trek*' tend to be presented on 'special occasions' like anniversaries, which become 'excuses' for both programme makers and audiences alike to 'wallow' in the 'knowing' pleasure of recognising references to the 'classic text'. In the fifth season *DS9* episode *Trials and Tribble-ations* (made in 1996 as a 'thirtieth birthday *Star Trek* 'special') Captain Sisko and his crew travel back in time to the time of the original series' much celebrated comic episode *The Trouble With Tribbles* in order to prevent the 'time line' being changed by an assassination attempt on Captain Kirk. Thanks to modern filmic and computer-imaging techniques, the *DS9* characters are able to interact visually with the 'legendary' figures of the original crew. The episode is full of ironic humour which 'plays' on audience knowledge of the original 'text', setting up a 'knowing' self-referential discourse between Sisko's crew – who are placed in the 'fan-fantasy' position in relation to 'classic *Trek*' – and the audience. In one scene, Sisko and Dr Bashir are confronted with a 'Kirk-era' female Starfleet officer who flirts coquettishly with them in the manner of many female characters in the original series. Similarly, *DS9*'s highly assertive female science officer, Jadzia Dax, takes a clearly ironic delight in donning the 'micro-skirt' worn by original-series female officers. The episode not only points out the differences between 1990s and 1960s *Star Trek* but also works as a humorous commentary on the differences between the 'politically correct' 1990s and the 'sexist' 1960s.

One particular moment in *Trials and Tribble-ations* illustrates well the modern *Star Trek*'s ability to make such 'knowing' comments on its own past. Dr Bashir, Chief O'Brien and the Klingon Worf are sitting at a table in a bar in a space station, about to witness the original-series bar brawl between the Klingons and Starfleet officers. In the 1960s series, Klingon 'makeup' consisted merely of thick, swarthy-looking eyebrows and sinister-looking droopy moustaches. During the 1980s movies and in subsequent 'new *Trek*' shows, Klingons were portrayed as having a series of thick ridges in their foreheads and a very distinctive facial structure, including particularly jagged teeth. This is one of the most obvious 'continuity glitches' between the original series and modern *Star Trek*. But instead of attempting to side-step the issue or explain the difference in any 'scientifically credible' way, writers Ronald D. Moore and Rene Echevarria turn the 'problem' into a hilarious 'postmodern' joke. O'Brien and Bashir are shocked at the Klingons' 'sixties look' and demand an explanation from Worf as to how his race could have changed appearance so much in 80 years. Worf, with his impenetrable Klingon 'cool', deadpans 'we do not discuss it with outsiders'. As 'privileged' viewers we, of course, are 'in' on the joke.

Star Trek's writers can now trade upon a rich tapestry of inter-connected stories in which each new episode will take its place. The significance of each event in the *Star Trek* universe is amplified by its resonance with the body of stories that precedes it. The remainder of Part I, which describes the evolution of *Star Trek* through its series and movies, demonstrates how its writers have succeeded in 'stretching' the apparently rigid boundaries that delineate the medium of TV and in doing so have established a new aesthetic for the medium itself.

Chapter 2
Adventure and utopianism: the original series

I guess it was the thought that under the terrible restrictions of television it might be a way to infiltrate my ideas, and that's what it's been all the time. You see, it's difficult for people to understand that even in the barren vineyards of television you might do these things. Actually you can do them better because you reach more people with more impact ... The power you have is in a show like *STAR TREK*, which is considered by many to be a frothy little action-adventure – unimportant, unbelievable and yet watched by a lot of people. You just slip ideas into it ...

(Gene Roddenberry, quoted in Asherman, 1986, p. 78)

In *Star Trek: The Making Of The TV Series* (1968) Gene Roddenberry describes his difficulties in getting the NBC network to back the concept of a science fiction show that would reflect his vision of a utopian, egalitarian future. SF was largely thought of by TV programmers as low-budget 'kids stuff'. The most successful SF show before *Star Trek* had been *Captain Video and His Video Rangers*, an extremely juvenile drama with very simplistic 'black and white' morality and unexplained science which ran for six years between 1948 and 1954. This series established SF TV as a children's medium, and was followed by similar productions as *Tom Corbett, Space Cadet* (1950–2), *Buck Rogers* (1950–1), *Johnny Jupiter* (1953–4) and *The Adventures of Superman* (1951–7). More recent adult-orientated SF shows such as *The Twilight Zone* (1959–64) and *The Outer Limits* (1963–5) had achieved some success, but these series were anthologies of different stories. The idea of launching a more 'serious' SF show with regularly recurring characters was thought to be both a risky and an expensive one, and Roddenberry's insistence that his cast would include at least one alien character as a regular member of the Starship crew seemed to some network executives to be a recipe for disaster. Yet Roddenberry had a proven track record as a TV writer and producer, and the network had enough confidence in him to fund him to produce a pilot for the series. Working with Lucille Ball and Desi Arnaz's production company, Desilu (which was eventually taken over by Paramount in 1968), he scripted and produced the first version of *Star Trek, The Cage.*

The Cage (which was later 'cannibalised' for the first season episode *The Menagerie*) is a fascinating curio from today's perspective. The story, in which the *Enterprise's* Captain Pike is subjected to a series of illusory states by telepathic but ultimately sympathetic aliens who are attempting to learn about humans by testing them to their limits, sets the initial pattern for *Star Trek* as a primarily psychological drama rather than a purely action-orientated series. Already there is a display of garish colour onscreen in terms of lighting and costume, anticipating the eventual series' visual style. In terms of casting, however, the pilot is quite different from the later series. In contrast to the very physical and demonstrative Kirk, Jeffrey Hunter's Captain Pike is a thoughtful and sensitive explorer. Pike's highly assertive female second-in-command, known only as 'Number One' (Majel Barrett) is cold and unemotional. The one familiar figure to modern eyes is Spock (Leonard Nimoy), who is given only a peripheral role and has yet to develop his unemotional character or Vulcan identity. Indeed, the existence of Starfleet and the Federation is not formulated until some way into the series' first season.

Although network executives applauded *The Cage*, they pronounced it to be 'too cerebral' for the mass TV audience. Roddenberry, however, was extremely persistent and was convinced that his basic idea was sound. He continued to lobby for a second chance, until NBC agreed to the (virtually unprecedented) step of allowing the series to have a second pilot. But in order for this to happen he had to agree to some of the network's demands for changes in casting. The character of Number One was removed in response to network insistence that audiences would not accept a strong, assertive female character on the bridge and female crew members were now attired in 'eye-pleasing' micro-skirts. Number One's 'emotionless' qualities were transferred to Spock, a character whom Roddenberry successfully managed to retain, despite network fears relating to his supposedly 'satanic' appearance. Jeffrey Hunter was not available for the second pilot and the more 'physical' William Shatner was cast as Captain Kirk. Other key features such as the famous 'These are the voyages of the Starship Enterprise ...' voiceover were also added. The second – and far more action orientated – pilot, *Where No Man Has Gone Before*, in which a crew member develops extra-sensory perception and finally turns into a crazed 'superbeing', finally won network approval, and the series went into production.

The original series of *Star Trek* was thus essentially a compromise between Roddenberry's desire to 'infiltrate' his ideas into mainstream TV and the demands of the networks for constant helpings of action and romance. The initial episodes, in which the final cast had not yet taken full shape, tended towards network-pleasing action-adventure stories with conventional plot resolutions. In *The Corbomite Maneuver* Kirk establishes his 'maverick' style when he bluffs his way out of an alien threat by claiming to be armed with 'corbomite', a purely fictional substance. In *The Man Trap* he kills a shape-shifting salt-devouring creature which turns out to be the last of its race with an equanimity that would have shocked later *Star Trek* captains. In the comic *Mudd's Women*, conman Harry Mudd arrives aboard ship with three beautiful young mini-skirted women whose presence causes the predominantly male crew to become virtually hypnotised. However, without the 'Venus drugs' supplied by Mudd the women revert to their previous state of 'plainness'. But in the fifth episode, *The Enemy Within* – which effectively reworks the Jekyll and Hyde theme in space – the series begins to take on its distinctive narrative shape. A transporter accident divides Captain Kirk into two men – one aggressive and lustful, the other passive but ineffectual. Although the aggressive Kirk is the 'baddie' of the story, the 'good' Kirk finally embraces him in the transporter beam as they are reunited. In *The Naked Time*, the first exposure of Spock's emotional side, we are introduced to the Vulcan 'backstory'. The planet Vulcan, we are told, was formerly ravaged by internal wars until the Vulcans adopted a culture of dispassionate 'logic', involving strenuous exercises in self-control to block out 'illogical' emotions. Spock himself is only half Vulcan, as he has a human mother, and has had to undergo tough mental training to cut off his 'human side'. The psychological disruptions in *The Enemy Within* and *The Naked Time* are *Star Trek*'s first exploration of one of its most basic themes, the question of what it is to be human. It was these two stories, rather than their more conventional predecessors, which first registered large-scale audience interest.

In the early days of *Star Trek*, Gene Roddenberry was a dominant influence on its storylines. Determined to place his own authorial 'stamp' on the series, he personally produced rewrites of the first 13 episodes, and supervised all aspects of their production. Once the series was proving its popularity to the network, he felt able to 'slip in' some of the moral and ethical dilemmas that were to further define its dramatic qualities. *Balance of Terror*, which introduces the Romulans, touches on issues of inter-species racism and *Miri* casts the ethics of genetic engineering in a planetary setting. *Dagger of the Mind* features a deranged psychologist whose methods of 'treatment' amount to a form of mind control. In *The Conscience of the King* Kirk is confronted by a former war criminal, opening up the controversial ethics of the potential redemption of such figures which would later be examined in a number of episodes of *DS9*. *The Squire of Gothos* introduces Trelane, an 'omniscient' being who captures members of the *Enterprise* crew for his own entertainment. It remains a major plank of the *Star Trek* universe that there are beings in the universe that have evolved beyond matter to become virtually 'gods'. Yet Trelane, on whom *TNG*'s Q is largely modelled, is conceited, wilful and vain. His omniscience is contrasted with the greater compassion of the relatively powerless Starfleet crew. Roddenberry's rewriting of scripts ensured that each episode was centred on a consistent – if sometimes simplistic – humanistic moral position.

By now Spock and Dr McCoy (DeForrest Kelley) had become established, with Kirk, as the central characters of the series. Although Chief Engineer 'Scotty' Scott (James Doohan), Lieutenant Uhura (Nichelle Nichols) and Commander Sulu (George Takei) appeared on a weekly basis, they were invariably confined to supporting roles. Many early episodes focused on developing the character traits of the principals. *The Galileo Seven* features Spock in command, forced into making an 'illogical' last-minute decision to save himself and the crew of a lost shuttlecraft. In *Arena* Kirk fights the Gorn, a ferocious monster, for the entertainment of 'superior' aliens, the Metrons. Demonstrating his compassionate nature, he refuses to kill the creature, which impresses his watchers. Here, as elsewhere, the Starfleet crew are called upon to demonstrate to higher civilisations the human capacity for compassion. Other early episodes tend more towards the fantastical. *The Alternative Factor* is an encounter with 'Lazarus', a being who (like Kirk in *The Enemy Within*) has 'good' and 'bad' versions of himself, the 'bad' version here being from an 'anti-matter universe'. Kirk has to prevent the two universes colliding and obliterating each other. The 'Alice in Wonderland' pastiche *Shore Leave* features an 'amusement park' planet where the thoughts of visitors produce illusions that appear to be real.

A number of the series' first draft scripts were submitted by well-established science-fiction writers like Theodore Sturgeon (*Shore Leave*), Robert Bloch (*What Are Little Girls Made Of?*) and Harlan Ellison (*City on the Edge of Forever*), and Roddenberry's rewriting frequently caused much to the chagrin to their authors. Ellison's original script for *City On The Edge Of Forever* (which puts *Star Trek*'s characters in a real historical environment – Depression America – for the first time) actually won a Hugo Award, and he publicly denounced Roddenberry for his 'censorship'. Roddenberry later insisted that the original script would have been far too expensive to produce. Certain plot elements, particularly the presence of a drug addict on the *Enterprise*, were deemed unsuitable, and indeed would probably never have got past NBC's censors. It soon became apparent that the kinds of stories that worked in SF literature did not always fit into the *Star Trek* format.

Midway through the first season, Roddenberry 'stepped back' from the full duties of day-to-day production to become the series' executive producer. The new 'line producer' Gene Coon became the original series' most prolific scriptwriter, writing 14 episodes over its three seasons and, like Roddenberry, providing rewrites for many others. Under Coon's influence the latter episodes of the first season developed much of the political background and ideology of the Federation and the social customs and traditions of alien races. Coon also put more emphasis on the humorous elements within the show, particularly focusing on the sarcastic interplay between McCoy and Spock. Whereas Roddenberry's inclination was to produce stories that featured the crew constantly encountering new aliens, Coon's contribution was to place the Federation in a galactic political context.

Four of Coon's first season stories were to have much influence on the future development of *Star Trek*. *Errand of Mercy* features the first meeting with the Klingons, who are attempting to conquer the planet Organia. But any conflict between the Federation and the Klingons is prevented by the 'omniscient', peace-loving Organians, who disarm both sides and force them to sign a peace treaty. Although the Klingons are portrayed here as ruthless totalitarian conquerors, the episode hints at a strong mutual respect between the Klingon leader, Kor, and Captain Kirk. In *Space Seed* the ship is taken over by Khan Noonian Singh, a 'genetic superman' who had been frozen in stasis since the 'eugenics wars' of the late twentieth century, the first suggestion that the utopian society of Kirk's day has only been achieved after a period of planetary chaos. *A Taste of Armageddon* is one of the first stories to refer to contemporary political dilemmas. It features two constantly warring races who, instead of wasting valuable resources in fighting, have agreed to allow a computer to select an equal number of people from each side of the dispute to die. Here the ethical problems of the nuclear stand-off of the Cold War, as well as that of over-reliance on computers, are clearly signposted. In *The Devil in the Dark* the crew investigates a number of deaths of miners on the planet Janus IV, which have been caused by a 'rock creature', the Horta. But Spock refuses to destroy the creature. Instead he 'mind melds' with it and learns that it is in fact a mother trying to protect her young. Having established communication, he negotiates a mutually agreeable arrangement between the Horta and the miners, whereby the Horta will assist in the mining operation in exchange for being left alone. This episode establishes clearly the *Star Trek* view of morality later encapsulated in the 'Vulcan' phrase 'Infinite Diversity In Infinite Combinations' – that any sentient being has a right to live and be respected.

Dorothy ('D. C.') Fontana (originally Roddenberry's secretary) also emerged as a key *Star Trek* writer in the first season. She provided a much-needed female perspective, and her stories (which usually eschewed violent confrontations) tended to focus on contemporary social and psychological issues. *Tomorrow is Yesterday*, in which the *Enterprise* travels back to the 1960s and inadvertently picks up a US Air Force pilot, is the first of many *Star Trek* 'time paradox' stories, dealing with the possible consequences of 'pollution of the time line'. *Charlie X* (co-written with Roddenberry) features a 'space orphan' in a story about teenage alienation. *This Side of Paradise* is the first episode to reflect the contemporary drug culture, when Spock's emotional side is revealed through the narcotic effects of a plant that has obvious parallels with LSD. With McCoy, Scotty and the rest of the crew also succumbing to the 'trip', only Kirk can supply the 'logic' that will save the situation. The episode clearly communicates the idea that drugs provide a 'false paradise'. The episode sets a precedent for the many *Star Trek* episodes in which characters experience 'altered states' of perception.

At the end of its first season *Star Trek* was nominated for five Emmy Awards, including best dramatic series and best supporting actor in Leonard Nimoy. Yet according to NBC's stringent standards its performance on the all-important Nielsen ratings 'charts' was considered poor. Only a concerted effort of letter-writing by fans and a group of the most prominent SF writers (including both Ray Bradbury and Isaac Asimov) known as 'the Committee' prevented the series being cancelled. Fans were even prepared to stage marches and demonstrations to save the show, phenomena that were completely new to bewildered network officials unused to an audience that was so obviously 'pro-active'. But although production began on a second season of *Star Trek*, the series was allotted a new Friday night slot which ensured that, with its mostly young viewers engaged in other pursuits, ratings were likely to fall even further.

This situation was satirised in the second season episode *Bread And Circuses* (co-written by Roddenberry and Coon), in which a planet is discovered which has had parallel development with Earth, except that the Roman Empire still exists. Gladiatorial combats are still the main form of entertainment, but here they are *televised*. As the gladiators fight the TV commentators get highly excited, pushing buttons marked 'APPLAUSE', 'CHEERS', 'BOOS', 'HISSES' and 'CAT CALLS', only pausing to deliver a message from their sponsors. Their show invites viewers to win a cash prize if they 'NAME THE WINNER!' There is no 'real' audience for the contest. One of the guards threatens a gladiator by saying 'you bring our ratings down, and we'll do a SPECIAL on you ...'. Here Roddenberry and Coon are venting their spleen on the networks, and the whole commercial system that limits artistry and social comment in the TV medium. The implication is that the stations will show *anything* if it increases their viewing figures, and that 'audience responses' are manipulated to achieve that all-important effect. In this context the gladiators themselves resemble 'warring' TV producers, ready to 'kill' if necessary to get their show on the networks, which are providers of 'bread and circuses' – supposedly giving the people 'what they want'.

A new introduction in the second season was the young ensign, Pavel Chekov (Walter Koenig), whose 'Beatle cut' hairstyle made him resemble Davy Jones, lead singer of US TV's 'Beatle clones' The Monkees. Undoubtedly the main reason for Chekov's addition was an attempt to attract younger female fans, although Roddenberry was also responding to an article he had read in *Pravda* complaining that there were no Russians aboard the *Enterprise*. Chekov's addition stresses that by the twenty-third century the cold war is long gone, although like the other minor characters he is rarely featured in anything but a supporting role.

The second season developed much of the political backstory of the *Star Trek* universe, mapping out the balance of power between the

Federation, the Klingons and the Romulans in episodes such as *The Deadly Years*, where the presence of the Romulan 'Neutral Zone' is established. The Federation Doctrine of the 'Prime Directive', whereby the Federation is prohibited from interfering with the development of less advanced cultures, is also given prominence in two of Roddenberry's own stories, *A Private Little War* and *The Omega Glory*. In *A Private Little War*, the Klingons have violated the Prime Directive by arming one side in the conflict on the primitive planet Neural with weapons. In order to create a balance of power, Kirk reluctantly decides to arm the other side. In *The Omega Glory* Kirk has to deal with the effects of a previous Prime Directive violation by a 'rogue' Starfleet captain who has sided with a tribe called the 'Kohms' against their opponents, the 'Yangs'. Both episodes make very specific references to the Cold War, with *A Private Little War* being a clear Vietnam parallel.

In contrast to the warlike Klingons, the Vulcans are the epitome of Roddenberry's view of the 'sacredness' of empirical rationalism, one manifestation of his belief that the future development of science can lead to the kind of 'utopian' society achieved on Federation planets. In *Amok Time*, Theodore Sturgeon supplied a story in which Spock begins to experience the effects of 'ponn farr', the Vulcan mating cycle. When Vulcans are seized by the 'ponn farr' they begin to experience extreme emotions, and must return to their home planets to complete their mating ritual or die. Kirk is so determined to save his friend that he disobeys Starfleet orders and takes Spock to Vulcan. But the mating process is far from the 'logical' ritual which Kirk expects. In fact the ponn farr appears to be one of the few occasions on which Vulcans revert to their brutal and emotional origins. Spock's 'intended', T'Pring (to whom he has been betrothed since childhood), invokes her right to have Spock fight to the death against a 'champion' of her choosing. T'Pring's choice turns out to be none other than Kirk. In the episode's climactic scene, Spock and Kirk fight with primitive weapons and Spock, seized by the 'fury' of the Ponn Farr, appears to 'kill' Kirk. Overwhelmed by grief, he loses the mating urge and returns to the ship. When he discovers that Kirk is alive – having been given a shot of a drug by McCoy which produced the appearance of death – he is overjoyed. *Amok Time* is the episode which perhaps best utilises the dramatic power of the device of giving Spock an emotional release. The unexpected emotions he does experience here are very powerful ones: lust, murderousness, grief and finally joy.

Another 'Vulcan story' that investigates the price that the half-human Spock pays for his emotional repression is D. C. Fontana's

Journey To Babel, which introduces his Vulcan father, Ambassador Sarek, and his human mother, Amanda. Although the episode contains some cloyingly sentimental scenes in which Amanda relates how the young Spock was 'picked on' by other Vulcan boys, its portrayal of the relationship between Spock and his father (who have been estranged for 20 years since Spock opted to join Starfleet) is a memorable study in the effects of such repression. As if to 'prove' his Vulcan nature to his father, Spock refuses to respond to Sarek's grave illness and devotes all his attention to the mission at hand. While *Amok Time* stresses Spock's Vulcan background, *Journey to Babel* provides perhaps the fullest picture of his divided nature. The popularity of Spock – easily the original series' most fully realised and distinctive character – had by now fully justified Roddenberry's insistence on retaining him.

The second season also sets up further key elements of *Star Trek*'s dramatic 'universe'. In *Mirror, Mirror* the concept of parallel universes is introduced, as the crew meet parallel versions of themselves in a universe in which the Federation is a corrupt organisation at war with the Klingons and bent on galactic domination. The device of temporarily 'repositioning' the characters, which had proved so successful in *The Enemy Within* and *The Naked Time*, was to be used in many forms throughout *Star Trek*'s history. In *The Changeling* Kirk has to 'persuade' a probe that had been launched in an earlier century from Earth not to destroy humanity, a plot that was largely reproduced in the first *Star Trek* movie. In *Metamorphosis* we are introduced to Zephram Cochrane, legendary inventor of the warp drive that has made interstellar travel possible and a key figure in the *Star Trek* chronology. Cochrane will later feature in the second *Next Generation* movie, *First Contact*.

Other episodes feature further encounters with 'higher powers'. In *Who Mourns For Adonais?* the ancient Greek Gods are identified as powerful aliens who depend on the worship of humans. Kirk's characteristically steadfast refusal to 'bow down' to the 'god' Apollo establishes *Star Trek*'s classically humanistic position on religion, where what appear to be 'gods' are in fact shown to be more evolved creatures with greater technology. The implication is that the human race has evolved past the need for worshipping any kind of deity. Similarly, Kirk maintains a defiant attitude to the 'all-powerful' aliens who capture him in *The Gamesters of Triskelion*. A certain 'suspicion' of technology is also featured prominently in several episodes. The experiment in *The Ultimate Computer* in which human control of the *Enterprise* is ceded to a computer fails disastrously. *The Apple* features a society kept in an artificial state of 'innocence' by a controlling computer, Vaal, which attacks the *Enterprise* in an attempt to drain its power. In *The Doomsday Machine* Kirk must destroy a planet-threatening destructive device created by a long-extinct alien race. Whether set against 'superior beings' or 'superior technology', the value of the 'human factor' is constantly emphasised.

Another feature of the second season is the divergence of *Star Trek* into different generic fields. Several episodes incorporate elements of the horror genre. In the 'halloween'-themed *Catspaw* Sulu and Scotty are transformed into 'zombies'. The villain of *Wolf in the Fold*, in which Scotty is wrongly accused of murder, turns out to be an evil being known as 'Redjac', who in another century had taken the form of Jack the Ripper. *Obsession* features a 'vampire'-like cloud creature and in *By Any Other Name* powerful aliens turn almost the entire crew into small tetrahedral blocks. Other stories place the crew in a variety of generic situations. The time-travel story *Assignment Earth*, in which the crew again return to the 1960s, ventures into the 'spy' genre by featuring Gary Seven, a slick 'secret agent' from the future. In *A Piece of the Action*, the crew discovers a planet which has adopted the lifestyle of 1920s gangsters. In *Patterns of Force*, a rogue Starfleet captain has created a facsimile of Nazi Germany. These episodes tend to be centred around the comic juxtaposition of the Starfleet 'heroes' being placed in unfamiliar situations and 'colourful' costumes. But the most effective comic episode of the second season is undoubtedly David Gerrold's *The Trouble with Tribbles*, in which the Klingons are wittily repositioned as effective comic foils when a 'plague' of rapidly-reproducing 'cute' furry creatures threatens to engulf the entire ship. *Tribbles* has proved to be one of the most popular *Star Trek* episodes and features a cleverly underplayed performance by Shatner, who often seems most at home in comic scenarios. Such second season episodes clearly established the importance of humour in *Star Trek*.

By the end of the second season, a number of NBC executives were again demanding the cancellation of the series. Despite clearly having a very vocal and committed following, its Nielsen ratings still indicated that it was a 'minority' show. Another letter-writing campaign saved the day, but NBC subsequently announced that they were rescheduling *Star Trek* into an even later slot on Fridays (10 p.m.). Following the departure of Gene Coon, Roddenberry wished to assume a more 'hands on' role in the production process again but refused to do so unless the network provided a better slot. The network refused, and Roddenberry's role as executive producer became ever-more distant. Effective control was handed over to new producer Fred Frieberger, an experienced professional but not a creative writer-producer like Roddenberry or Coon. In the subsequent third (and last) season, the stories lack the originality and the psychosocial focus of those in the first two seasons, and without Roddenberry's guiding hand scientific credibility is virtually abandoned. Particularly galling for 'serious' fans was the series' opener, *Spock's Brain*, where Spock's brain is removed yet, rigged up to an electronic device, is still capable of 'talking'.

Many of the season's episodes trade on previously-established ideas. As mentioned earlier, the device of allowing Spock to emote is used rather indiscriminately. *Plato's Stepchildren* reworks the 'Roman planet' theme again and *Spectre of The Gun* is more, rather contrived, genre-hopping – this time in a Wild West setting. The shipboard encounter with the Klingons in *Day of the Dove* mirrors almost exactly the story of their original meeting in *Errand of Mercy*, with both sides being disabled by a 'higher power'. *Whom Gods Destroy* features another 'double Kirk' and in *Turnabout Intruder* Kirk's body is again taken over, this time by a jealous woman using an alien 'mind control' device. In both *The Empath* and *The Savage Curtain* the crew are again captured and experimented on by powerful aliens. One story, *Let That Be Your Last Battlefield*, explores the theme of racism. But the plot, involving a half-black/half-white humanoid engaged in a lifelong hunt for his half-white/half-black counterpart years after every other member of both of their races has been wiped out, is contrived in the extreme and its moralism blatantly obvious.

A series of 'romantic' stories (from which much of the original series' reputation for simplistic sexism originates) feature 'syrupy' music to introduce female characters who are supposed to 'overawe' the audience with their beauty. *Is There in Truth No Beauty* (where members of the crew appear to 'fall in love' at first sight with the visiting Dr Miranda Jones), *For the World Is Hollow and I Have Touched the Sky* (where a supposedly dying McCoy falls in love), *The Lights of Zetar* (where Scotty protects a young woman who is 'possessed' by an energy storm), *Elaan of Troyius* (where Kirk falls in love with a young woman intended for an arranged marriage to unite two warring peoples) and *Requiem for Methuselah* (where Kirk falls in love with an android whose 'circuits explode', killing her, when he and her creator fight) are typically overheated TV SF melodramas.

Two episodes from the early part of the season do, however, manage to enlarge the scope of *Star Trek*. In D. C. Fontana's *The Enterprise*

Incident Kirk is sent on a mission to the Neutral Zone to steal a Romulan cloaking device and is surgically altered to resemble a Romulan. Here the morals of galactic politics are questioned, in a way that would presage the rather ambivalent treatment of Starfleet's 'official morality' in later episodes of *TNG*. In *The Paradise Syndrome*, an amnesiac Kirk is stranded for several months on a planet whose inhabitants resemble a primitive Native American tribe. Having revived a dying boy with the 'kiss of life' he is at first taken to be a god. He also acquires a wife, who becomes pregnant, but who is later killed by angry villagers when they realise the limitations of Kirk's powers. Here, the series appears to break out of its usual 'time constraints' and allows Kirk to show unfulfilled sides to his character. The 'anthropological' issues dealt with rather crudely here will be examined in much greater depth in a number of episodes in the new *Trek* series.

As William Shatner points out in his memoir, *Star Trek Memories*, cancellation at the end of the third season came as no surprise to the cast. Lodged in its late night slot, the show's ratings had fallen drastically. Its last episode, *Turnabout Intruder*, was first broadcast on 3 June 1969, ironically less than three weeks before Armstrong and Aldrin first walked on the moon. Viewed from today's perspective, and especially in comparison with the newer *Trek* series, much of the original series appears to suffer from an innate 'corniness' and predictability. Levels of plot credibility, character backstory development and dialogue are certainly much less developed than in the later series, as are levels of realism in acting styles, settings and special effects. However, the original series was a unique phenomenon in television history. It marked the first real attempt on mainstream US TV to create a popular series with a narrative framework that would allow comment (albeit in a way that was filtered through its generic codings) on contemporary socio-political and ethical issues. A handful of the episodes – particularly *City on the Edge of Forever*, *Amok Time*, *The Devil in the Dark*, *Journey to Babel* and *The Trouble with Tribbles* – are still compelling television and provided strong dramatic models on which future *Trek* series would be based. The triumvirate of Kirk, Spock and McCoy remains a remarkable fusing of elemental human characteristics, which subsequent series have struggled to match. The character of Spock in particular became one of television's main twentieth-century icons and the imaginative concepts and repeated 'slogans' of the series – such as the apocryphal phrases 'Live long and prosper' and 'Beam me up, Scotty', the Prime Directive, the Vulcan philosophy of 'Infinite Diversity in Infinite Combinations', and

Spock's 'devices' such as the Vulcan hand signal, the 'neck pinch' and the 'mind meld' – passed into widespread general currency. Despite their origins in the restrictive environment of 1960s TV, the best episodes of *Star Trek* presented a model of the possibilities of what TV series might achieve in the future. The original series thus touched a particular nerve in its audience which helped it transcend the 'classical' form of US commercial series TV.

Chapter 3

Pastiche and nostalgia: the 1980s movie series

Although there was to be a gap of an entire decade before the first *Star Trek* movie was released, the 'legendary' status of the series continued to build throughout the 1970s. After cancellation the series was sold into syndication on the American and international markets. Though most shows at this 'repeat' stage would be seen by ever-declining audiences, *Star Trek*'s ratings actually increased over the years. Evidence began to emerge of the existence of a huge and dedicated fan base. In June 1972, 2000 people attended the first *Star Trek* Convention, a forum for star guests and series-related merchandise. By 1975 conventions were attracting numbers of up to 8000. A series of novelisations of episodes of the series sold extremely well, and many fanzines began to circulate among the audience. The market for *Star Trek* 'spin-offs' continued to increase. Clearly, although *Star Trek*'s initial ratings had not put it in the front rank of popular shows, it had attracted a fan base large and dedicated enough to preserve it as a continuing phenomenon. The long hiatus in production between the original series and the movies only encouraged the development of a 'cult' audience, as each re-run episode became well known to fans.

The first major concession to the fans was the creation in 1973 of an animated series. Most animated versions of a major live action series or movie tend to be trivial, exploitative, and aimed at children. Production is rarely taken on by the original staff. Yet already Paramount executives were able to recognise the value among *Star Trek* fans of preserving the 'authenticity' of the *Star Trek* product. Thus, the original cast (minus Walter Koenig as Chekov) were employed to do voice-overs of their animated selves. Many of the original series' writers were drafted in. As associate producer and story editor, D. C. Fontana was in effective control of the series, while

Roddenberry functioned as 'executive consultant', making sure that the new series fitted with the parameters of the *Star Trek* universe. Though the series was short-lived, and the episodes are not generally seen as part of the *Star Trek* 'canon', the scripts were literate enough to lift the series above the usual Saturday-morning animated fodder and to help keep interest in *Star Trek* alive.

By 1975, Paramount had begun negotiating with Roddenberry for the return of *Star Trek* in some form and he began to work on a new TV series, *Star Trek II*. As many as 12 scripts were written, but the sudden and resounding success of the movie *Star Wars* in 1977 changed the thinking of Paramount executives. As Hollywood studios clamoured to climb on the *Star Wars* bandwagon, the plan for a second series was abandoned and a *Star Trek* movie went into production. *Star Trek: The Motion Picture* (1979) (produced by Roddenberry and directed by Hollywood veteran Robert Wise) was based on a typically 'Roddenberryesque' plot line, whereby an apparently 'evil' alien entity eventually turns out to be a being which, when fully understood, is sentient and capable of moral choices. Frustrated at being 'tied to a desk job' at Starfleet headquarters, Kirk reassembles the original crew and assumes control of the *Enterprise* to prevent a mysterious 'alien cloud' destroying Earth. The 'cloud' turns out to be controlled by a machine that has become a living entity as the result of a collision of alien intelligence with one of NASA's original *Voyager* probes. Heavily laden with special effects and lingering shots of the new *Enterprise*, the film's approach seems caught between that of *2001: A Space Odyssey*, emphasising the 'grandeur' of space travel, and *Star Wars*-type action adventure.

Although the movie recouped a large profit of some $175m. on its initial investment of $44m. Paramount's 'suits' were well aware that much of this was merely due to fan enthusiasm following the long hiatus in *Star Trek* production. Although committed to a sequel, they felt disinclined to rely on a (potentially ageing) TV audience and moved towards a movie series on a less grandiose (and thus smaller-budget) scale that could attract a broader public. In the process Roddenberry was increasingly sidelined. Writer-producer Harve Bennett, who had considerable film experience but no previous *Star Trek* connections, was appointed in his place and Roddenberry was reduced to the rather nominal role of 'Executive Consultant'. David Alexander's biography of Roddenberry, *Star Trek Creator*, recounts his years of growing frustration as his influence on the films decreased and the films themselves increasingly incorporated elements that he considered to represent a betrayal of his original vision. Roddenberry's had always wanted to use the 'surface' of action-adventure as a 'cover' for the posing of ethical questions. But in a movie culture then dominated by the 'ironic' action-adventure ethos of such films as the *Raiders of the Lost Ark* Indiana Jones saga, this conception was to be submerged under action-adventure plots which either emphasised the 'larger than life' dimensions of the major protagonists or engaged the characters in 'knowing' pastiche of the original series.

In the wake of the success of the sequence of three *Star Wars* films, and with the proliferation of sequels being made of popular 'blockbusters', especially in the now-dominant generic fields of horror and science fiction, Hollywood movies were beginning to appropriate some of the episodic and repetitive qualities of the TV series that were often being made by the same studios. In this climate of the 'merging' of TV and cinematic forms, *Star Trek* was a natural choice for a continuing film saga. The 'movie trilogy' consisting of *The Wrath of Khan* (1982), *The Search for Spock* (1984) and *The Voyage Home* (1986) features a continuous story arc in which each film ends with the suggestion of a sequel to follow. In *The Wrath of Khan* the *Enterprise* is attacked by Khan Noonian Singh, the 'genetic superman' from the original series episode *Space Seed*. Khan's purpose is to commandeer Project Genesis, a device designed for the regeneration of barren worlds, in order to dominate the galaxy. Naturally, Khan is foiled, but at the cost of the 'death' of Spock, who sacrifices himself to save the ship and its crew. Spock's body is dispatched to the planet below, just as the Genesis device begins to work. In *The Search For Spock* Kirk and his crew disobey Starfleet orders and steal the *Enterprise* in order to return to the Genesis planet to regenerate Spock, whose consciousness has been temporarily housed in Dr McCoy. En route they clash with a group of Klingons who are searching for the secrets of the Genesis device. Kirk is forced to allow the *Enterprise* to be destroyed and escapes in a captured Klingon Bird of Prey, taking a 'reborn' Spock back to Vulcan for 'reintegration'. In *The Voyage Home*, with the Earth threatened by another mysterious probe, they travel back to San Francisco in 1986 in order to locate a humpback whale. In the twenty-third century humpback whales are extinct, but the probe will only turn back from destroying Earth if it can communicate with such a creature. Much of the film is played for laughs as the familiar *Enterprise* crew interact with twentieth-century characters.

Creatively, the movie trilogy was dominated by three figures – Bennett, who produced the third and fourth movies, wrote the screenplay for *The Search for Spock* and co-wrote *The Voyage Home* and *The Wrath of Khan*; Leonard Nimoy, who directed *The Search for Spock* and directed and co-wrote *The Voyage Home*; and Nicholas Meyer, who directed *The Wrath of Khan* and co-wrote *The Voyage Home*. Bennett and Meyer were both inclined to treat *Star Trek* as light popular entertainment, although Nimoy brought a vital understanding of Roddenberry's ethos which preserved some of the substance of the original series. Yet although the events of the films are sometimes referred to in the new *Trek* series, some commentators have argued that their frequent disregard for Roddenberry's ethics excludes them from the true *Star Trek* 'canon'.

If any one movie can be called 'uncanonical' in this way it is the fifth *Star Trek* film *The Final Frontier* (1979), directed and co-written by William Shatner. The *Enterprise* is commandeered by Spock's 'long-lost brother' Sybok, who manages for a time to convert both Spock and McCoy to his cause of journeying to the 'Great Barrier In The Centre of the Galaxy' (a scientifically rather ludicrous concept) to find the planet 'Sha Kee Ree', the legendary 'home of God'. Sybok certainly makes an unlikely villain (and an even more unlikely Vulcan), and even many loyal fans found the plot melodramatic in the extreme. Roddenberry, by now fully engaged with *TNG*, found his protests against the film's many violations of what he considered to be the ethos of *Star Trek* largely ignored. For the final movie featuring the original cast, *The Undiscovered Country*, Meyer returned to direct a story developed from an original idea by Nimoy. The plot centres around a definitive peace treaty with the Klingon Empire and Kirk's efforts to prevent it being undermined by a conspiracy led by the villainous Klingon general, Chang. The film has a grand political theme, but the parallel which is set up between the Klingon–Federation peace treaty and the ending of the Cold War is made blatantly obvious, with Chang hissing 'in space all warriors are cold warriors'. Following the mode of the most commercially-successful movie, *The Voyage Home*, the script is full of very pointed self-referential jokes, with Kirk casually bemoaning that he has to 'save the galaxy once again' and Chancellor Gorkon rather unforgettably claiming that the only way to understand Shakespeare is to 'read it in the original Klingon'.

The original-cast movie series largely abandons the Roddenberryesque world of *Star Trek* in favour of action-adventure/pastiche. But as the years went by the participation of the ageing cast in 'action scenes' came to look increasingly ridiculous and was widely lampooned. Also, sub-plots had to be devised to engage the minor characters, which tended to add a rather ponderous element to the scripts – there is always the sense that they are merely being 'paraded' in front of the fans. However, the interconnectedness of the movies presaged the movement of the new *Trek* series towards the serial form. They were also instrumental in developing the chronology which would inspire the new series, and proved decisively to Paramount's executives that the market for *Star Trek* was an ever-expanding one.

Chapter 4

Diplomacy, family, destiny:
The Next Generation

In 1987, when Paramount announced the launch of *The Next Generation*, the appointment of Gene Roddenberry as its executive producer was a key part of its marketing strategy. Whereas the film series was directed at a broad cinemagoing public, *TNG* was projected at an audience with the kind of auteur-consciousness that was rapidly spreading from fans of the cinema to those of TV. A new *Star Trek* series made by anyone else but its 'original creator', who by now had become perhaps the most famous writer-producer in the history of television, would have lacked credibility among the fans. After the years of declining influence during the 1980s film series Roddenberry was now given virtually free rein to demonstrate his 'authorial' qualities and was provided with a generous budget of over $1m. per episode.

The initial impetus and creative ideas behind the new series came largely from members of the original series' production team. Roddenberry had a number of meetings with original *Trek* co-producers and writers Bob Justman, David Gerrold, Eddie Milkis and D. C. Fontana. Out of these 'brainstorming' sessions came the scenario for the new series, which was to be set some 80 years after Kirk's time. *TNG* was to feature an 'ensemble' cast (in the style of such series as *Hill Street Blues*, *Thirtysomething* or *St Elsewhere*), allowing for eight or nine leading characters to be developed and enabling the frequent reappearance of a number of 'guest' characters who come to play a significant role in the series' overall story arc. The twenty-fourth century was initially seen as a more peaceful era, with the *Enterprise*'s mission being primarily diplomatic rather than military. Families would live aboard the *Enterprise*, which now became a floating 'city in space'. A crucial new innovation was the holodeck, where any given fantasy world could be played out, both for rest and recreation for the crew and for effective simulations in training exercises.

Under Roddenberry's control, *The Next Generation* stayed consistent with his idealistic conception of the *Star Trek* universe in a way that the films had patently failed to do. But although acting skills, levels of sophistication of plotting and dialogue and the show's 'look' were all clearly superior to the 1960s series, in its first two seasons there was an almost constant turnover in writing and production staff that reflected the search for a distinctive identity. Roddenberry himself was over 70, his health was failing and he was aware that the excessive physical demands of producing a long TV series were likely to be too much for him. He needed an 'heir apparent', someone on his production staff who shared his vision of *Star Trek* and who could 'nourish' and defend it against the forces of trivialisation and commercialism so prevalent in American TV. During the preparations for the first season, an encounter with Rick Berman, a young but already well-seasoned TV producer with considerable experience in the field of mini-series and TV movies, had led to a meeting of minds, which Roddenberry later jokingly described as 'love at first sight'. By the end of the first season Berman had been promoted to co-executive producer and by the third season he was effectively in control. Under Berman's leadership, a 'next generation' of young writer–producers was eventually to transform *Star Trek* into a multifaceted and uniquely 'televisual' creation.

In terms of the range of main characters, the 'international' element in casting was expanded into an 'inter-species' one. The science officer was an android, Data (Brent Spiner). Perhaps the most surprising addition to the crew was the Klingon bridge officer, Lieutenant Worf. As well as Michael Dorn as Worf, another black actor, LeVar Burton, was cast as Geordi, the ship's blind engineer, who sees by means of a sophisticated device known as a VISOR. Female characters featured more prominently, with Denise Crosby as the highly assertive security officer, Tasha Yar; Marina Sirtis as Deanna Troi, the ship's counsellor from the telepathic Betazoid race; and a female doctor, Beverly Crusher (Gates McFadden). Wil Wheaton, one of the teenage stars of the film *Stand By Me*, was cast as her son Wesley. As first officer, Jonathan Frakes as Commander Riker played the nearest thing to a 'Kirk' role, often leading landing parties while the captain remained with the ship, and cultivating a romantic eye for females of all species in the Kirk tradition. In casting the brilliant British Shakespearean actor Patrick Stewart as Captain Jean-Luc Picard, Roddenberry made the biggest leap into the unknown. Even in the age of 'televisuality', having a bald, middle-aged captain was regarded by many as a considerable risk. But Picard, as a far more reserved and intellectually cultivated figure than Kirk, was a fitting captain for the new 'diplomatic' *Enterprise*.

Perhaps Roddenberry's most enduring creation in these initial episodes – and one which would provide a regular recurring presence and an often ironic philosophical perspective over the entire run of *TNG*, is Q, a 'rogue' member of a race of highly advanced beings known as the 'Q continuum' whose evolution has progressed so far that they can achieve virtually any feat through the projection of their will and can travel to any place in space and time without the aid of spaceships. Played in an arch, slightly camp way by John De Lancie, the 'omniscient' jester Q is Picard's nemesis. He generally displays a mocking contempt for the human race, regarding them as 'mere mortals' whose lives are dominated by trivial concerns. In the series' feature-length pilot *Encounter at Farpoint* (written by Roddenberry and D. C. Fontana), while the crew is involved in trying to solve the mystery of how the apparently underdeveloped Bandii race could have built the sophisticated Farpoint space station, Q suddenly transports Picard to the scene of a twenty-first century 'kangaroo court' where he places humanity 'on trial' for the crimes of its past. To Q, the progress the human race has made towards a utopian society has occurred in what to him is merely a brief instant in time. He tells Picard that the history of the human race is one of barbarism – referring particularly to the wars of the twenty-first century – and that he doubts whether he should allow their exploration of space to continue. In his vigorous defence of humanity Picard assures Q that the human race has evolved beyond its 'barbarian' phase.

A dubious Q then returns Picard to Bandii space, where it is discovered that the Bandii city has been attacked by a mysterious spaceship. But the crew is able to discern that the 'spaceship' is actually a sentient life-form which is attacking the Bandii to free its mate from them. It seems that the Bandii had enslaved the spaceship's mate to force it to build the station. Picard acts decisively to allow the two beings to leave the planet, forcing Q rather reluctantly to concede that humanity is not quite as 'primitive' as he thought. He tells Picard that – for the time being – their voyages can continue.

TNG's pilot develops grand Roddenberryesque themes that will eventually encompass the entire series. *Star Trek*'s central tenet, that by the twenty-fourth century humanity has evolved into a 'higher state', is emphasised. By implication, the voyages of the new *Enterprise* (which Q will be constantly observing) will comprise a continuous 'trial', in which humanity must match up to certain ethical standards in order to be able to continue its expansion. In this way *Encounter at Farpoint* embodies the ethical qualities of the original series, adopting a seriousness of tone and purpose in a way that the 1980s film series never approaches. The encounter with 'higher beings' harks back to such original series' 'humanist' episodes as *Who Mourns for Adonais?* or *The Squire of Gothos*, in which the 'god-like' figures who capture the *Enterprise* crew are characteristically decadent and vain, so much so that they can be defeated by human ingenuity. At the same time the 'sentient spaceships' plot develops the 'infinite diversity' theme as epitomised in *The Devil in the Dark*.

With veterans of the original series taking charge of *TNG*, in its initial stages it often veers towards imitation of its famous predecessor. As with the first season of the original series, Roddenberry worked exhaustively on the first half of the season, rewriting the first 13 episodes himself. He was determined to establish the new *Star Trek* as a more serious, 'adult' development of the 1960s show, and the dramatic presentation of the show reflected this. But most of the first season's episodes betrayed a sensibility that was still more attuned to traditional TV storytelling models. A number of the first season episodes reworked elements of 'classic *Trek*' in a very blatant way that caused consternation among some fans, who feared that Roddenberry had merely produced a 'retread' of the original series. *The Naked Now* and *Where No One Has Gone Before* (which features another, more benevolent 'higher being', the Traveler) were very deliberate 'tributes' which virtually replicated the plots of *The Naked Time* and *Where No Man Has Gone Before*. In an 'evil twin' story that strongly recalls *The Enemy Within*, *Datalore* introduces Lore, Data's identical android 'brother' whom Data is eventually forced to dispatch into space after he attempts to take over the ship. *Too Short a Season* reiterates the themes of *A Private Little War* by being set on a planet that had been plunged into continuous conflict by a Starfleet admiral who had violated the Prime Directive by supplying the natives with arms 40 years before.

Much of the first season portrays a ship patrolling the galaxy on a largely diplomatic mission, and frequently encountering ethical problems connected with the Prime Directive. In the style of the original series, these episodes are self-contained stories with 'neat' resolutions and the long-term effects of Federation intervention are rarely explored in any meaningful way. *Justice* focuses on a race whose apparently 'idyllic' lifestyle is maintained by a system of draconian punishment, resulting in Wesley Crusher being sentenced to death for a minor legal infringement, yet Picard still succeeds in having him released. Similarly, in *Code of Honor* Picard uses his diplomatic skills to free Tasha Yar, who has been 'taken' by the local chieftain as a new wife. In *When the Bough Breaks* Picard convinces the Aldeans to release a group of children, including Wesley, whom they have kidnapped in a bid to perpetuate their race. In *Angel One* Riker's intervention helps to change the nature of an oppressively matriarchal society. Although the importance of the Prime Directive is constantly quoted, in these episodes the *Enterprise* crew still seems able to intervene in the cultural affairs of a range of societies without apparently causing much damage. The element of 'galactic politics' later developed as the inspiration for *DS9* and *Voyager* is still an occasional concern. In fact, alien races featured in the original series are largely avoided. The main 'threat' is posed by the newly-created Ferengi, later to become stalwarts of *DS9* but presented here in *The Last Outpost* and *The Battle* as greedy, unscrupulous but somewhat unconvincing villains. Roddenberry's approach seems to be to present each new alien race as a vehicle for comment on a particular social issue, but this inevitably leads to the Federation crew regularly 'solving' the problems that are encountered. Such an approach, while it may propose 'solutions' to important social issues, is dramatically predictable and often shallow.

It is only towards the end of the season, ironically as Roddenberry began the process of relinquishing control, that the series began to evolve its own distinctive character. *Skin of Evil* breaks completely new ground by featuring the death of Tasha Yar, the first time a starring character has been 'killed off'. The death itself is handled in a surprisingly low-key manner, but the episode signifies *TNG*'s first real breakthrough into the serial format and will have continued implications throughout the entire run of the series. Two episodes develop a continuing plotline – in *Coming of Age* and the later *Conspiracy* Picard works to expose a covert attempt by certain members of its higher echelons to take complete control of Starfleet. In this case Starfleet turns out to have been infiltrated by an alien presence, but these episodes begin to lay the groundwork for further stories of corruption in Starfleet that will come later. The stylish *The Big Goodbye* is the first full-scale 'holodeck story', in which Picard becomes trapped in the narrative of a 'holonovel' based on a piece of 1940s pulp detective fiction. As the holodeck characters begin to question their own existence, the holodeck emerges as a site for innumerable 'stories within stories' and for plots centred around questioning the nature of reality. Such philosophical questions will later come to dominate much of the later seasons of the series. The season ends with another diplomatic stand-off after the rediscovery of the Romulans following a 50-year silence in *The Neutral Zone*, giving a further hint of the darker political intrigues to come.

The second season brought a number of changes in casting. In an attempt to 'toughen up' the female characters, Beverly Crusher was replaced by Dr Pulaski (Diana Muldaur), a somewhat cynical figure in the crusty 'Dr McCoy' mode, who was to prove rather unpopular with the fans. A new location, The Ten Forward lounge, featured as a rest room, bar and social meeting area for the crew. It is run by Guinan, an enigmatic member of an ancient race who is several hundred years old, and who acts as a kind of 'alternative counsellor', giving rather more brusque advice than the empathic Deanna Troi. Guinan is played by Hollywood star Whoopi Goldberg, whose request for a part in the show was initially met with incredulity by the *Star Trek* production staff when she declared herself willing to take a part in the series at standard TV actors' rates. Her appearances are sporadic, and often feature her in interaction with only one character (presumably so that she could be shot separately to fit in with her film commitments), but she provides a beguilingly ambiguous presence on the ship.

With an ailing Roddenberry increasingly taking a 'back seat' in the second season's production, Berman sought to put together a more stable writing team to create a more distinct identity. But the season was again characterised by a rapid process of turnover in the writing staff, and often displays signs of being in an awkward 'period of transition'. Further problems were caused by a writers' strike in spring and summer 1988 which delayed the start of the season, forced the studio to cut the number of shows from 26 to 22 and made it necessary for some of the episodes to be based on old unused scripts. The rather fantastical opener *The Child*, where Deanna becomes 'miraculously' pregnant with a child that grows up in a matter of hours and which turns out to be an alien entity who wishes to experience the human condition, is a revamped version of a script written for the aborted *Star Trek II* series from the 1970s. The closing episode *Shades of Grey* appears to consist mostly of a hastily-assembled montage of previous episodes under the guise of Riker's dream-fantasy.

A number of episodes still continue to imitate the model of the earlier series, using often crudely drawn 'representative' alien races and entities to make 'statements' about various contemporary social themes. In the 'social class' parable *Up the Long Ladder* Picard eventually succeeds in persuading the Mariposians, an ascetic and snobbish 'higher culture' (consisting entirely of clones of five explorers who crash-landed many years before) to breed with the Bringloidi, a quaintly stereotyped group of 'Irish simpletons'. In the 'disability' allegory *Samaritan Snare*, the Pakleds, who request help in repairing their ship, appear to be rather mentally 'slow'. At first the crew treats them with a certain amount of condescension, but when they kidnap Geordi and demand that Picard supplies them with all the *Enterprise*'s computer data it transpires that they merely use a restricted language code. Picard finally outwits the Pakleds by threatening them with a 'crimson force field', a piece of bluff which recalls Kirk's similar use of the non-existent 'corbomite' in *The Corbomite Maneuver*. Both episodes feature rather 'heavy-handed' plot resolutions which rework the 'appearances are deceptive' motif that already threatens to become a *Star Trek* cliché.

Despite rather one-dimensional nature of such stories, a number of episodes in the second season still feature a noticeable shift in direction. In *Time Squared*, the first *TNG* 'time-paradox' story, Picard encounters a version of himself from a few hours in the future and has to work to prevent the *Enterprise* being trapped in a 'time loop'. In *Q Who*, the first 'Borg story', Q (who regards the Starfleet crew as somewhat complacent about the safety of the Federation) transports the ship to a distant area of the galaxy where they are threatened by the Borg, half-human, half-machine beings with a single collective mind dedicated to 'absorbing' other cultures. Q's role in the story is, as ever, rather ambivalent. Although he genuinely intends to warn humanity about the future threat they may face, and rescues the *Enterprise* at the last moment, his actions also alert the Borg to the existence of humanity. The episode is a dire warning of things to come. *Q Who* is one of the first *TNG* stories to hint at future consequences, continuing the series' emerging tendencies towards the serial mode.

In other episodes, the 'discovery of new races' mode begins to be succeeded by a more character-based approach. Several stories focus on Data, whose status as an android creates many narrative possibilities. These are often comic, as in the scenes in *The Outrageous Okona* in which he uses the holodeck to practice his attempts at telling jokes. In *Elementary, Dear Data*, another story of sentient holograms, he assumes the role of Sherlock Holmes. These episodes allow Spiner to exercise his considerable talents as a mimic, and establish Data as a charmingly 'eccentric' figure. Like his predecessor, Spock, Data has a particular 'deadpan' quality which often makes him an effective comic presence. But, as with Spock, his 'semi-human' status allows for the exploration of more serious ethical issues. As Data is the first android to serve in Starfleet, there are few legal precedents in Federation law to indicate whether Data can be considered an individual or Starfleet 'property'. In the tense courtroom drama *The Measure of a Man*, when a Federation scientist wishes to be allowed to disassemble Data for experimental purposes, Picard has to prove that Data is an independent and sentient being. This is finally proven by Data's display of his holographic 'keepsake' of the late Tasha Yar, whom he had actually 'made love' to in *The Naked Now*. Yet in many ways Data is an 'old style' *Star Trek* character who, despite his growing understanding of humanity, remains somewhat 'fixed' as 'the android who wants to be human'.

In contrast, the episodes which develop the 'dark sides' of Riker and Worf begin to explore characters who will experience considerable growth during the series. Riker had been somewhat bland and 'underwritten' in the first season, but in *A Matter of Honor*, in which he takes part in an 'exchange programme' that places him on the bridge of a Klingon vessel, his hearty if somewhat cynical character begins to emerge. In order to survive the experience he has to assert himself in the 'macho' Klingon pecking order, a task he performs with some gusto. In *The Icarus Factor* his troubled family background is revealed as we see him in conflict with his father, a Starfleet admiral. The ritual nature of Klingon culture is explored in the same episode, in which Worf experiences a holographic representation of the Klingon 'Rite of Ascension'. In *The Emissary* we meet Worf's half-Klingon lover, K'Ehleyr, whose contempt for Klingon traditions provides the first of Worf's challenges to his rather idealised view of Klingon ethics. These stories presage the development that each character will experience in later seasons.

The third season saw *TNG* finally stepping out of the shadow of the original series and establishing its own dramatic parameters. Much of this was due to the appointment of Michael Piller, a former producer of *Simon and Simon*, as new head of the writing team. From the third season onwards, Piller was to form a close and productive partnership with Rick Berman that would steer the series towards new levels of consistency, originality and depth. Piller's approach represented a definite refinement of the Roddenberryesque ethos that had dominated the first two seasons. Under his supervision, *TNG* stories gravitated far more towards morally ambiguous resolutions. This was perhaps demonstrated most clearly in two of the episodes Piller himself wrote for the third season, *The Best of Both Worlds* and *The Enemy*. In *The Best of Both Worlds*, the 'dehumanisation' process that takes place as the Borg temporarily assimilate Picard is presented in a far more psychologically realistic way than previous mental 'takeover' stories. There is a real sense in which we feel that Picard's experience will change him permanently, and the rest of the series will confirm this. In *The Enemy* Geordi La Forge is stranded underground on an inhospitable planet with a wounded Romulan, and the two have to overcome mutual prejudice to survive. This is contrasted against a parallel situation on board the *Enterprise*, where another Romulan is dying. Crusher's researches reveal that only a blood transfusion from Worf can save him but Worf, whose parents were murdered by Romulans, refuses to help – despite 'humanistic' pleas from Picard, Riker and Troi. This was perhaps something of a 'shocking' moment for *Star Trek* fans, but a decisive one in terms of the series' direction. For the first time, we see a major 'hero figure' make a morally questionable decision which instigates real conflict between the main characters.

This new stress on the imperfection of the characters is emphasised by the introduction in *Hollow Pursuits* of a new 'recurring guest', Lieutenant Reg Barclay, who is so insecure and paranoid that he has to create a holodeck program featuring 'passive' versions of the main ship's officers in order to fulfil his 'control fantasies'. In *Booby Trap*, when the *Enterprise* is trapped by an energy-draining device that is the remnant of an ancient war between long-dead races, the psychological effects of the holodeck are given a disturbing new twist when Geordi La Forge creates a hologram of renowned Starfleet scientist Dr Leah Brahms to help him solve the problem. Geordi finds himself becoming increasingly attracted to his version of Dr Brahms, but this is a 'woman' who is of course programmed to serve him, with whom he can never, of course, conduct a 'real' relationship. The episode points out particular flaws in Geordi's character, as well as the psychological dangers of the holodeck (and, by implication, any form of 'virtual' interactive culture). Both Barclay and Geordi are seen to participate in 'unethical' uses of the technology in order to assuage their own sense of insecurity.

Sarek is the first story which features the return of an original series character. (discounting a brief cameo by McCoy in *Encounter at Farpoint*). Spock's father is suffering from the effects of Bendii

Syndrome, a condition which has echoes of Alzheimer's disease. The illness makes Sarek unable to conduct vital diplomatic negotiations which are intended to establish peaceful relations between the Federation and the Legaran race, with whom they have been at odds for centuries. Picard agrees to undergo the traumatic experience of a mind meld with Sarek in order to take over his role and manages to conclude the negotiations successfully. Up to this point the portrayal of Vulcans had been largely avoided, in an effort to avoid duplicating stories which were too close to episodes of the original series like *This Side of Paradise* and *Amok Time*, but here the writers succeed in using original-series elements in a way that enhances the characterisation of members of the new crew, rather than merely 'exploiting' them as pre-established plotlines. For, Picard, 'merging' with Sarek has a profound effect on him which will be reflected in future episodes, and he attains a new insight into the complex Vulcan psyche.

Prominent amongst the new young staff writers Piller introduced were Rene Echevarria and Ronald D. Moore, both of whom proved capable of supplying the kinds of stories that could move *TNG* into 'new realms'. Echevarria's writing tends to focus strongly on intimate and unusual personal relationships, an approach which is epitomised by his third season contribution, *The Offspring*, where Data's initially secret experiment in building an android 'daughter' fails when the 'child's' circuits overload and 'kill' her when she begins to experience emotions. The ethics of Data's 'rights' to reproduce are questioned, in a development of themes suggested in *The Measure of a Man*. Again, ethically dubious Starfleet scientists attempt to appropriate the new android as if she were Starfleet property.

Moore's work was soon to advance him to a leading position in the *Star Trek* writing hierarchy. Though his writing contains a consistent strain of ironic humour, he also proved particularly effective at developing the backgrounds of the major alien races in a way that often emphasises their cultural backgrounds. In *The Defector* he provides the first really sympathetic portrayal of a Romulan, as Admiral Jarok defects to the Federation in order to prevent what he expects to be a ruinous and futile war. Throughout the story, Jarok emphasises that he is a Romulan patriot who has chosen certain exile and estrangement from his entire family in order to follow his conscience. When he discovers that he has really been used as part of a Romulan plot to provoke war over control of the Neutral Zone, he commits suicide.

Two of Moore's other stories reposition the Klingons in a new light and place much emphasis on the 'nobility' of aspects of their culture.

In *The Bonding*, we see Klingon ethics in a newly positive way, as Worf's 'joining' with an orphaned boy in the 'R'ssstai' bonding ceremony helps the boy come to terms with his mother's death. In *Sins of the Father* Worf voluntarily returns to the Klingon homeworld to stand trial for his late father's alleged treachery. If convicted he may be executed, but he is prepared to face up to this in order to uphold his family honour. Yet when, with Picard's help, he discovers that the Klingon High Council have manufactured the evidence of his father's treason, he opts to accept 'discommendation' – the dishonouring of himself and his family – to avoid the escalation of a dangerous political situation that could cause civil war in the Klingon Empire and threaten the stability of the Klingon–Federation peace. Ironically, this is the most 'honourable' choice Worf can make, and he learns that 'honour' itself – that most prized Klingon virtue – is very much a matter of interpretation. From here onwards Moore becomes the main writer for 'Klingon stories'.

Under the guidance of Piller's writing team, *TNG* was to move decisively from being a purely episodic series towards a number of story arcs that would create the 'serial' mode eventually to dominate *DS9* and *Voyager*. Partly as a consequence of this, the third season episodes began to veer away from a definite sense of 'closure'. The convention of 'closure' – whereby each story's narrative threads are neatly tied up in a 'definite ending' – dominated both Hollywood cinema in its 'studio system' era and network TV in its hegemonic period. But one of the key elements of the new era of 'televisuality' was the abandonment of the insistence on closure in TV series drama. This came particularly into focus at the beginning of the 1990s with the emergence of the 'surrealist soap opera' *Twin Peaks*, with its highly ambiguous patterns of narrative and of the first season of the paranoid–UFO conspiracy series *The X-Files*, in which almost every episode ended without any definite resolution. Such TV series had begun to take on more and more of the qualities of 'serious' drama, wherein formulaic 'feelgood' endings are generally avoided. Though it is true that a few episodes – such as *The Most Toys*, where the self-obsessed Kivas Fajo, who kidnaps Data for his 'collection', resembles similar figures from the original series (like Harry Mudd and Apollo); *Allegiance*, – where Picard is kidnapped by powerful energy beings who (in an echo of *The Savage Curtain*) subject him to a behavioural experiment; and *A Matter of Perspective*, which features Riker being put on trial for murder (recalling Scotty's trial in *Wolf in the Field*) – tend to follow the earlier model of closure, most of the series' episodes tend towards very ambiguous resolutions.

Increasingly, members of the crew are faced with situations which counterpose their 'utopian' Federation ideals against the often intractable political and social realities of various alien societies. In *The Ensigns of Command* Data has to persuade a stubborn leader of a doomed colony to order the evacuation of his people. Finally he realises that he can only achieve this by a demonstration of force, destroying the aqueduct which is the colony's 'lifeline'. In *The Survivors* Picard can do nothing to punish 'Kevin', a pacifistic 'super being' who in his rage once used his powers to wipe out an entire race and can only leave him to wrestle with his conscience. The situation depicted in *The High Ground*, where Beverly Crusher (who has now returned to replace Pulaski) is captured and held hostage by a terrorist group, is a thinly-veiled allegory for the 'troubles' in Northern Ireland, and as such was banned from *TNG*'s initial British run on BBC 2. Significantly, though Crusher is extricated from her predicament, Picard's intervention does nothing to resolve the conflict. Under Berman and Piller's guidance, the moral certainties of the Roddenberry era have been replaced by a new open-endedness which gives *TNG*'s stories more resonance and depth. In perhaps the most memorable episode of the season, the complex and witty 'time paradox' story *Yesterday's Enterprise*, we are suddenly and shockingly transported to a new time line in which the Federation is at war with the Klingons and in which Tasha Yar is still alive. Although the 'normal' time line is ultimately restored, the episode proposes that ultimately any apparent 'resolutions' that *Star Trek* may appear to present are subject to the vagaries of the space–time continuum, which creates an infinite number of possible futures – a dramatic space in which all the stories are potentially 'open-ended'.

With the *Star Trek* writers having broken new ground by introducing the morally ambiguous stories of season three, the main focus in season four is now on the emotional lives of the central characters. Many episodes now include sub-plots, often with a similar theme that reflects on that of the main story, allowing stories which incorporate more fully all the members of the 'ensemble cast'. The most striking narrative innovation of this season is the number of episodes that deal with personal relationships and the characters' family backgrounds. In *Galaxy's Child* the sexually reticent Geordi meets the real Leah Brahms, who (to his great embarrassment) turns out to be a very different personality from the hologram that he became attracted to in *Booby Trap*. In *The Host* Beverly falls in love with a member of the Trill race, who are symbiotic creatures consisting of a human 'host' and a worm-like 'symbiont'. When her lover dies but is given a new female host, she decides she cannot pursue the relationship. It could be said that in these stories *Star Trek* begins to take its characters' sexuality seriously for the first time, and in *The Host* even 'flirts' with gay issues.

Much of the season concentrates on the family backstories of the major characters, continuing a trend begun in the third season's *The Offspring* and *Sins of the Father*. Some episodes incorporate narrative elements more characteristic of soap opera than adventure-series drama. In Moore's *Family* we see Picard (still recuperating from his ordeal with the Borg) on vacation in his native France and attempting to build bridges with his estranged brother, René. In a comic sub-plot, Worf's adoptive human parents appear on board the *Enterprise* and proceed to embarrass him at every opportunity. In *Reunion*, Worf's former lover, K'Ehleyr, presents him with his son, Alexander. Later in the episode she is killed and he faces the prospect of single parenthood. In Rick Berman's *Brothers* Data's creator, Dr Noonian Soong, whom he regards as his 'father', creates an 'emotions chip' for him which is stolen by Lore, his evil 'brother'. In *Future Imperfect* Riker is given an 'imaginary family' by his Romulan captors as part of an elaborate attempt to get him to reveal secret information. These 'family' stories rarely depict harmonious situations and their portrayal of characters who are 'married to their careers' is largely devoid of sentimentality.

A different kind of 'family crisis' is the focus of *Suddenly Human*, in which Jono, a teenage human whose real parents were killed when their planet was attacked by the ruthlessly militaristic Talarians, is captured by the *Enterprise*. Jono has been raised by the Talarians and regards himself as one of them. Though appalled by their militaristic values, Picard eventually has to respect the boy's wishes and return him to his adoptive father, despite the physical abuse which it seems the boy has been subjected to during his upbringing. As a galactic 'diplomat' Picard often has to demonstrate his respect for other cultures, even if in doing so he has to override his Federation values. In such episodes Roddenberry's utopian liberalism is placed in a more challenging context. The 'neat' resolutions which characterised episodes in the first two seasons are no longer available.

The fourth season saw the addition of three important new writers – Brannon Braga, Joe Menosky, and Jeri Taylor. Each was to bring particularly distinctive qualities to the series. Braga, who with Moore was to become the most prolific writer in *TNG*'s final seasons, demonstrated a predilection for stories which are influenced by the horror genre, often fused with elements of high-camp 'weird science'. In his *Identity Crisis* – perhaps the nearest *Star Trek* has got to a 'zombie' story – Geordi is almost 'absorbed' by the 'ultraviolet light beings' of Tarchannen III. Menosky's stories often deal with elaborate deceptions or extraordinary psychological states. His contributions to the fourth season show examples of both tendencies. In *Legacy*, Tasha Yar's sister manipulates the sympathy of the crew to double-cross them in an internal power struggle on her planet. In *Nth Degree* an energy surge from an alien probe temporarily causes the insecure Barclay to become a 'genius', newly self-confident in his abilities. Taylor's stories tend more towards political and social realism. In *The Wounded* – which introduces new 'villains', the Cardassians – a 'rogue' Starfleet captain attacks and destroys several Cardassian ships in an attempt to provoke a Federation–Cardassian war and Picard is forced to help the Cardassians track him down. In *The Drumhead* a 'show trial' is 'staged' of a crew member who has covered up his Romulan ancestry and thus has been linked with sabotage. The trial is conducted by the 'hard-line' Starfleet admiral, Norah Satie, whose paranoia and power-fixation suggests parallels to the McCarthyite 'witch hunt' trials of the 1950s. In an important move away from the naïve idealism often displayed in earlier episodes, it is established that – despite its officially tolerant ethics – the Federation itself is being compromised by its constant engagement in the intrigues of galactic politics.

The season's 'political' episodes begin to develop the *realpolitik* ethos which will later come to dominate *Deep Space Nine*. In the more complex moral universe that is now being depicted, Picard and his crew often have to accede to varying alien viewpoints in intractable situations. In *Clues*, when the isolationist Paxans demand that the entire crew's memory is wiped to keep their existence a secret, Picard has no choice but to grant their wishes. In *First Contact* a surgically-altered Riker is sent to 'observe' the Malcorians, a culture which the Federation is studying in order to consider whether to make formal contact. Riker becomes embroiled in internal Malcorian politics, which involve a strong belief that Malcorians are the only sentient beings in the universe. Finally it is clear that Malcorian society is not yet politically evolved enough to have contact with the Federation and the ethics of such covert attempts at intervention by the Federation are rigorously questioned. As the key diplomatic figure in maintaining the delicate balance of power, Picard's liberal-humanitarian credentials are frequently held up to investigation. He has to defend the Federation's pacifistic, tolerant, culturally relativistic values while committing himself to a position of military strength that will enable him to maintain the negotiated peace with its aggressive rivals. As such he has to contend with various subterfuges from both sides, and finally to stand in defence of Federation values against the forces of internal decay. In Echevarria's *The Mind's Eye* he has to enact some delicate diplomacy when Geordi is captured by Romulans who are plotting to break the Federation–Klingon treaty. In Moore's two-part 'Klingon epic', *Redemption*, Worf temporarily leaves Starfleet to participate in the power-struggle for control of the Klingon Empire. Again Picard plays master-diplomat, becoming the arbiter of succession to the Chancellorship.

The emphasis of the stories in the fifth season shifts towards social and psychological themes. The season's only major 'political' episode is the two-part *Unification* (written by Jeri Taylor, Rick Berman and Michael Piller), which features the return of Leonard Nimoy as Spock, now living 'under cover' on Romulus, where he is working with the dissident movement. At first there is suspicion that Spock has defected and the first half of the story concerns Picard's own 'search for Spock'. It transpires that Spock is in fact working with the Romulan 'underground' as part of a movement that hopes to reunite Romulans and Vulcans, who are genetically virtually identical but who diverged centuries ago, with the Vulcans following the path of 'logic' and the Romulans forming an aggressive military empire. In the role he frequently assumes as 'go-between', Picard helps to heal the split between Spock and his father by sharing the 'mind meld' he had carried out with Sarek in the third season episode of the same name. Inevitably the main focus of the episode is on the psychological 'link' this creates between 'old' and 'new' generations of *Star Trek* characters. The political situation on Romulus characteristically remains unresolved.

Three episodes focus on the problematical ethics of first contact and the Prime Directive. *Darmok* is a 'linguistic thriller' in which Picard has to decode the entirely metaphorical language of the Tamarians in order to make effective contact and avoid violent conflict. In *The Masterpiece Society* the *Enterprise* intervenes to prevent a planet with a 'perfect' genetically-engineered population which has remained isolated for many generations being destroyed by a stray fragment of a star, but this results in social destabilisation as key members of the society opt to leave the colony. Here Picard is caught between the principle of the Prime Directive and the Federation's equally strong belief in the rights of the individual. Rene Echevarria's *The Perfect Mate* is an 'updated' version of the original series' *Elaan of Troyius*, with Picard rather than Kirk falling in love with a 'princess' being transported on the *Enterprise* for an arranged marriage that will guarantee political stability between warring races. Again the Prime Directive precludes the Federation intervening in a process that clearly violates its notions of individual rights. Following the Directive is seen more and more as a 'messy', difficult business, one which frequently results in unpleasant 'side-effects'.

Here, as in a number of other episodes that serve to deepen our understanding of the main characters, there is renewed (if less direct) focus on 'family' themes. In Joe Menosky's bizarre psychological drama, *Hero Worship*, Data becomes a 'surrogate father' to a bereaved young boy who temporarily decides he is an 'android'. In *New Ground* Worf's son Alexander comes to live with him on the *Enterprise* and Worf has to cope with the pressures of raising a child caught between Federation and Klingon values who has little interest in following 'the path of the warrior'. This produces some memorable comic scenes as Worf attempts in vain to maintain his 'cool' demeanour, but it also provides considerable insight into Worf's internal struggle to balance human and Klingon values. In the ground-breaking *The Inner Light* a probe launched by a long-extinct species causes Picard to mentally experience an entire lifetime as a member of their race, during which time he attains the happy family life which as a Starship captain he has never been able to have.

Though these episodes all transmit essentially affirmative messages about the characters, other stories continue to challenge the Roddenberryesque ideal of 'perfect' Starfleet officers. In *The Game* almost the entire crew becomes addicted to a (highly dangerous) new computer game. *The First Duty* shows how even the 'clean cut' Wesley Crusher can allow himself to be compromised, when he becomes involved in a 'cover up' after the death of a colleague at Starfleet Academy. In *Conundrum*, when the crew lose their memories (and thus are temporarily stripped of their Starfleet ethics), they jostle competitively for power. *Ensign Ro* introduces a new character of that name who is often belligerent and insubordinate to senior officers. Under Piller's tutelage the new writing staff have by now redefined the nature of the treatment of character in *Star Trek*, so that the *Enterprise* now appears to be a community full of essentially fallible individuals.

Other stories with 'darker' psychological themes include *Violations*, which deals with the 'mental rape' inflicted on Troi by a telepathic alien; and another one of Moore's powerful explorations of Klingon mores in *Ethics*, in which an apparently dying Worf, preferring death to paralysis after a severe accident, asks his son Alexander to assist him in ritual suicide. These episodes, however, have relatively 'positive' resolutions, whereas others end in disappointment and even despair. In Echevarria's *I, Borg* the crew rescue a solitary Borg, who gradually comes to acquire some individuality and even a name, 'Hugh'. But Picard has no option but to return Hugh to the collective, where he will be 'reassimilated'. In Taylor's *The Outcast* (whose scenario closely resembles that of Ursula Le Guin's classic SF study of ambivalent sexuality, *The Left Hand of Darkness*) Riker falls in love with a member of an androgynous race who is secretly 'female'. He plans to help her escape from the 'reprogramming' that is planned for her, but finds he is too late. The 'woman' rejects him, having been successfully 'reconverted' to a genderless state, and Riker is left distraught.

An increasing proportion of episodes feature parallel dimensions and time-line distortions. In *The Next Phase* Ro and La Forge are shifted by a transporter accident into another dimension, which causes them to become temporarily invisible. In *Cause and Effect* the ship is caught up in a 'time loop', of which at first only Beverly is aware. Each sequence of the loop ends in the *Enterprise*'s destruction, and Data has to use his initiative to break the chain. In *A Matter of Time* Rasmussen, a 'scientist' who claims to be from the twenty-sixth century, arrives and causes much irritation to the crew as he attempts to 'observe history' without interfering. However, Rasmussen turns out to be a conman from the twenty-second century who has stolen the twenty-sixth century time ship. In *Time's Arrow* Data's head is discovered in an excavation of nineteenth-century artefacts under San Francisco and he is forced to return to that time period (where he comes into contact with a younger Guinan and authors Mark Twain and Jack London) in order to uncover an alien plot to sabotage the stability of established time lines. These stories take varying approaches to the notions of time paradox first developed in *Time Squared* and *Yesterday's Enterprise*. The existence of an apparently infinite multiplicity of time lines now suggests a 'multiverse' in which there may be any number of possible consequences of a particular action. As far back as *Who Mourns for Adonais?*, *Star Trek* had always rejected fixed notions of destiny, so taking up an existentialist position which stresses the importance of human choice over 'gods' or 'cosmic forces'. But as the sophistication of individual stories grows, so does the range and complexity of possible choices the characters face.

With a settled writing team in place, the sixth season demonstrates a remarkable narrative range, ranging from the (increasing) elements of comic parody in the stories to some very serious psychological explorations. Moore, Braga, Menosky and Echevarria now dominate the writing process, with over two-thirds of the writing credits in their names. With the backstories of the major characters now well established, the action flows more naturally from their interplay. There is less emphasis on the 'family' themes of the last two seasons and the evocation of 'social themes' is less 'pointed' than before. The season includes some of the most challenging drama ever presented in *Star Trek*. In Braga's disturbing 'play inside a play' story, *Frame of Mind*, Riker is captured by aliens and projected into various false realities which he has to mentally break through to escape. In Echevarria's *Second Chances* Riker is confronted with a 'real-life' double of himself created by a transporter accident some years earlier. Yet this 'duplicate Riker' is not a typical *Star Trek* temporary double, but a person who must live out his life in the shadow of his more successful 'other self'. In Moore's philosophical conundrum *Tapestry*, Picard 'dies' to confront Q in the 'afterlife' and is given a series of choices that will crucially affect the development of his future. Increasingly, what may be reality and what may be fantasy, illusion or hologram projection is seen as a matter of perspective. This is perhaps most powerfully realised in *Chain of Command* (written by Moore and Frank Abetemarco), in which a number of scenes graphically portray the torture of Picard by the Cardassian, Gul Madred. By the end of the torture process, Picard is ready to agree to whatever construction his torturer puts on reality.

One of the major developing themes of the series seems to be the appropriately Einsteinian one of 'relativity', with the stories increasingly featuring varying perspectives on the nature of reality. Indeed, 'Einstein' himself appears in the season's final episode, *Descent*, engaged in a holodeck poker game with Data, 'Isaac Newton' and the (real-life) Stephen Hawking. In *Star Trek*, relativity is as much psychological as spatial and temporal. Several episodes present the characters with new 'relative' perspectives. In Moore's unashamedly nostalgic homage, *Relics*, the original series' engineer Scotty is discovered frozen in stasis and has to adjust his perspectives to a new century. In *Rascals*, when a transporter accident temporarily turns Picard, Ro, Guinan and Keiko into 12-year olds, Ro – who like Kira in *DS9* was brought up in a Bajoran refugee camp – is able to experience elements of a happy childhood for the first time. In *True Q* Amanda Rogers, a young

Starfleet trainee, suddenly discovers she has undreamed-of powers which, after Q's arrival, lead to her leaving the ship to join the Q continuum. In *Realm of Fear* (a characteristic Brannon Braga episode with horror genre overtones) Barclay's perception of 'creatures' he encounters in the transporter beam is thought by other members of the crew to be a paranoid delusion brought on by the phenomenon of 'transporter psychosis'. But when – surprisingly – the 'creatures' turn out to be real, Barclay's inner fears are dispelled.

In the season's two 'Klingon stories', Worf himself has to adjust and develop his perspectives on Klingon culture. In Braga's two-part *Birthright* he takes leave to penetrate a former Romulan prison camp to search for his late father, whom he has heard may still be alive. Surprisingly, this proves to be a false rumour, and Worf's attempt at heroic rescue is subverted when he discovers Romulans and Klingons, having now intermarried, living together peacefully. In Moore's *Rightful Heir* Worf has a vision in which the legendary Klingon 'spiritual leader', Kahless, reappears, so causing a crisis in belief in the whole Klingon empire. But this Kahless is a genetically engineered clone whom Worf eventually persuades the Klingon leader Gowron to install with the honorary (and long-defunct) title of 'Emperor' in order to unite the spiritual and political sides of the Empire. In both stories Worf's idealised Klingon beliefs are counterposed against the rationality of his human upbringing and his Starfleet training.

After the death of Tasha Yar, *TNG* had been criticised for keeping its main female characters in 'caring' roles. A number of episodes in this season focus on making both Beverly Crusher and Deanna Troi more assertive. In *Suspicions* Crusher risks her life by piloting a shuttlecraft into a sun's corona to prove the efficacy of a new shielding device. In Echevarria's *Face of the Enemy* Troi is kidnapped by members of the Romulan underground and made to impersonate a member of the Tal Shiar, the powerful Romulan 'secret service'. In order to maintain the illusion, she has to act with an uncharacteristic ruthlessness. In *Man of the People* a 'mind link' with a Lumerian ambassador ages her and temporarily changes her personality. She randomly picks out and seduces a young ensign and violently attacks several crew members. Yet the sudden 'transformation' of these characters into 'action heroes' is not always a convincing one, as their personalities seem bound by their 'caring' nature.

As the end of the series begins to draw close, there is something of a return to more 'traditional' *Star Trek* themes. In the action thriller *Starship Mine* Picard takes on the 'Kirk' role of 'action-hero' when he is stranded alone on the *Enterprise* and has to prevent a group of terrorists taking it over. In the 'infinite diversity' story *The Quality of Life* Data fights for the rights of the exocomps, machines developed as tools for repairing computers which have 'evolved' into sentient beings. In *Lessons*, the dilemmas and loneliness of command are again stressed when Picard falls in love with a subordinate officer and is forced to order her into dangerous situations. He finally realises that the relationship will be untenable, and accepts the situation with his usual stoicism. There is also renewed focus on the holodeck. In *A Fistful of Datas* a holodeck malfunction traps Worf and Alexander in a spoof 'western' setting in which all the 'baddies' become holographic images of Data. In *Ship in a Bottle* the hologram of Professor Moriarty, who became self-aware in the first season's *Elementary, Dear Data*, re-emerges.

By the time of the production of *TNG*'s seventh and final season *DS9* had completed its first season, plans were already underway for *Voyager* and the *Next Generation* crew were now being 'lined up' to take the place of the original series' stars in a new movie series. Control of the movies, as of all three TV series, was to rest with the same team, led by Berman and Piller. The final season of *TNG* consciously seeks to 'tie up loose threads' while still leaving narrative options open for the planned films and succeeding series. There is also a considerable attempt to define the series as a 'cosmic drama', within which the theme of human destiny is always prominent. The format of the series as originally devised by Roddenberry made romantic inter-crew relationships very difficult to fit into plot lines, but as *TNG* takes on more and more elements of the serial mode this restriction begins to disappear. Both *Attached* and *Eye of the Beholder* break the established *Star Trek* mould by suggesting ongoing relationships between crew members. In *Eye of the Beholder*, Troi begins a relationship with Worf. In *Attached*, Picard and Crusher are kidnapped and bonded together by a device that causes them to experience a telepathic link. Unable to suppress his feelings in the usual way, Picard reveals the love he had for Beverly when her husband Jack was alive, and his subsequent feelings of guilt.

A number of episodes re-emphasise 'family' themes, but the 'family members' who appear mostly turn out to be 'fakes' or 'ghosts': in *Bloodlines* Picard is provided with a 'son' (actually the son of a former lover whose DNA has been altered in a 'revenge plot' by the Ferengi, Dai Mon Bok); in *Firstborn* a mature Alexander returns from the future to prevent the murder of his father Worf; in *Homeward* Worf encounters his adoptive human 'brother', Nikolai Rozhenko; in *Dark Page*, an unusually tragic 'Lwaxana story', we learn of Lwaxana Troi's heartbreak over the death of her first daughter, which up till now she had kept secret from Deanna; in *Interface* Geordi has to face up to the death of his mother; and in *Inheritance* we meet Data's 'mother' – the 'wife' of his creator, Dr Juliana Soong – who, unknown to herself, is actually another android.

Other episodes, particularly those contributed by Braga, emphasise the fantastical element, with allusions to the horror genre, that becomes prevalent at this stage in the series. In *Genesis* members of the crew 'de-evolve' into 'wild beasts' and in *Emergence*, the holodeck becomes the scene of a surreal collision of elements from different holoprograms as the *Enterprise* itself begins to evolve on its own embryonic intelligence. In *Sub Rosa* Beverly Crusher is 'haunted' by the ghostly 'lover' of both her mother and grandmother. In the case of Data, who had often been exploited as a source of comic relief, this leads to darker and more ambiguous stories. In Moore's *Thine Own Self* he accidentally poisons a village on a primitive planet with radiation. In Menosky's extraordinary *Masks* he absorbs the memory of an entire ancient civilisation and begins to speak in various alien 'tongues'. Although as a character he is essentially unchanged, in these stories Data is far from the unthreatening 'Pinocchio' figure of the early seasons.

As the series moves towards its climax, the overall 'galactic politics' story arc is re-emphasised. *Gambit* is an adventure story linked to inter-species intrigue and conspiracy, in which Riker and Picard infiltrate a mercenary ship engaged in a hunt for an ancient Vulcan thought-weapon. Both *Journey's End* and the penultimate episode *Pre-Emptive Strike* specifically link *TNG* to *DS9* by describing the consequences of the treaty between the Federation and the Cardassians which has secured peace following the Cardassians' withdrawal from the planet Bajor. In Moore's *Journey's End*, Picard is faced with an ironic and distasteful historical parallel as he is forced to demand that Durvan III, a planet settled by a group of Native Americans, be evacuated under the terms of the treaty. Eventually the settlers opt to stay under Cardassian rule, despite somewhat dubious assurances that they will be left alone. Durvan III is just one of the planets in the 'demilitarised zone' on which Federation colonies had been established. By the time of *Pre-Emptive Strike* resistance against Cardassian rule by these colonies has reached the stage of armed rebellion in the form of the Maquis, a group of terrorists who oppose the Federation–Cardassian treaty. The action in *Pre-Emptive Strike* is seen very much from Ro's point of view. Ro is dispatched by Picard to infiltrate the Maquis, but later defects to them. This defection is portrayed as entirely honourable and the Maquis are shown to have an extremely worthy cause. In creating the Maquis–Cardassian–Bajoran story arc, the position of the Federation as an unambiguous force for good in the galaxy is challenged. Although the Federation has made a treaty with the Cardassians with the worthy intention of ending a bloody war, the colonists in the demilitarised zone have certainly become victims as a result.

Three episodes also make further strong challenges to established notions of the Federation as morally 'righteous'. *Force of Nature* features a cautionary ecological parallel, when it is revealed that warp drive – the key element in all twenty-fourth century space travel – has in fact been 'polluting' areas of space for some time, and a new 'maximum warp' speed has to be set. In *Homeward* Picard's decision to allow the entire population of a primitive planet to be wiped out rather than break the Prime Directive and attempt to save them is seen to be somewhat callous. In Moore's *The Pegasus* Riker is forced to choose between his loyalty to Starfleet protocols and his loyalty to Picard, when he becomes involved in a plot by his former captain, Admiral Pressman, to develop a Federation cloaking device. Again, senior elements of Starfleet are depicted as being morally suspect.

Ultimately, *TNG* is not, however, a 'political drama' as such. It combines its perspective on 'galactic politics' with a sense of the mutability of destiny, both on a 'cosmic' and on an individual scale. *TNG*'s ever-mutable 'alternative time lines' are used to focus and develop *Star Trek*'s liberal-humanist ethos by showing that neither political nor personal histories are fixed. This attitude is epitomised in Braga's *Parallels*, in which Worf finds himself 'sliding' between various parallel universes. The episode ends in an extraordinary climax as the different parallel universes intersect and thousands of identical '*Enterprises*' appear. Inside each of these *Enterprises* is a crew composed of parallel 'versions' of the characters we know. Each ship comes from a different political 'reality', in one of which the *Enterprise* is about to be destroyed by the Borg. The implication is that the *Star Trek* universe contains all possible futures.

In the final episode, the feature-length *All Good Things* (written jointly by Braga and Moore), Picard similarly finds himself shifting between various time periods – the beginning of his command on the *Enterprise*, the present, and 25 years into the future. *All Good Things* culminates the entire *Next Generation* story arc begun in the pilot episode *Encounter at Farpoint*. Supervising the proceedings as Picard experiences the 'timeshifts' is Q, who has returned to see the final outcome of his 'trial' of humanity. Q returns Picard to the moment that life began in a primordial swamp on Earth, to demonstrate that he must act to prevent a time anomaly growing that will threaten the existence of humanity in the past as well as the future. In the future time Picard (now a retired admiral) and Beverly (now a starship captain) have been married and divorced; Geordi has left Starfleet to become a successful novelist; Data is now a professor at Cambridge University; Deanna Troi is dead, for unknown reasons; Worf and Riker, still torn by jealousy over Deanna, are bitter rivals; and Riker himself has become embittered and positively dislikeable. But, as ever, it is stressed that this somewhat grim scenario is just one possible future. The *Star Trek* audience is thus given a 'false ending' which fits with the main humanistic message of *TNG*: that individuals, not 'gods' or 'cosmic forces' choose their own destiny. In *Star Trek's* Einsteinian universe, destiny, like space and time, is always relative.

The Next Generation stands as a television landmark – a series launched outside the aegis of the major networks that produced seven years of consistently high ratings and two further 'spin-off' series. After its beginnings as a virtual homage to the original series, it develops a unique identity of its own, expanding towards the complex political scenario that would later dominate *DS9*. Though much of the idealism of Roddenberry's original vision is retained, a far more realistic view is taken of the imperfections of, and potential for conflict between, individual characters. In the worlds of *DS9* and *Voyager* that followed, humans would become increasingly outnumbered and the ideals and goals of the Federation itself would be vigorously challenged. Although Roddenberry's humanist principles would still be respected, the 'human factor' would no longer be the only formula for solving the problems that would be encountered.

The release of the first *Next Generation* movie, *Generations* (1994), followed swiftly on from the end of the series. With Berman as producer, Braga and Moore as co-writers and experienced *TNG* director David Carson behind the camera, there were none of the production battles that plagued the 1980s movies. Yet, partly due to its need to 'bridge the gap' between old and new casts, the film never matches up to the imaginative possibilities explored in the later seasons of *TNG*. *Generations* is basically an action-adventure movie with a very conventional villain, the 'mad galactic genius', Dr Tolian

Soran (played with over-the-top relish by Malcolm McDowell). Although there is a strong 'fantasy' element, with Picard meeting Captain Kirk in a 'timeless' zone known as the Nexxus, this is again rather conventionally presented, and lacks the sense of generic experimentation the audience had seen in recent TV episodes. The treatment of Kirk by the *Next Generation* writers is, like that of Spock in *Unification*, somewhat over-reverent, and lacks the sense of self-reflexive irony displayed in Scotty's return in *Relics*. The story centres on Picard having to locate Kirk and seek his assistance in stopping Soran, during which, in perhaps the film's most sentimentalised scene, Kirk dies a suitably heroic death, declaring that he had 'made a difference' one more time. Kirk's death scene seems a somewhat contrived way of finally ending the original series' era. The rest of the *Next Generation* cast are given somewhat peripheral roles in the film, although Data's experiments with his new 'emotions chip' provide an entertaining sub-plot. Despite being produced by the *TNG* 'team', *Generations* has perhaps more resemblance to the 1980s *Star Trek* movies than it has to the TV series.

Star Trek: First Contact (1997), however, makes use of many of the elements that lifted *TNG* above the level of the both original series and the 1980s movies. Directed by Jonathan Frakes and again co-written by Moore and Braga, it has a grand cinematic sweep which enlarges on the themes of human and individual destiny that had dominated the last few seasons of *TNG*. The device of travel into the past to 'save' the future had been used in *Star Trek* before, but here the obvious clichés of sending the crew back to the present are avoided. Instead *First Contact* focuses on the murkiest period of *Star Trek's* future chronology, the twenty-first century, which from the time of the original series had been referred to as an era of global devastation. The plot centres around an attempt by the Borg to prevent legendary inventor Zephram Cochrane launching Earth's first warp-drive ship. The launch is a crucial moment in Earth history which will bring about Earth's first contact with aliens, without which the progress towards the utopian society that will be in place by Kirk's time, 200 years later, would be impossible. The crew know that if they fail, they face a future in which the Borg will completely control humanity. If they succeed, the impetus provided by the 'first contact' will eventually unite the human race into a utopian world culture without racism, sexism, poverty, starvation, religious divisions or war – in which materialism and greed for individual possessions have been abandoned.

The climax to the movie provides a priceless moment for *Trek* cognoscenti. The great moment of 'first contact' nears as the friendly alien ship lands near Cochrane's camp. We see the ship's doors open and a figure emerges, clad in a long, white, hooded robe. Cochrane approaches the alien, somewhat nervously. Then the alien pushes back his hood, to reveal his pointed *Vulcan* ears. He raises his hand in a gesture familiar to all *Star Trek* fans and opens his mouth to deliver the inevitable 'Live long … and prosper'. The bemused Cochrane, like a first-timer at a *Star Trek* convention, attempts but cheerfully fails to make the distinctive Vulcan hand-sign. Here the ironic, 'knowing' humour that was often overplayed for cheap laughs in the 1980s film series is used in the service of a sophisticated self-referential narrative. The revelation of the 'Vulcan ears' – the iconic element that first defined *Star Trek* – creates a 'sense of wonder' which is simultaneously 'real' and 'tongue-in-cheek'. It presents itself as a 'key' that unlocks a crucial 'secret' of *Star Trek* future history and implies that, in order to achieve their utopia, the human race *needed* to absorb the Vulcan rationalistic viewpoint that Dr McCoy would so often mock in the original series. Poverty and prejudice are, after all, 'illogical'. This admission is a measure of the extent to which *The Next Generation* had shifted the emphasis of *Star Trek* from the naïve humanism of Roddenberry's day to a far more relativistic stance.

Chapter 5

Intrigue, prophecy, Armageddon: *Deep Space Nine*

Deep Space Nine, which was launched in January 1993 with Berman and Piller as both creators and executive producers, provides a parallel narrative to the last two seasons of *TNG* (which were broadcast simultaneously). Its major writers, Ira Steven Behr, Robert Hewitt Wolfe and Peter Allan Fields, had all contributed to a number of *Next Generation* episodes and were thus very familiar with the 'rules' of the *Star Trek* universe. Behr, Wolfe and Fields all proved adept at the 'political' stories that dominate the series, with Behr – an accomplished comic writer who had provided comic pieces such as *Qpid* for *TNG* – also specialising in the regular 'Ferengi stories'. Michael Piller made frequent contributions to the writing in the first two seasons, with more occasional contributions from Rick Berman, Jeri Taylor and Naren Shankar. After season two, when *TNG* came to an end, the addition of Ronald D. Moore and Rene Echevarria gave the team added depth. As the product of a settled and experienced group of writers, *DS9* maintains a consistency of themes and storylines that no previous *Star Trek* series had been able to achieve. Many episodes were co-written by several members of the team, with the result that, at least until Moore and Echevarria's arrival, it is harder to distinguish the style of any one writer.

From its inception, *DS9* was conceived of as a 'darker' version of *Star Trek*, in deliberate contrast to the optimism of the original series and much of *TNG*. This is reflected in its visual tone, which eschews the 'clean', brightly-lit look of the Starfleet ships and uses subdued lighting in the form of a diffusion filter, as well as a great deal of high-contrast shadow. According to production supervisor Dan Curry:

> *Deep Space Nine* has a darker look. The stars are printed in a little bit

darker and the contrast ratio is a little bit greater. If you'll notice, the shadow side of the *DS9* station is much darker than the shadow side of the *Enterprise* under most circumstances. Part of it is that we took our look from NASA orbital shots – real photographs of the space shuttle and other space vehicles. What we ended up with might be termed a grittier look. (Dillard, 1994, p. 169)

Even in its lighter moments *DS9* is always primarily a *political* drama, centred upon a former Cardassian space station which has recently been occupied by the Federation in the wake of the withdrawal of Cardassian occupation forces from Bajor. After the discovery of the wormhole which allows access to the 'Gamma Quadrant' (a previously unreachable area of space) from the more familiar 'Alpha Quadrant', *DS9* becomes a key strategic location in the galactic balance of power. The Federation have been called in as protectors of Bajor, a planet with a highly theocratic tradition which is now riven with internal strife in the wake of the ending of the 40-year occupation. Many Bajorans hope that they can soon join the Federation, but there is understandably strong suspicion of outsiders. At first the Federation's role is that of a 'peace-keeping force' but as the series progresses it becomes a major player in a long and complex series of political intrigues and shifting alliances that eventually threaten to lead to a galactic 'Armageddon'. Meanwhile, the spiritual traditions and prophecies of Bajor form a constant backdrop to the action and a continual challenge to the scientific humanism of the Federation.

DS9 fulfils the desire of Berman and Piller – which had become apparent in the latter seasons of *TNG* – to create a version of *Star Trek* that is more oppositional and more psychologically realistic than earlier formats allowed. Now the serial mode dominates, in a way that enhances both plot and character development. While the social and political ramifications of the unfolding of the overall story arc of the series grow ever more complex, the characters are allowed to grow in a way that was never possible in the more episodic earlier series. Whereas *TNG*, with its many 'family' orientated stories, emphasised the characters' backstories, *DS9* concentrates more on the growth the characters experience as a result of the unfolding narratives of the series itself. In the earlier series the characters' roles and relationships were clearly defined by their status as members of a crew that is, short of various forms of alien intervention, always loyal and co-operative. *DS9* takes the radical (for *Star Trek*) step of setting up certain main characters in opposition to each other. The series also focuses on aliens more than ever before, with humans actually in a minority. Increasingly, human values are weighed against those of other races and cultures, and are not always found to be superior.

The series features another multi-racial ensemble cast and each of the main characters is first introduced in terms of the initial dilemmas they face, leaving much room for character development. As Commander Benjamin Sisko, Avery Brooks is *Star Trek's* first African-American 'leading man'. At first Sisko is a very reluctant hero, deeply embittered after the death of his wife Jennifer in the Borg attack depicted in *TNG's The Best Of Both Worlds* (for which he still blames Captain Picard) and he is initially unenthusiastic about taking on the assignment of commanding DS9. He has a teenage son, Jake (Cirric Lofton), whose role in the series grows in importance as he gets older. In contrast to the largely 'caring' roles of Troi and Crusher in *TNG*, the two female leads – Nana Visitor as Kira and Terry Farrell as Dax – are assertive, combative women who take leading roles in action sequences. The science officer, Lieutenant Jadzia Dax, is a beautiful young Trill who has recently been physically and mentally 'joined' with a symbiont creature that has experienced several lifetimes in both sexes. As the series opens she must adjust to her new status, as well as to a new relationship with Sisko, who had been an intimate friend of her last host, Curzon Dax (an often undisciplined, woman-ising old man who had been a leading Federation diplomat). Major Kira Nerys, the Bajoran envoy and second in command on the station, was one of the leaders of the Bajoran resistance movement which fought for many years against the Cardassians. Born in a refugee camp, her harsh experience of life has made her, at least on the surface, rather bitter and cynical. Fiercely proud of her Bajoran origins, she is at first rather suspicious of the Federation's motives in occupying the station, fearing that they could become another occu-pying force like the Cardassians. She must overcome her mistrust of Starfleet's motives in order to function fully in her post. At the same time, she has to learn to allow her emotional side to express itself after years of repression conditioned by anger against her oppressors.

The station's doctor, Julian Bashir (Siddig El Fadil) is a brilliant – if often rather socially inept – young man who has a rather romantic view of the 'frontier medicine' he will practise on DS9. His initial attempts to start a relationship with Jadzia are clumsy and ineffectual, showing that despite his advanced academic achievements he has much to learn in terms of how to conduct himself. The other major Starfleet character is Irish Chief Engineer Miles O'Brien (Colm

Meaney), who had been a minor character on the *Enterprise* in the first five seasons of *TNG*. O'Brien is also a somewhat embittered veteran of the Cardassian wars. He brings with him a family, consisting of his wife Keiko (Rosalind Chao) and their small daughter Molly. O'Brien is perhaps *Star Trek*'s most down-to-earth character, and faces the practical challenge of adapting the Cardassian-built station for Federation purposes. Bashir and O'Brien are initially at loggerheads but soon begin to develop a friendship built on a certain competitive rivalry.

The two other major characters are permanently set in opposition to each other. Both have remained in their roles on the station despite the Cardassian withdrawal. Odo (René Auberjonois) is the station's chief of security, or – to give him his popular nickname – 'constable'. He is a shape-shifter who can turn into any object at will, a plot device responsible for some of the series' most imaginative special effects. Although most of the time he exists in humanoid form, when he requires sleep he reverts to a liquid state. As yet Odo, who had been discovered by the Bajorans as a 'child', has no idea of his origins, the revelation of which will later motivate one of the major story arcs of the series. Odo is permanently suspicious of the station's Ferengi bar owner, Quark (Armin Shimerman). This is hardly surprising, as Quark is, like a 'true Ferengi', obsessed with the accumulation of profit. He is constantly involved in illegal activities, particularly the smuggling of various commodities, and is scathing about the morals of the Starfleet crew, whom he sneeringly refers to as 'hoo-mans'. Odo continually tries to catch Quark in his nefarious activities, but usually finds that Quark is one step ahead of him. The conflict between the two develops through the series into an often comic 'love–hate' relationship which is reflected in their different characters – Odo is very 'stiff' and psychologically repressed, whereas Quark is sexually expansive and capable of 'charming' himself out of almost any situation.

DS9 further redefines the nature of the various humanoid races in the *Star Trek* universe. The Ferengi are portrayed as the galaxy's ultimate capitalists, whose obsession with profit dominates their entire culture to such an extent that they even have a 'religion' based on belief in the 'Rules of Acquisition' – a set of 'commandments' which praise greed and deception as virtues. Their version of the afterlife is known as the 'Divine Treasury'. Each season has at least two 'Ferengi stories', which often gravitate towards rather farcical comic extremes. The development of the Klingon culture continues, particularly after Worf is added to the cast in season four. Key members of the Klingon hierarchy originally seen in *TNG*, such as Chancellor Gowron, have recurring 'guest' roles. Although Klingon ethics are increasingly romanticised as part of a 'warrior tradition', Klingon culture itself is also seen as decaying and essentially backward-looking. The Klingons who inhabit Quark's bar in the early part of the series are boorish, drunken and aggressive, whereas Worf (whom we come to see more and more as a very atypical Klingon) remains self-possessed, enigmatic and capable of a uniquely dry wit.

Cardassian society is portrayed as rigid and totalitarian, with a 'justice system' in which sentences are passed before trials begin and every sentence is a 'guilty' one. The Cardassians culture follows the classic pattern of fascist regimes, with 'weak' individuals such as the disabled being disposed of at birth. The political hierarchy keeps control of the population through a mass media that purveys constant propaganda. But the Cardassians are never one-dimensional 'fascists'. As the series progresses we see that dissident elements are struggling against the hierarchy, and even the former 'war criminal', Gul Dukat (Marc Alaimo), the former overlord of DS9 in its Cardassian days, is seen to have a 'charming' personality. The Cardassian 'tailor', Garak (Andrew Robinson), who lives in exile on the station and develops a strong friendship with Dr Bashir, is another extremely enigmatic figure, who may or may not be a former Cardassian spy and as such becomes one of *Star Trek's* most ambiguous characters.

The after-effects of the Cardassian occupation of Bajor are a major concern of the series. The 'holocaust' which caused the death of 15 million Bajorans has obvious parallels with that of the Jews in the Second World War. The Bajorans themselves – Kira included – are an intensely religious people, though the planet is extremely faction-alised in the wake of the Cardassians' departure. The Bajoran religion is focused on 'the prophets', divine beings who live in a 'celestial temple' and are said to protect Bajor and its inhabitants. The leading figures of the Bajoran priesthood – the 'saintly' Kai Opaka; her schem-ing, manipulative successor, Kai Winn; and Kira's sometime lover, Vedek Bareil – play important roles in the many episodes of the series that focus on Bajoran issues.

DS9 creates a new kind of 'inter-species' environment, which becomes a kind of cultural melting pot. The station itself is the site of meetings and intrigues between many different races from both sides of the wormhole. These take place in various locations on the Promenade, the 'shopping mall' of the station, and particularly at Quark's bar. In contrast to the rather 'squeaky clean' social environ-ment of *TNG's* Ten Forward lounge, Quark's has gambling tables that operate a game similar to roulette known as Dabo. He also offers all-comers access to pornographic holodeck programmes with names such as 'Vulcan love slave'. It is hardly surprising that Quark, like Q in *TNG*, regards Starfleet as staid and puritanical. Thus, while making Roddenberry's universe more politically and socially complex, *DS9* also lampoons the 'innocent' preconceptions that were built into the original series. Starfleet itself remains an honourable, idealistic institution, but the naïvety that was built into its original formulation is constantly exposed. This is partly achieved through the series' comic episodes, which balance the seriousness of the main story arcs with very broad satire that is often stretched to farcical extremes, particularly in the case of the Ferengi stories and in those set in *DS9*'s own distopian 'mirror universe'.

The opening pilot, the feature-length *Emissary* (written by Berman and Piller) opens up many of the key themes of the series. Soon after Sisko is assigned to the station, an artificially constructed stable wormhole is discovered. Inside the wormhole Sisko encounters its creators, a race of pure energy beings who exist outside time and who subject him to a series of 'visions' that send him back to two key moments of his life – his meeting with Jennifer and her death in the Borg attack. This forces him into finally shaking off the state of depression he has been caught in since his wife's death. Supplied with 'spiritual sustenance' he returns and embraces his position as head of DS9 with renewed confidence. On his return, he discovers that his meeting with the wormhole aliens has been interpreted by the Bajorans as the fulfilment of an ancient prophecy concerning an 'Emissary' who will meet with the prophets in the 'celestial temple' and become Bajor's spiritual guide. As the product of the humanistic Federation culture, Sisko is initially horrified that he is suddenly regarded by the Bajorans as a 'god-like' figure. But with the political situation in Bajor in turmoil and strong elements within Bajor calling for the expulsion of the Federation from DS9, he is finally reluctantly persuaded to accept the title. That a Starfleet commander is prepared to make such a compromise says much about the equivocal values of the series and the direct challenge to *Star Trek*'s traditional humanism that it represents. Whereas in *TNG*'s pilot, *Encounter at Farpoint*, Picard's meeting with a 'higher being' had stressed the value of the 'human factor' against the vanity and capriciousness of Q, here Sisko's encounter with the 'prophets' is the prelude to a series that will give increasing credence to the 'reality' of Bajoran spiritual beliefs.

The majority of the first season's episodes concentrate on establishing the main characters, and on building up a picture of their still-evolving (and not always harmonious) relationships. Two strongly character-driven episodes feature murder trials, a rather well-worn plot device in *Star Trek* but one which generally provides immediate psychological insights. In *Dax* Jadzia is put on trial for a murder originally committed by her last host, Curzon. As her defending counsel, Sisko has to argue that she is not responsible for Curzon's actions. But to protect the 'honour' of a high-ranking general's wife, with whom Curzon had been spending the night at the time of the murder, she refuses to defend herself. Though she is eventually exonerated, the story provides much detail of her Trill nature and establishes in her the high regard for 'honour' which also attracts her to the Klingons. In *A Man Alone*, Odo is framed by black marketeers who wish to use the station to conduct their business and his stoical reaction provides an initial insight into his stern, emotionally repressed but essentially good-hearted personality.

Many of the situations encountered tend to amplify the communication problems that initially exist between the principals. In *Dramatis Personae*, a 'telepathic matrix' is brought aboard the ship that affects the consciousness of the crew and turns the main characters against each other, so amplifying the tensions which already exist between them. In *Babel* the station is beset by a virus that makes normal speech impossible. The stories are linked by continuing 'soap opera'-type subplots such as Bashir's ineffectual attempts to romance Jadzia, Sisko's difficulties with his adolescent son, Jake, and Odo's continual pursuit of Quark. It is emphasised that DS9 is a multicultural community in which there will be less focus on the 'military' life of Starfleet as seen on *TNG's* *Enterprise*, and in which relationships between characters will be less bound by their rank and position.

The first season episodes which build up a picture of Bajoran society and politics in the aftermath of the Cardassian withdrawal naturally focus on Kira. After years as a Resistance fighter, she is forced to learn a series of difficult lessons about the realities of wielding real power. In *Past Prologue* she is at first deceived by a former colleague in the Bajoran resistance who has come to DS9 with a plan to destroy the wormhole for his own rather dubious political ends. In *Progress* she is forced to evict an old Bajoran farmer from one of Bajor's moons, which the Bajorans intend to make uninhabitable by tapping the power of its core. In *Duet*, she is charged with interrogating a Cardassian, who deceives her into thinking he is Gul Darhe'el, a former mass murderer during the occupation. Kira herself is a strong devotee of the Bajoran religion. As a consequence, she regards Sisko – the 'Emissary' – with a certain degree of awe. At the same time she is very scientifically minded and logical, which occasionally brings a clash with her faith. In many ways her personal dilemmas symbolise the clashing forces on Bajor itself, as well as the conflict between scientific and spiritual explanations that becomes a major theme of the series.

Captive Pursuit, which stresses O'Brien's compassionate nature, is something of an old-style *Star Trek* morality tale (concentrating on the morals of hunting) as O'Brien befriends the Tosk, a fully sentient humanoid creature being chased by members of the race from beyond the wormhole that created it. O'Brien risks his life to help the Tosk escape, but the Tosk itself has been genetically engineered to be hunted and the only meaning in its life is to continue to prolong the chase as long as possible until it is eventually caught and killed. The story gives a foretaste of the genetically engineered races that will be encountered later in the series and hints at a very different moral approach to such matters among the races of the still-mysterious Gamma Quadrant. Perhaps the most inventive comic episode in the first season is *Move Along Home*, which features a bizarre First Contact encounter with the Wadi, a race of inveterate game players from the Gamma Quadrant who – when they find that Quark's Dabo table is loaded – involve Sisko, Dax, Kira and O'Brien in what is apparently a 'game of life and death' by reducing them to figures in a game of their own.

Although Quark's presence is felt in every episode as bartender and perpetual schemer, *The Nagus* is the first *DS9* story to develop the background to its tongue-in-cheek depiction of Ferengi culture, which is dominated by an ultra-capitalistic ethos and gross sexism. Here Quark is shocked to discover that the Grand Nagus, the leader of Ferengi commerce, has chosen him as his successor. But Quark is a perpetual 'loser' who is never destined to achieve the vast profits he craves. Although for a while he almost believes that fantastic good fortune has come his way, his installation as Ferengi leader is finally revealed as a mere device by which the scheming Nagus can temporarily draw the fire from his enemies who are trying to bankrupt him.

The final episode of the first season, *In the Hands of the Prophets*, concerns the beginnings of the contest for the accession to the post of Kai between the moderate Vedek Bareil and Vedek Winn, a member of an orthodox sect which believes in the 'purity' of Bajoran beliefs. In

In the Hands of the Prophets Vedek Winn demands that Bajoran children be withdrawn from DS9's school because Keiko O'Brien is teaching them a conventional scientific explanation about the origins of life which contradicts the Bajoran sacred texts. Vedek Winn represents a section of the Bajoran population which, in an obvious echo of the Biblical fundamentalists, holds that their creation myths are fact. Yet despite the intolerance of Winn and her followers, the Bajoran religion is generally portrayed as compassionate and openminded. Bajor is depicted as a society whose traditional foundations have been shattered by 40 years of occupation and one which contains many isolationist elements.

The second season begins with a series of episodes that indicate dramatic developments in the Bajoran political situation. In Behr and Taylor's *The Homecoming*, Kira rescues Li Nalas – a legendary Bajoran resistance fighter whom she feels could potentially unite the planet's factions – from a Cardassian labour camp. But her political naïvety is underlined when Nalas protests that he is reluctant to enter the intrigues of Bajoran politics. As a result of her actions she is replaced as the Bajoran representative on DS9 by Nalas himself. In Fields' *The Circle* Kira discovers that the fundamentalist terrorist group, the Circle, whose isolationist 'Bajor for the Bajorans' policies place them in opposition to Federation values, are being led to Minister Jaro. In Piller's *The Siege* the Circle takes DS9 by force and Nalas is killed in its defence. When Kira exposes the Circle as being supported by the Cardassians (who hope to use it as a new 'puppet government'), Jaro is discredited, the Circle collapses, DS9 reverts to Federation rule and Kira is returned to her old job. The resourceful Vedek Winn, however, manages to distance herself from events. *The Collaborator* focuses on the election of the new Kai. Vedek Bareil, the most popular candidate and Kira's lover, has his name tarnished by accusations that during the occupation he gave the Cardassians information about the whereabouts of a rebel Bajoran base. In fact Bareil is protecting the reputation of the former Kai, Opaka, who reluctantly gave the Cardassians the information to prevent a huge massacre of civilians. Rather than have Opaka exposed, Bareil withdraws from the contest and Vedek Winn – who has cleverly manipulated the whole situation – becomes the new Kai. There is nothing that the DS9 crew can do to prevent this development, although it certainly endangers future prospects of Bajor joining the Federation.

Political realism becomes the main ethos of *DS9*, as the Starfleet crew's idealism has to be tempered by a need to preserve what is still a very delicate peace. In order to honour its treaty obligations, the Federation sometimes even has to co-operate with the fascistic Cardassians, a development which naturally makes Kira very uneasy. In the two-part *The Maquis*, when Gul Dukat is captured and held hostage by the Maquis rebels, Sisko has to work with the Cardassians for his release. Yet, as contemporaneous *TNG* episodes such as *Pre-Emptive Strike* had established, the Maquis are seen to have a very valid cause. Much of the Bajoran–Cardassian political situation which the Federation now has to deal with is centred on the after-effects of events which took place before the Federation came on the scene. Disinformation and conflicting versions of what happened during the occupation are rife. Wolfe's labyrinthine character study *The Wire* focuses on Garak, who offers Bashir a number of possible versions of his past. By the end, we are still unsure whether Garak was formerly a major player in the Cardassian hierarchy or merely a very clever liar.

Fields and Piller's deliberately exaggerated comic melodrama *Crossover* is *DS9*'s first major 'tribute' to the original series, and caustically points out the effects of the 'interventionism' that Kirk practised so blithely. An accident in the wormhole causes Kira and Bashir to be transported into the same politically corrupt parallel universe that Kirk entered in *Mirror, Mirror*. Here, Sisko appears as a rogue 'pirate captain', Odo as a vicious military controller and Kira as a ruthless and sadistic political 'dominatrix'. The 'alternative Kira' informs 'our' Kira that as a result of the previous crossover the 'alternative' Spock led the 'Terran Empire' into a newly peaceful era which subsequently left them defenceless against the combined forces of the Cardassian–Klingon–Bajoran Alliance. Consequently, 'Terrans' have now become a subjugated 'slave race'. Kira and Bashir finally escape back to the wormhole after persuading the alternative Sisko to begin a rebellion against the Alliance.

DS9's leading characters continue to face hard choices and intractable moral dilemmas, which add a personal dimension to the *realpolitik* ethos of the series. In *Sanctuary*, when an exiled race from the Gamma Quadrant come through the wormhole and claim Bajor as their mythical home, Kira is reluctantly forced to communicate the provisional government's refusal of their request to settle. In *Paradise* Sisko is temporarily stranded on a planet occupied by an idealistic group of survivors who follow a 'back to basics' philosophy, but his conscience forces him to rebel against the group's authoritarian leader. A number of episodes develop O'Brien's long-suffering nature. In *Armageddon Game* he is gravely injured and is barely kept alive by

Bashir in the midst of a war zone, and in *Tribunal* he is placed on trial by the Cardassians for supposedly supplying weapons to the Maquis. In *Whispers*, the O'Brien whose narration we have been following turns out to be a *Blade Runner*-style 'replicant', designed to sabotage a diplomatic conference. Such deliberate 'disinformation' in the narratives mirrors the many rumours and half-truths that surround the whole political situation in which the Federation is caught and further stresses the moral ambiguity of the series.

The episodes which focus on Dax establish that Trill culture, like that of Bajor, has many morally ambiguous aspects. In *Invasive Procedures* the Trill Verad (assisted by mercenary Klingons), having been rejected from the symbiosis programme, forces Bashir to remove the Dax symbiont from Jadzia's body and transfer it into himself. The rescue plan, during which Quark displays some rare heroism, succeeds just before Jadzia's body is about to give out. It emerges that those who are 'joined' form something of an elite in Trill society and that only a small proportion of Trill ever attain the honour. In *DS9*'s first fully fledged 'Klingon show', Fields' *Blood Oath*, Dax herself exhibits a questionable sense of morality by taking part in a Klingon 'revenge pact' sworn to by her previous host, Curzon Dax. The story itself is something of a tragicomic burlesque, featuring the reuniting of three 'legendary' Klingon warriors – Kor, Koloth and Kang (all veterans of the original series). After the murderous fulfilment of the pact (which results in Kor and Koloth being killed), Dax returns to *DS9*, where in the closing scenes the disapproval on the faces of Kira, Bashir and others is palpable. The conflict this points to between human and non-human perspectives, which recalls Worf's refusal to donate blood to a dying Romulan in *TNG*'s *The Enemy*, is one of the major sources of tension in the series.

Towards the end of the season, the beginnings of *DS9*'s epic depiction of the coming crisis in galactic politics are emerging. The discovery of the wormhole, to which the Bajoran priesthood gave such significance, turns out to be a 'Pandora's box' for the Federation. Although initial contacts with Gamma Quadrant civilisations are largely friendly and some colonisation is undertaken, throughout the season various rumours circulate about a huge empire in the Gamma Quadrant known as the Dominion and its semi-mythical leaders, the Founders. The closing episode of the season, *The Jem' Hadar*, opens up the new political and military crisis scenario that will dominate the rest of the series. The Jem' Hadar, reptilian creatures which the Dominion has genetically engineered to be its soldiers, and who are kept under control by their addiction to a drug known as 'ketracel-white', destroy the Gamma Quadrant Federation colony of New Bajor. The season ends on a chilling note, as Sisko realises that a Dominion invasion could be possible at any time and that, if it comes, DS9 will be the site of the first battle.

The third season brought a number of significant changes to *DS9*. With *TNG* now at an end, various members of its production team could be assigned to the new series. Some *TNG* writers, notably Braga, Taylor and Piller, were to concentrate their efforts on *Voyager*, whose launch (in January 1995) was imminent, but other writer–producers – particularly Ronald D. Moore and Rene Echevarria – became important contributors to *DS9*. The series also becomes more action-orientated as DS9 acquires its own starship, the *Defiant*, and Sisko is promoted to captain. The stories are highly diverse, developing both already established and new story arcs. The most unusual and most directly political episode is *Past Tense* (described in detail in Chapter 9), one of *DS9*'s few ventures into time travel, in which the crew are sent back to the twenty-first century and have to work to preserve the integrity of the 'Federation time line'.

The season opens with the two-part *The Search* (written by Moore, Behr and Wolfe), in which Odo discovers that the Founders, legendary leaders of the Dominion, are in fact his own race. The shape-shifting Founders share the Great Link, a mental and physical bond that unites them, but have ensured their survival by ruthlessly suppressing and controlling other races and by creating the Jem' Hadar, who are programmed to protect them at all costs. Appalled by the Founders' lack of concern for other beings, Odo makes the painful decision not to join them. Throughout the season, the Dominion remains an ever-present background threat. In *The Abandoned* Odo attempts to 'reform' a captured Jem' Hadar boy, but his genetically-programmed violent nature proves to be immutable. In *Heart Of Stone*, an 'accident' in which Kira is encased and apparently almost killed by a growing crystalline formation she encounters in a cave turns out to be a trick by the Founders to try to entice Odo back to their homeworld. Here Odo, thinking that Kira is about to die, reveals his long-suppressed love for her. In *Improbable Cause* an alliance against the Dominion is formed between the Romulans and Cardassians, but by the next episode *The Die is Cast* this already lies in ruins. In the season's final episode, *The Adversary*, the *Defiant* is taken over by a shape-shifting saboteur who attempts to lure the Federation into a war with the Tzankethi homeworld as a preparation for a Dominion attack. By the end of the season the suspicion is also growing that the Founders, using their shape-shifting powers, may be infiltrating key positions in the governments of various Alpha Quadrant powers. We are left with a strong suspicion that none other than the Klingon leader Gowron has been replaced by such a shape-shifter.

The Bajoran–Cardassian–Maquis story arc further develops in episodes such as Moore's *Life Support*, where Vedek Bareil insists on completing peace talks with the Cardassians despite suffering from a serious injury. As a result of his stubbornness he dies, leaving Kira grief-stricken. In *Shakaar*, the consequences of Kai Winn's rise to power are explored. Now the First Minister of Bajor's provisional government, her application of power has become increasingly totalitarian. Kira finds herself caught up in an armed rebellion by a group of former members of her resistance cell, whose attempts to become independent farmers are being suppressed by Winn, and plays a leading role in forcing Winn to step down as political leader. In Wolfe's *Second Skin* Kira's Cardassian captors (who have surgically altered her to look Cardassian) try to convince her that she is in reality a Cardassian spy whose memories of her Bajoran upbringing were implanted in her. In the process she forms a strong relationship with Ghemor, a Cardassian politician who thinks he is her father and who later turns out to be a member of the Cardassian 'underground'. In Moore's *Defiant*, Thomas Riker (separated from Will in *TNG*'s *Second Chances*) appears on the station, disguised as Will Riker, and exercises his considerable charm upon Kira. But Thomas is now a member of the Maquis and is merely manipulating her to gain access to the *Defiant*, with which he proposes to attack Cardassia. Again Starfleet has to co-operate with the Cardassians to prevent him triggering a new war. The 'alternative' Riker emerges as a thoroughly insecure character who is desperately seeking to find his own identity.

The character-driven episodes in this season tend to focus on the inner states of the featured principals. In *Visionary* O'Brien is exposed to a form of radiation which causes him to see 'visions' of events as they are likely to unfold in the future, allowing him to prevent both his own death and the destruction of the station. After an alien attack in *Distant Voices* Bashir goes into a coma and the main action of the episode takes place in his mind, with the familiar characters of Sisko, Kira, Dax, O'Brien, Quark and Odo appearing as various facets of his personality. Similarly, in Echevarria's *Facets* the crew members agree to temporarily house the 'spirits' of Dax's former hosts as part of the Trill Rite of Closure. In *Equilibrium* she is shocked by her sudden recall of the memories of a previous host – supposedly an 'unsuitable' candidate for 'joining'- whose existence as one of her 'forebears' had been suppressed by the Trill authorities.

Among the lighter episodes, *Fascination* features a 'plague' on DS9 brought on board by Lwaxana Troi. This causes various characters to develop unexpected 'crushes' on other inhabitants of the station. In Echevarria's *Explorers* Sisko takes Jake on a nostalgic voyage in an ancient Bajoran sail-powered spaceship, in a 'Kon-Tiki'-type attempt to prove that the ancient Bajorans had space travel before the Cardassians. *Through the Looking Glass* is another visit to *Crossover's* 'mirror universe', with Sisko leading a successful rebellion against the Alliance. There are also three 'Ferengi stories': in *The House of Quark*, Quark is forced into a 'convenience' marriage with Grillka, a very striking Klingon widow; in *Family Business* we meet 'Moogie', Quark and Rom's mother, who has violated Ferengi codes by wearing clothes and conducting business herself; and in *Prophet Motive* Quark has to work to restore the Grand Nagus – who has suddenly become a philanthropist – to his normal greedy self.

The fourth season of *DS9* features a new emphasis on action-orientated stories. In part this was undoubtedly a response by the producers to a decline in ratings which threatened the continuing existence of the series. There was a perceived need to 'beef up' the stories with elements that would draw in more viewers. Most obvious among these were the addition of Worf to the cast and the return of the Klingons as Federation enemies. With his cross-cultural background and frequently divided loyalties, Worf's character fits well into the multicultural ambiguities of *DS9*, and his presence makes the insertion of 'Klingon stories' more natural. In Behr and Wolfe's *The Way of the Warrior*, which opens the season, we see the first of a series of major political realignments as the Klingons attack Cardassia. This shatters the well-established peace between the Federation and the Klingon Empire. Worf has been sent to DS9 as a possible bridge between the Federation and the Klingons but – having in *TNG's Sins of the Father* suffered official 'discommendation' from Klingon society – is regarded by most Klingons as a traitor. Several 'Klingon stories' examine the effects of this.

Ronald D. Moore continues his exploration of Klingon culture in *Rules of Engagement* – where Worf faces extradition to the Klingon homeworld when falsely accused of causing the death of 400 people on a transport ship. In *Sons of Mogh* Worf's brother Kurn, who has been 'dishonoured' in the family-centred world of Klingon politics by

Worf's 'treason', comes to DS9 to ask Worf to kill him. Eventually Kurn's memory is erased as an alternative, further increasing Worf's sense of alienation from his homeworld. Worf, however, never rejects his Klingon heritage. In Hans Beimler's witty morality play, *The Sword of Kahless* (essentially a piece of 'Klingon pastiche'), he and Dax join with Kor in a quest for the legendary sword, the Klingon 'holy grail' which they believe will unite the Empire. But the sword brings only disunity, giving both Worf and Kor dreams of dominating the Empire, and – rather like the ring of power in Tolkein's *Lord of the Rings* – it finally has to be destroyed, in this case by being dispatched into space. Beimler's stories, particularly the later *Rapture*, put much emphasis on 'spiritual' themes.

The Dominion story arc develops throughout the season. There are several encounters with the Jem' Hadar, such as in *Starship Down*, where Sisko is injured in their attack on the *Defiant*. In *Hippocratic Oath* Bashir and O'Brien are captured by Jem' Hadar soldiers, who force Bashir into an unsuccessful attempt to find a cure for their addiction to ketracel-white. In Behr and Wolfe's *To the Death* Starfleet combines with the main Jem' Hadar command to search for Jem' Hadar rebels who are on the point of developing a weapon that could make them invincible. The Jem' Hadar – though they are ruthless killers without sentiment – emerge as pathetic figures, 'junkie soldiers' whose lives are completely manipulated by the Founders. The two-part story *Homefront/Paradise Lost* (written by Behr, Wolfe and Moore) enlarges on the Dominion story arc by giving us a very rare glance of twenty-fourth century Earth. Sisko is manipulated into supporting what is an effect a military coup when Starfleet itself assumes control of the home planet. Fear and irrational paranoia about infiltrating shape-shifters is seen to affect even the 'paradise' of the Federation's homeworld. In *DS9* even the Roddenberryesque 'utopia' of Earth is shown to be vulnerable. Thus a further challenge to *Star Trek*'s traditional utopian optimism is posed.

The new emphasis on the galactic balance of power still leaves room for stories about the Bajoran–Cardassian–Maquis situation, which often focus on clashing moral values. In *Accession* a Bajoran poet who disappeared 200 years before returns from the wormhole and claims to be the Emissary. Sisko is at first relieved and agrees to renounce his position, but later changes his decision when the poet calls for the reinstatement of the ancient Bajoran caste system. In Moore's *For the Cause* Sisko is horrified to discover that his lover, freighter captain Kassidy Yates, has been supplying the Maquis with provisions; and that a senior member of his crew, Commander Eddington (featured in a minor supporting role in a number of previous episodes) is a Maquis spy. Yates is imprisoned, but Eddington escapes to become one of the Maquis' leaders.

In *Indiscretion* Kira is dispatched with Gul Dukat on a joint Federation–Cardassian mission to locate a Cardassian ship containing prisoners of war which had crashed several years before. The resistance compatriot whom Kira hoped to find is dead, but Ziyal, a teenage girl who is revealed to be Dukat's daughter by his Bajoran mistress, is found alive. Dukat swears he will kill the girl as the revelation of her existence would destroy his family life and lead to his public disgrace and humiliation, but when confronted with her he is unable to do so. This is a surprising twist, 'humanising' the wily Dukat's character and forcing the naturally antagonistic Kira to confront her preconceptions about him. By the time of the follow-up story, *Return to Grace*, Dukat has been demoted to the lowly position of freighter captain as a result of his disgrace. He is assigned to take Kira to a peace conference with Bajoran and Cardassian officials, but on reaching the planet where the conference is to be held they discover that Klingon raiders have killed the entire group. Kira and Dukat combine to destroy the Klingon ship. A strong affinity develops between the former leader of the occupation forces and the former terrorist, to the extent that Kira opts to become Ziyal's guardian when she comes to live on DS9.

There are a number of powerful character-based stories in the fourth season. Behr and Beimler's *Shattered Mirror* features another, more serious, visit to *DS9's* parallel universe, with Sisko crossing over to recover Jake, who has to learn to understand that the 'mirror' version of Jennifer is not his real mother. Echevarria's interest in psychological stories leads him towards developing the complex character of Odo. In *Crossfire*, Odo's frustration at being unable to express his love for Kira is showcased when he is assigned to protect Kira and Bajoran First Minister Shakaar, her current lover. In the moving *The Muse* (co-written with Majel Barrett), when a pregnant Lwaxana Troi appears on the station, Odo nobly goes through a marriage ceremony with her to prevent her losing custody of the child. In order to protect them he kills a shape-shifter who has come to DS9 to kill Shakaar. This represents an agonising moment for him, as no shape-shifter has ever previously killed another. In the season's final episode, Behr and Wolfe's *Broken Link*, Odo is brought back to the Founders' homeworld and tried for his 'crime'. In a dramatic final twist to the season, the Founders deprive him of his shape-shifting powers.

In the disturbing *Hard Time*, O'Brien is given a mind implant which provides him with the experiences and memories of a 20-year prison sentence, an experience from which will take him some time to recover. Another remarkable example of character development is seen in *The Visitor*, which cleverly uses a time-paradox conundrum to presents an alternative 'life story' for Jake Sisko, now emerging as one of the series' major characters. Moore and Echevarria's *Rejoined* is the most subtle and daring story yet of Trill ethics, featuring Dax's heart-breaking encounter with a Trill who had been 'her' wife in a previous host's body. Whereas in *TNG*'s first Trill story, *The Host*, Beverly Crusher balked at a relationship with another woman, here there is little doubt that the issue of Dax's lover being of the same sex is irrelevant to her. *Rejoined* is evidence of the greater confidence in its storytelling abilities that *DS9* has now gained. Themes of sexuality that were only touched upon in the previous series can now be explored in greater depth.

Again there are several distinctly comic episodes. Moore's *Our Man Bashir* is a holodeck story that develops into a 1960s spy spoof, with Bashir enacting the 'Bond' role. Wolfe and Behr provide three comic 'Ferengi stories'. In *Bar Association* Quark's brother leads his over-exploited staff in a strike for better pay in conditions, in Ferengi terms a 'sacrilegious' act, while the rest of the DS9 crew watches in amusement. In *Body Parts* (during which a pregnant Keiko O'Brien is badly injured and her baby 'rehoused' in Kira) Quark is told he has an incurable disease and, in keeping with Ferengi tradition, sells his remains in advance for a profit. When he finds out that the prognosis was a mistake he needs to break his contract, a violation of the Rules of Acquisition. *Little Green Men* is probably the most successful Ferengi comedy of the entire series. En route to transport Nog to Earth, where he is (much to Quark's chagrin) to join Starfleet, an accident causes Quark, Rom and Nog to crash land at Roswell, USA, thus 'explaining' the famous 'Roswell Incident' where, according to many UFOlogists, a real 'alien encounter' was covered up by the US government. This kind of 'reassigning' of history was a common practice in the long-running BBC SF serial *Dr Who* (1963–91) – one example was in an early episode called *The Chase*, where the Daleks are seen to be responsible for emptying the famous ghost ship, the *Mary Celeste*. Yet such 'easy options' had generally been avoided in *Star Trek*. Here, though, the premise works as comedy because the entire episode – including the characterisation of the army officers and scientists who confront the Ferengi – is presented as a pastiche of a low-budget 1950s SF film.

The stories in the fifth season of *DS9* range from the richly comic to the genuinely tragic. With a few notable exceptions – such as *Ferengi Love Songs*, a rather formulaic 'Ferengi comedy' featuring a 'love affair' between 'Moogie' and The Grand Nagus; and *The Assignment*, in which Keiko is possessed by an 'evil alien' who forces Miles to sabotage the station – the stories avoid established clichés. Ronald D. Moore is again largely responsible for three outstanding comic pieces, all of which make use of well-established character traits, but each of which allows us to see those characters from a new angle. *In the Cards* centres on an attempt by Jake (assisted by Nog) to attain a rare 1951 baseball card as a gift for his father, during the course of which they encounter the paranoid scientist Dr Gieger, who is working on an 'immortality machine' known as a 'cellular regeneration and entertainment chamber'. *Trials and Tribble-ations* (co-written with Echevarria, Wolfe and Behr) is a hilarious pastiche of the original series. In *Looking for Par'mach in All the Wrong Places* the longstanding *Star Trek* joke about Klingon sexuality – which goes back to the Worf's muttered boast in the *TNG* first season episode *Hide and Q* that human women would be 'too fragile' for him to have sex with – is exploited to full comic effect. The episode centres mainly around Worf, who, after being 'lovestruck' by the arrival on the station of Grillka – the Klingon woman Quark had married for convenience in *The House of Quark* – rather indignantly agrees to help Quark 'charm' her. Worf enlists Dax to assist him in teaching Quark Klingon ways. The 'Cyrano de Bergerac'-type intervention is successful and Quark (who for once has no interest in profit) finally wins Grillka's 'heart'. In the process Dax finally reveals her feelings to Worf. Both couples later appear rather sheepishly in sickbay, highly dishevelled (and injured) after 'vigorous' Klingon trysts.

The season's more tragic themes are worked through in a number of episodes that focus on Odo's emotional development and the effects of his loss and eventual regaining of his shape-shifting powers. In *The Ascent*, when the newly 'solid' Odo and Quark are stranded together on an inhospitable planet, he has to rely upon Quark's uncharacteristically heroic efforts save them. In the tragic and oddly moving *The Begotten* a 'baby' changeling is discovered floating through space in its liquid state. Odo attempts to 'raise' the creature by teaching it to shape-shift. It is weak and eventually dies, but not before 'integrating' itself with Odo, so restoring his shape-shifting powers. In the time-paradox episode *Children Of Time* we glimpse an emotionally developed 'alternative Odo' as he would be in hundreds of years time, now fully capable both of expressing his love for Kira and of making the ultimate sacrifice – of negating his own existence – for her. Odo's character development is thus 'stretched' into one possible future, just as *TNG*'s characters were in *All Good Things*.

Many of the stories in this season concentrate on making us see the principals in new ways, with a particular focus on their 'dark sides'. In the harrowing *Empok Nor* the effects of a Cardassian drug turn Garak into a murderer, and he kills several Starfleet officers. Although Garak is judged to be 'innocent' of any crime, the drug itself has been designed merely to amplify existing Cardassian feelings of xeno-phobia, not to create them. In *Doctor Bashir, I Presume* when Bashir's parents visit the station it is finally revealed that the brilliant Bashir's intelligence was genetically enhanced as a child. *Things Past* explores the guilt Odo feels at allowing two innocent Bajorans to be executed when the station was under Cardassian rule. Echevarria's *Nor the Battle to the Strong* details how the idealistic Jake Sisko loses his youthful illusions and discovers his own 'dark side' in the heat of battle. The story is set during the short period that the Federation is at war with the Klingons. When Jake and Bashir arrive at a Federation colony in order to provide medical assistance, he has a somewhat romanticised view of the war and hopes that the 'excitement' of the experience will provide 'inspiration' for him in his budding career as a novelist. But when confronted by the actual reality of trying to care for the wounded without sufficient medical facilities, he becomes genuinely frightened. While he and Bashir are returning from a mission to retrieve a generator from their ship, they are shelled by Klingons. In the confusion, Jake panics and abandons Bashir to his fate. For much of the episode he is haunted by guilt over this. Finally he saves a number of Starfleet personnel during the Klingon attack, but it is pure fear rather than any kind of 'nobility' which motivates him to fire the phaser which keeps the Klingons at bay. The episode is *Star Trek*'s most eloquent statement of the horrors of war. The story becomes all the more poignant when it turns out that the skirmish served no political ends and was merely a strategic prelude to another Federation-Klingon pact.

An equally disturbing episode in its own way is Fields' *For the Uniform*, in which Sisko's desire to capture Starfleet 'traitor' Eddington, who defected to the Maquis in *For the Cause*, becomes so obsessive that he threatens to irradiate one of the Maquis planets – making it uninhabitable for 50 years – in order to force Eddington to surrender. Eddington is convinced that Sisko is bluffing, but is shocked when Sisko carries out his threat. Sisko has finally come to the realisation that the only way to defeat the terrorist Maquis is to 'play dirty', as the Maquis tactics appear to rely on the Federation acting in an 'ethical' manner. Sisko's absolute determination to crush the Maquis seems to come from an irrational source but may well be connected with the 'visions' he has received from the 'prophets'. Yet his actions appear to violate many of *Star Trek*'s moral principles. Just as 'baddies' such as Dukat tend to be progressively 'humanised' for much of the series, so the series' heroes are increasingly seen to have the capacity to exhibit a very questionable morality.

Kira, who in *The Begotten* gives birth to the baby she has been carrying for Miles and Keiko, is again the focus of a number of 'Bajoran stories'. In Moore's thriller *The Darkness and the Light* she discovers that her former friends in the Shakaar resistance cell are being murdered. Though still pregnant, she travels to confront the killer, a former Cardassian servant, Silaran Prin, who was disfigured in a resistance attack during the occupation. The morality of guerrilla war tactics is searchingly examined, with Prin seeing himself as an innocent victim of Bajoran terrorists now taking justifiable revenge. But Kira is capable of eloquently defending her past actions. In *Ties Of Blood And Water* the dying Ghemor (Kira's 'surrogate father' in *Second Skin*) appears on the station, having finally defected from Cardassia. When it is revealed that Ghemor took a minor part in the suppression of Bajor, Kira is deeply shocked. But by being forgiving enough to sit with Ghemor while he dies, she is able to make some personal atonement for her feelings of guilt about her absence at the death of her own father. Again, the theme of the need for forgiveness and reconciliation after a war is over is given great prominence. The most powerful 'Bajoran story' of all, *Rapture* (written by Hans Beimler and L. J. Strom) focuses on a series of 'revelations' Sisko has after an accident in which he receives an electric shock causes him to experience a state of heightened perception. This leads him to take his role as Emissary more seriously and delays Bajor's planned entrance into the Federation. That the revelations are not 'explained away' in the usual 'scientific' manner underlines the new respect for spirituality which *DS9* demonstrates – an attitude which further distances it from Roddenberry's original secular humanism.

A series of episodes chart the rapidly accelerating progress that seems to be occurring towards an oncoming galactic war. In Behr and Wolfe's season opener, *Apocalypse Rising*, Sisko and his team embark on a mission to the Klingon homeworld in order to expose Gowron, the Klingon leader, as a shape-shifter. In fact it is General Martok, his first minister, who is revealed as the changeling. In *Let He Who Is Without Sin* we see that even on the 'pleasure planet' of Risa there are political groups whose paranoia about the growing Dominion threat makes them call for a military/totalitarian response, just as Admiral Leyton did with Earth in *Homefront/Paradise Lost*. Another crucial 'double header' In *Purgatory's Shadow/By Inferno's Light* outlines a series of key realignments of the balance of power. Gul Dukat has engineered a *coup d'état* by negotiating an 'alliance' between Cardassia and the Dominion, in which Cardassia is by far the weaker partner. The alliance, however, allows the combined Klingon and Jem' Hadar fleets both to drive the Klingons out of Cardassian space and to utterly destroy the Maquis. In response Gowron signs a new treaty making the Federation and the Klingons allies once more. The (genuine) General Martok is stationed on DS9 as the official Klingon representative. The new treaty naturally puts Worf in a very different position, and in Moore's *Soldiers of the Empire* he is able to act as temporary first officer for Martok. His heroism on their mission against the Jem' Hadar leads to Martok accepting him as a member of his family, which gives Worf back much of his lost status in Klingon society. In the final episode of the season, Behr and Wolfe's *A Call to Arms*, increasing numbers of Jem' Hadar ships come through the wormhole headed for Cardassia, and the Romulans (with whom the Federation has been hoping to form an alliance) sign a non-aggression treaty with the Dominion. Sisko's desperate response is to mine the entrance to the wormhole, an act that he is well aware will lead to a Dominion–Cardassian attack. The dramatic battle that ensues ends in defeat for the Federation. DS9 is abandoned, and Gul Dukat arrives to reclaim the station. But in the season's final shot we see the *Defiant* and Martok's *Rotarran* making a rendezvous with a huge Starfleet–Klingon fleet, promising that all is not lost.

Deep Space Nine stands as *Star Trek*'s major dramatic achievement. Whereas the two preceding series were basically episodic, using more-or-less 'fixed' characters and relationships, *DS9* interweaves its continuous political story arcs with strong character development. The movement away from 'closure' of narratives that had begun during the third season of *TNG* reaches its climax in a series which continually presents its characters with challenging political and personal choices, emphasises the relative perspectives of different alien races, and grasps the 'epic' form in a way unparalleled in TV history. While the utopian idealism of Roddenberry's conception of *Star Trek* remains as a constant reference point, the political and psychological realism of *DS9* gives it a constant 'edge' that redefines *Star Trek* as a strikingly cohesive product of the modern 'televisual' age.

Chapter **6**

Romance, isolation, return: *Voyager*

The fourth *Star Trek* series was launched some seven months after the final episode of *TNG* and inherited a large proportion of its production team. Again the series was under the overall control of Berman and Piller, with co-creator Jeri Taylor joining them as *Star Trek*'s first female executive producer. While Berman remained mainly in an overall supervisory role, Piller and Taylor were highly active members of the writing team in the first two seasons. They were joined by *Voyager*'s most prolific writer, Brannon Braga, who contributed 18 stories in the first three seasons. Another *TNG* veteran, Joe Menosky, later came 'on board', along with new staff writers Kenneth Biller and Lisa Klink. With Moore, Fields and Echevarria joining the *DS9* writers, the *TNG* writing team had now split into two units with fairly distinctive writing styles. Not surprisingly *DS9* had attracted the more politically inclined writers, whereas Braga and Menosky, who tend to concentrate on a more fantasy-based approach, gravitated to *Voyager*.

The disparity between the two newest *Star Trek* series is illustrated by their respective 'looks'. Whereas *DS9* uses dark lighting and images with a slightly grainy texture, *Voyager* is brightly lit in a way that sometimes recalls the original series. From the outset *Voyager* was envisaged as a 'romantic' contrast to the more 'hard-edged' political and psychological drama of *DS9*. Whereas in Kirk's day space was an almost 'empty' place where the unexpected could be encountered at any moment, by the time of *TNG* and *DS9* the Alpha Quadrant, is divided into various shifting zones of influence which restrict exploration. By setting the newest series on a smaller, more manoeuvrable ship stranded in the faraway Delta Quadrant, the creators of *Voyager* reinstated the 'encounter with the unknown' factor that had been largely lost in its two predecessors. In the desperate situation in which

Janeway and her crew find themselves, following the strictly ethical 'Starfleet protocols' that proved so restrictive to Picard often becomes impossible. Janeway thus has to rely on the same mixture of bluff, cunning and bravado that characterised Kirk's earlier 'frontier' voyages.

Yet despite its deliberate positioning as a 'romantic' alternative to DS9, Voyager is still very much a product of the 'televisual' 1990s. Its basic scenario places it more firmly in the serial mode than any previous version of Star Trek. Again there is an ensemble cast, within an overall story arc structure that builds in elements of conflict between the main characters. The Delta Quadrant also turns out to have its own political culture which is as complex (if generally less technologically developed) as that of the Alpha Quadrant. From the outset Federation ethics are counterposed against those of a range of alien cultures, and the ship's presence frequently has an effect on the balance of power in whatever sector of space they are transversing.

As with DS9, the highly serialised mode of Voyager allows characters to develop and change as the series progresses. Female characters are ever more prominent. For the first time there is both a female captain, Kathryn Janeway (Kate Mulgrew), and chief engineer, B'Elanna Torres (Roxann Biggs-Dawson). Janeway is strong-willed and sometimes impulsive, with a strong sense of Starfleet ethics, which she takes pains to preserve despite being so far from home. Torres, a former Starfleet 'dropout', is a brilliant and resourceful but undisciplined engineer who has learned much about the art of improvisation under pressure while serving as a member of the Maquis. She is half-Klingon, but has little knowledge or understanding of Klingon culture and traditions. Commander Chakotay (Robert Beltran), another former Maquis who becomes Voyager's first officer, is a Native American who hails from the planet ceded to the Cardassians in TNG's Journey's End. Lieutenant Tuvok (Tim Russ) is a (full-blooded) Vulcan who, like Spock, is dedicated unswervingly to the path of logic and who had been serving on the Maquis ship as a Federation infiltrator.

Lieutenant Tom Paris (Robert Duncan MacNeil) is another Starfleet dropout who had also been very briefly in the Maquis and who had been serving time in a Federation prison before Janeway requested his presence on Voyager. Like B'Elanna he is highly talented (in this case as a pilot) but essentially undisciplined, and he tends to lapse back into feelings of inadequacy. Ensign Harry Kim (Garrett Wang) is an earnest young Asian-American officer on his first Starfleet mission. Kes (Jennifer Lien) is a member of the Ocampa race which Janeway rescues in the series' pilot, *Caretaker*. As an Ocampan she has a life span of only nine years, but can develop and learn at a very fast rate. She also has some form of (as yet largely unrealised) telepathic powers. At the beginning of the series she has a relationship with the colourful Talaxian, Neelix (Ethan Phillips), another native of the Delta Quadrant, who joins the crew as a guide and negotiator. Neelix is a largely comic character with a tendency to bluster his way through situations. He becomes the ship's cook and 'morale officer'. The Doctor (Robert Picardo) is a hologram who is at first confined to sickbay. After the death of the original ship's doctor he is called into service. Imbued with much of the tetchiness of his creator, Dr Lewis Zimmerman, he gradually develops a strong character of his own. Picardo is a highly skilled comic actor who provides many of the series' most effective comic moments.

Voyager's pilot, the feature-length *Caretaker* (written by Piller, Taylor and Berman), sets up the ethical dilemma that forces Captain Janeway to allow the ship to become stranded in an area of space from which it will take – at Starfleet warp speeds – some 70 years to return 'home'. Like Roddenberry's original pilot, *The Cage*, and the pilots for both *TNG* and *DS9*, it features an encounter with 'higher beings'. While in pursuit of a Maquis ship commanded by Chakotay, both *Voyager* and its quarry are suddenly and unexpectedly transported 70 000 light years across space by a huge space array controlled by a powerful 'energy-being' known as the Caretaker. In the process both ships suffer heavy casualties, and the Maquis crew are beamed on board *Voyager* before their ship explodes. The planet around which the array is in orbit is the home of the Ocampa, a race who have no military defences and who are protected and sustained by the Caretaker. Janeway learns that the Caretaker is dying and that if they use the array to return to the Alpha Quadrant, this will leave the Ocampa race defenceless against the warlike sects of the Kazon race. She is thus forced to choose between returning home, which would entail abandoning the 'innocent' Ocampa to their fate, and remaining to protect them. In order to prevent the array from falling into Kazon hands she destroys it.

One of Janeway's rationalisations for her course of action is that she still hopes that another quick way home may be found. In two episodes partly written by Jeri Taylor, such opportunities do present themselves, but both (rather inevitably) end in disappointment. In *Eye of the Needle* Kim detects a wormhole that leads to the Alpha Quadrant, but which is too small for the ship to pass through. The crew plan to beam themselves onto the Romulan ship, but it is discovered that this wormhole moves through time as well as space and that the ship is from 20 years in the past. The crew opts to remain in the Delta Quadrant, knowing that a return would play havoc with the time lines. In *Prime Factors* the crew visits the Sikarian homeworld, where the inhabitants possess advanced technology which could allow the ship to return home, but the Sikarians explain that such an action would be prohibited by their own version of the Prime Directive. A disappointed Janeway appears to accept this, but a group of 'rebels' in the crew, consisting of the Bajoran Seska (who had previously been openly contemptuous about Janeway's earlier decision to abandon their chance to get home) together with Torres and (very surprisingly) Tuvok, ignore Janeway's orders and negotiate to swap the ship's database of literature for the device. When Torres attempts to activate the device it fails and almost destroys the ship. Janeway is naturally furious at what in normal circumstances would be regarded as virtually mutinous behaviour, but in the position in which she finds herself, she can do little to discipline the crew members. There is a recognition here that in *Voyager*'s extraordinary situation the normal ethical rules of Starfleet behaviour cannot apply in the usual way.

Such internal dissent within the crew is a major factor in the stories of the first season. Although the former Starfleet and Maquis crews now have a common purpose, they were previously enemies and had very different working methods. Whereas Starfleet officers are bound by a series of ethical rules and protocols, as terrorists the Maquis have learned to live on their wits. Janeway knows that both qualities are important in their situation, and she is determined to weld the crew into one unit. Much of the first season consists of character-based episodes in which these dynamics are worked out. In *Learning Curve* Tuvok attempts to instil Starfleet discipline and physical fitness into a group of former Maquis but meets considerable resistance and finds he must 'soften' his approach. In *Parallax* the hot-headed and rather cynical Torres (whose rather teasingly sarcastic nickname for the idealistic Harry Kim is 'Starfleet') is disciplined by Janeway for fighting with Carey, the senior engineer in the Starfleet crew. Janeway at first thinks Torres is too undisciplined to be made chief engineer, but when Torres shows her brilliance by rescuing *Voyager* from a temporal singularity she wins Janeway's confidence. In *State of Flux* it is discovered that a member of the crew has allowed the Kazon to have access to Starfleet's transporter technology. In a dramatic turn of events, Seska (a former lover of Chakotay's) is revealed not only to be the traitor but also to be a Cardassian spy who had been surgically altered to look like a Bajoran. In the meantime, Seska has left the ship to ally herself with the Kazon.

Other character-based episodes develop the backstories of the main players in a way that frequently pose further ethical and psychological questions. Yet a number of these tend to fall back on previously established *Star Trek* plotlines. *Faces* is an episode in the tradition begun by *The Enemy Within*, in which Torres, having been captured by the Vidiians, is split into two people – her human and Klingon halves. Both 'halves' have to co-operate to help her escape. *Ex Post Facto* sees Paris put on trial for murder, a device previously used to explore the characters of Kirk, Riker, Dax and Odo. In *Jetrel* (a story which echoes the *DS9* episodes that deal with the effects of the Bajoran holocaust) Neelix encounters the scientist responsible for the invention of the weapon of mass destruction which had caused the deaths of 300 000 Talaxians (including Neelix's entire family) some 15 years before. *Heroes and Demons* is the first *Voyager* holodeck story, in which (in what has by now become a somewhat clichéd premise) the holodeck 'safeties' fail during a program for the Beowulf story which Harry Kim runs. With the holodeck becoming too dangerous for humans, the Doctor is cast as the hero of a story that sees him involved in his first 'romance'.

A number of episodes in the first season are heavily influenced by Brannon Braga's orientation towards the horror genre. In *Phage* the crew encounters the 'gruesome', disease-ridden Vidiians, who are affected by the phage, a dreadful plague which gradually rots their bodies. In order to survive, the Vidiians steal organs from other species to replace their own. In *Emanations*, which focuses on a culture which believes in a literal, physical afterlife, Harry Kim is accidentally transported to a moon on which lie thousands of rotting corpses. *Cathexis* is another alien-possession story in which Chakotay's 'brain energy' is 'sucked out' by aliens who wish to extract the entire crew's 'neural energy' (or perhaps, in 'horror' terms, to steal their souls). The solution is found in a rather mystical manner by consulting Chakotay's medicine wheel.

The first season of *Voyager* already exhibits many of the contradictions inherent in its attempt to create a newly 'romanticised' version of *Star Trek*. Although it quickly creates a range of believable characters, those characters are too psychologically realistic to attain the 'mythic' status of Kirk, Spock and McCoy. Whereas Kirk's 'duplication' in *The Enemy Within* is believable because Kirk is a 'symbolic' character, Torres being split into two parts in *Faces* is arguably less so. In the original series (and in much of the early *Next Generation*) the closure of each story seems to come naturally within the dramatic conventions of the 'classical' form of the series. But in *Voyager* such closures can seem forced and inappropriate. A good example is the early story *Time and Again*, where several *Voyager* crew members are caught in a time loop which involves the wiping out of an entire planet's population. The paradox of the situation is that the *Voyager* crew members inadvertently cause the explosion that sets off the 'holocaust' by attempting to prevent it happening. Yet a 'solution' is found by merely sending the ship back in time before the situation can occur. Closure is thus achieved, but any deeper implications of the paradox itself are ignored.

In the second season, *Voyager* becomes embroiled in the political intrigues of the Delta Quadrant as it encounters the various warlike Kazon sects, who are continually engaged in a struggle for power with each other. *Voyager* is carrying more advanced technology than the Kazons possess, and is thus a considerable prize. In *Maneuvers* Seska, now allied to the Nistrim sect, sends a small boarding party onto *Voyager* to steal Starship transporter devices, which are unknown in the Delta Quadrant. In *Investigations* Paris fakes a defection to the Kazon so that he can uncover the identity of a *Voyager* crew member who has secretly been sending key strategic information to Seska and her Kazon allies. In *Alliances*, as the Kazon attacks increase, Janeway is forced to attempt to negotiate the first of *Voyager*'s politically expedient pacts with other races. To some extent, these manoeuvres (and their outcome) recall the *realpolitik* atmosphere of *DS9*. Janeway is even prepared to consider making an alliance with the Nistrim, but in deference to the Prime Directive is not prepared to surrender Federation technology. Finally she attempts to make an alliance with the Trabe, the Nistrim's former captors and oppressors. But the Trabe turn out to be even more untrustworthy, attacking a peace conference at which Janeway attempts to bring the Kazon sects together. Attempts to make alliances are – for now – abandoned. Although the Kazon lifestyle appears to resemble the warrior culture of the Klingons, the positive sides of that culture remain undeveloped and they remain somewhat one-dimensional villains.

Though the overall story arc of *Voyager* emphasises its 'voyage home' theme, many individual episodes confront the crew with unfamiliar situations in a manner that often reworks elements of the original series or well-established *Star Trek* plot devices. *Meld* recalls a number of Spock's scenes in the original series when Tuvok mind melds with the disturbed murderer, Suder, causing Tuvok to experience violent (and very un-Vulcan) emotions. *Elogium*, which features Kim entering her 'mating cycle', is reminiscent of Spock's similarly traumatic experience in *Amok Time*. In *Parturition* – a 'sanctity of life' story in the vein of *The Devil in the Dark* – Paris and Neelix's shuttle crashes on an unknown planet. As they wait to be rescued Neelix insists on defending a newly hatched creature despite the danger that its mother may return. These stories tend towards an over-reliance on their original models, although Kenneth Biller's *Tuvix* – another 'doppelganger' story in the mould of *The Enemy Within* – devises a new twist on the scenario which makes it one of *Voyager*'s most effective 'moral dilemma' shows. Here a transporter accident actually unites Tuvok and Neelix into one being, an amalgam of both personalities who becomes known as Tuvix. As work progresses on finding a way to restore the two original crewmen, Tuvix's quite different and independent personality begins to assert itself. When the 'reverse transport' process has been perfected and it is time for Tuvok and Neelix to be restored, Tuvix protests and accuses Janeway of sanctioning his murder. But after listening to arguments from all sides, she is forced to order the process to go ahead. It is to the episode's credit that no 'easy solution' is found as Janeway is forced to make the kind of unpleasant ethical decision that comes with her command role.

In *Resolutions*, the uneasy line between 'romantic' and 'realistic' dramatic modes which *Voyager* often treads is inventively exposed when Chakotay and Janeway have to be abandoned by *Voyager* as both have developed a virus which means they cannot return to the ship. As they begin to abandon hope of a cure being found, a romance begins to blossom which is immediately and unsentimentally curtailed on their return. In Brannon Braga's complex 'virtual reality play', *Projections*, the Doctor becomes trapped in a holodeck simulation of his own making, in which he is apparently human and the rest of the crew are holograms. In Lisa Klink's first contribution, the often moving *Resistance*, Janeway is rescued from captivity on a hostile planet by Caylem, an old man who believes she is his daughter. Klink's later *Dreadnought* focuses on Torres, who has to keep her cool under very difficult circumstances as she attempts to disarm a 'talking bomb' she had programmed herself many years before as a Maquis terrorist device. The plot rather stretches the viewer's credibility by explaining that this device somehow strayed into the faraway Delta

Quadrant, but the story cleverly focuses on Torres' characteristic attempts to control the fiery Klingon side of her personality. In another Klink story, *Innocence*, Tuvok's 'emotional side' is exposed when he acts as a guardian to a group of children who have apparently been abandoned by their parents. But, in a plot that recalls that of Philip K. Dick's satirical novel *Counter-Clock World*, it transpires that the 'children' are part of a race that lives its life in reverse and that they have come to the planet as part of their natural cycle to die.

There is an increasing tendency towards the fantastical in episodes like Joe Menosky's entertaining *The Thaw*, where Kim and Torres enter a 'virtual world' in which they are captured by a computer-generated 'clown' whose existence is built on the fears of those trapped in the program. In Michael Piller's *Death Wish*, *Voyager*'s first 'Q story', the ship is transported back to the moment of the creation of the universe, shrunk to the size of a subatomic particle and then expanded to the size of a present on a Christmas tree. In Braga's *Threshold*, perhaps his most outlandish story, Paris and Janeway 'super-evolve' into lizard-like creatures who then mate and reproduce. Braga here takes the 'horror' themes he developed in *TNG*'s *Genesis* to even more extreme lengths. In both of these episodes, two normally inventive and consistent writers seem to fall into the trap of allowing the apparently unlimited storytelling freedom of the *Star Trek* universe to 'run away with them'. These are not intended to be comic stories, but it is virtually impossible to take them seriously.

In the first part of *Basics*, which culminates the series of stories about encounters with the Kazon sects, *Voyager* is ambushed by the Kazon Nistrim and as the season ends, Kazon leader Culluh and Seska take over the ship and strand the entire crew on the planet below. This leaves many dramatic options open for the third season, but it seems rather unbelievable that the murderous Culluh would not kill the crew rather than merely abandon them. In the highly melodramatic third season opener, *Basics Part 2*, *Voyager* is recaptured thanks to a combination of the efforts of Paris (who still has possession of a shuttlecraft), the Doctor (who pretends not to care that the Kazon have taken over the ship) and the deranged Suder, who finally redeems himself with a heroic death after 'taking out' a number of Kazon warriors. *Voyager*'s leading 'villain', Seska, is also killed in the attack. This leaves the 'Kazon situation' largely resolved, and there is surprisingly little development of the main story arc in the third season, until the final episode – when *Voyager* finally enters Borg space. Whereas in *DS9* every 'political' action has consequences that help to build up a complex narrative structure, in *Voyager* the ship can avoid those consequences by merely travelling on. By now, serious conflicts within the crew are virtually absent. The only episode to touch on this area, *Worst Case Scenario*, begins rather shockingly by showing Chakotay and the former Maquis members (apparently disillusioned with what they see as Janeway's over-ethical approach) staging a mutiny. This turns out, however, to be merely an out-of-control holodeck program which Seska had left as a 'booby trap'.

With these important elements of its original story arc virtually extinguished, the stories of the third season tend to meander rather aimlessly. In the highly melodramatic *Warlord*, Kes's body is 'possessed' by a ruthless dying alien whom *Voyager*'s crew were attempting to save. The alien escapes, stages a *coup d'état* on 'his' home planet and plans to restore the dictatorial regime with which 'he' had controlled the planet in the past. But finally he finds that 'his' time has passed and that 'he' no longer has any support. Other episodes make use of rather clichéd plots which often strain credulity. In *Rise*, Neelix and Tuvok are stranded on a planet after (yet another) shuttle-craft crash and have to make their escape via a huge 300-kilometre high pole which extends into space. In two rather contrived action-orientated episodes the ship is threatened by various forms of 'take over'. In *Macrocosm* – another example of Brannon Braga's sometimes wildly undisciplined approach – the ship is threatened by a 'macrovirus' which takes the form of 'giant killer bugs' reminiscent of those in 1950s B-movies (though portrayed by vastly superior special effects).

Other episodes trade heavily on pre-established *Star Trek* themes. In *Flashback* Janeway mind melds with Tuvok, taking them both back to the time of *The Undiscovered Country*, when the young Tuvok was serving under Captain Sulu. Tuvok is still traumatised about Sulu's illegal trespass into Klingon space, but Janeway justifies Sulu's actions by arguing that the situation in the twenty-third century was a desperate one and that in this case, the ends justified the means. *False Profits* relocates the two Ferengi who were dispatched through a wormhole in *TNG's Profit and Loss* and who have now set themselves up as 'gods' to exploit the natives of a 'primitive' planet. *Blood Fever* revisits *Amok Time* territory again, as the young Vulcan ensign, Vorik, enters his ponn farr, which he (rather incredibly) 'transmits' to Torres, causing her to experience violent sexual cravings. *The Q and the Grey* features a supposed 'war' in the Q continuum (portrayed rather ludicrously in an 'American Civil War' setting) which Q hopes to resolve, for reasons the episode never successfully explains, by impregnating Janeway. The appearance of Q's jealous 'girlfriend' in the episode completes a very contrived 'cosmic farce'. Whereas Q played a crucial role in *TNG*, his 'guest appearances' in *DS9* and *Voyager* rarely make effective use of his high-camp whimsy. In the two-parter *Future's End* the crew is transported back to 1996. But whereas in the earlier time travel stories like *Past Tense* the threat being encountered is to the 'present day' of *Star Trek*'s twenty-fourth century utopia, here the crew are engaged in preventing a rather nebulous 'explosion that will destroy the entire galaxy' in the twenty-nineth century. Also, given *Voyager*'s situation, the presence of a time-travel story seems to strain credibility. It becomes hard to sympathise with a 'lost' crew if they can be projected through time and space with such apparent ease.

Among the more successful character-based episodes, Kenneth Biller's *Before and After* is an inventive story of possible alternate time lines, in which Kes first experiences her own death (as an 'old lady' of nine years), then 'travels backwards' through key experiences of her life, one of which involves a 'future' marriage to Paris resulting in a daughter who marries Harry Kim. Another features a possible future in which both Janeway and Torres have been killed. The episode provides intimations of a potential future in a similar way to *TNG*'s *All Good Things*. Perhaps the most impressive and serious character-based story of the season is *Remember*, where Torres has a series of vivid dreams which turn out to be real memories of a forgotten holocaust on the home planet of a group of apparently benevolent telepaths who are visiting the ship. Many of the more effective stories focus on the Doctor, who has emerged as *Voyager*'s most distinctive character. In Braga and Menosky's *Darkling* his attempts to integrate the strengths of various holodeck characters into his 'matrix' leads to the emergence of an 'evil Doctor' who kidnaps Kes and almost murders her. In the witty and ultimately moving *Real Life* he programs himself with an 'ideal family' on the holodeck. In *The Swarm* he begins losing his memory and has to be reprogrammed. In the process he risks losing the memories of the past two years, and thus his entire 'human' development so far.

A prelude to *Voyager*'s coming encounter with the Borg is staged in Biller's *Unity*, where an injured Chakotay discovers a colony of humanoids who, after an explosion destroyed their Cube, have managed to separate themselves from the Borg collective. As individuals they still have 'mind-linking' powers and the episode explores the positive possibilities of such 'unity'. By linking together with

Chakotay, a group of the former Borg cure him. Later they enlist his help in combining together to form a new 'mental collective' without the aggressive intentions of the Borg collective. Braga and Menosky's epic, often cinematic *Scorpion, Part 1*, which concludes the season in the same way as the third season of *TNG* – with an 'all-out' Borg story – is a promising climax. While *Voyager* seems at first to be helpless against the vast power of the Borg – whose space they must cross to make their attempt to get home at all possible – it is discovered that the Borg are themselves threatened by an even more powerful enemy, a non-humanoid race known only as 'Species 8472'. When Kim is attacked by this species and the Doctor finds an antidote, Janeway realises that this discovery could be used as a weapon against the new species. In a sudden moment of revelation, she decides that the only way forward is to make 'a pact with the devil' and ally *Voyager* with the Borg against Species 8472 by offering the Borg the antidote in exchange for unhindered passage through their space. This highly dangerous plan is being formulated just as Species 8472 attacks the Borg, destroying one of their planets and leaving *Voyager* with its most effective season-ending cliffhanger.

As we have seen, in the case of *TNG* the series did not really find its distinctive storytelling style until this point in its 'evolution' and *DS9*'s 'galactic war' scenario took several seasons to develop. But in *Voyager*'s first three seasons it finds a truly distinctive narrative 'voice' only sporadically. It may be that the encounter with the Borg and the return to an overall story arc that it represents will give the series more impetus. The success of the later seasons of *TNG* and the overall triumph of *DS9* indicate that modern *Star Trek* series work best when they can build on a structure of interwoven story arcs rather than merely a series of self-contained stories. If *Voyager* is to achieve its potential, it may need to change its approach in much the same way that *TNG* did. A television series needs to find an identity of its own to succeed. In the case of *Star Trek* series – which naturally build on the material from previous versions of *Star Trek* – this can at times be particularly difficult to achieve. *Voyager*'s attempt to recapture the 'romantic spirit' of the original series is largely a failure. Though its characters and the relationships between them are highly believable, it has often suffered from a lack of overall direction and a general confusion of purpose. It may well be that the structural differences in television production between the 1960s and the 1990s, and the changes in the broadcasting environment of which *Star Trek* has taken such positive advantage, preclude the creation of stories and characters that have the kind of mythic or iconic significance that was achieved by Kirk, Spock and McCoy. While the hard-edged realism and ironic comedy of *DS9* seems to fit perfectly with today's self-consciously postmodern era, the 'new romanticism' of *Voyager* – like the ship itself – appears to be rather out of place.

Part II
Star Trek, myth and ritual

[Popular TV drama is] ... not escapist but mythic ... it enables and encourages the reader to make a particular kind of sense of existence. The reader and the text are both active and the text becomes popular only when the activities are mutually supportive ...

(John Fiske, quoted in Tulloch, 1990, p. 77)

Television, because it is not written, does not communicate fixed and recoverable texts. Like ancient oral myth forms, the potentially endless play of generic formula create a memory ...

(John Tulloch, 1990, p. 15)

Chapter 7

Ritual and relativism: *Star Trek* as cult

> As TV viewers we are usually innocent of our inevitable part
> in the struggle for meaning. As we put our feet up in front of
> the TV, our mood is more likely to be relaxed than combative
> ... yet ... our regular encounters with the kaleidoscope of
> words and images that flow into our living rooms form an
> inexorable part of our semiotic universe ...
>
> (Justin Lewis, 1991, p. 42)

A TV series typically presents itself as a form of drama which offers a
unique *bond* with its audience. TV itself is an intimate, 'domestic'
medium' which the viewer experiences as part of the routine of everyday life', and the aim of the makers of a TV series is to win the 'loyalty'
of viewers so that they will be persuaded to integrate its characters and
situations into that routine. The experience of watching thus becomes
'ritualised' as part of a pattern of lifestyle. In the case of an action-
adventure-based series such as *Star Trek* viewers must, in a weekly
'ritual' of suspension of disbelief, accept narrative conventions such as
stylised fight scenes or last-minute dramatic escapes from danger. The
regular viewer of a TV series, who becomes 'privileged' with more and
more understanding of a show's characters and situations, naturally
learns to 'read' the 'text' of a TV series in a way that may elude more
'highbrow' critics. As Jane Feuer points out:

> observers from the high culture who visit TV melodrama occasion-
> ally in order to issue their tedious reports about our cultural malaise
> are simply not seeing what the TV audience sees ... They are espe-
> cially blind to the complex allusiveness with which the TV medium
> uses its actors ... (in Newcomb, 1994, p. 44).

The earliest studies of TV postulated it as a 'hypnotic' and rather dangerous medium in which individual segments were subsumed in what Raymond Williams (1966, p. 3) described as an endless 'flow' of programming. Viewers were portrayed as being highly susceptible to 'conditioning' by the manipulation of this 'flow'. These studies originated out of concerns about the supposedly 'damaging' effects of the medium, and they were mainly concerned with measuring the extent to which TV influenced behaviour, particularly among children. Much debate concentrated on what became known as the 'hypodermic' model of TV effects, whereby the showing of violent or antisocial behaviour was taken to indicate an 'injection' of such behaviour into society. But as TV grew and diversified as a medium researchers began to take a more sympathetic stance. In 1974, Blumer and Katz produced the theory of 'Uses and Gratifications', which concentrated on the notion of the TV viewer as an active rather than a passive participant who could 'see through' a programme's narrative conventions and thus: 'make sense of programmes in a way that is relatively unconstrained by the structure of the text, drawing instead upon his or her interests, knowledge and expertise' (quoted in Livingstone, 1990, p. 36).

Later developments in audience theory in the cultural studies school shifted to the notion of the viewer as an active producer of meaning. As Barwise and Ehrenberg (1988, p. 25) point out: 'the audience is not an indiscriminating crowd all watching the most popular fare. The average viewer watches only 2 or 3 of the top ten rated programmes in the week ...' This new emphasis on the TV audience as being selective in its viewing habits and creative in its interpretations has led to the activities of fans being taken far more seriously. Many recent studies have gravitated towards examinations of fan culture, of which *Star Trek* fandom soon presented itself as a key example. As we have seen, the *Star Trek* audience has played a key role in pressurising the TV companies to keep the various series and films going, and the *Trek* fan community has always displayed an unprecedented degree of internal organisation. Tulloch and Jenkins describe the growth of the *Star Trek* convention circuit, which they identify as a model for 'cult' organisation for other TV series. They also imply that the narrative mode of the series has encouraged an active fan response: 'the generic multiplicity and ideological contradictions of *Star Trek* invite fans to construct their own utopias from the materials it provides ...' (1995, p. 212).

Two fairly recent examinations of the TV audience – Jenkins' *Textual*

Poachers and Camille Bacon-Smith's *Enterprising Women* (both 1992) – concentrate on the ways in which *Star Trek's* fan culture has developed into an interchange between fans of various forms of 'rewriting' of the scenario presented in the original series. Both studies focus particularly on female fan writing as an 'oppositional' response to the male-orientated nature of these early stories. Bacon-Smith describes how female fans composed many variants on the basic theme of what became known as a 'Mary Sue' story – a story in which a young heroine joins the crew of the *Enterprise* and 'saves the day' when a crisis looms. Other common fan fantasies included 'Lay Spock' or 'Lay Kirk' stories in which the resourceful heroine has a sexual relationship with either of the main characters and 'slash' fiction – homoerotic stories featuring Kirk and Spock as lovers.

As a product of 1960s TV, the original *Star Trek* naturally avoided such stories, but many of the changes that have come about in the new *Trek* series can be seen as responses to the perceived shortcomings of the original series in dealing with more controversial issues. In the new media environment of the 1980s and 1990s the diversification of programming has led to a far greater diversity of cultural perspectives being represented in television shows. As we saw in previous chapters, *Star Trek* has 'modernised' its narrative viewpoints so that even 'gay themes' have been approached, especially in the stories centring on Dax and the Trill race. The main writers of the new *Trek* series were often fans of the original series in childhood, and thus their writing – like those of Bacon-Smith's female fans – is motivated by the need to fulfil the narrative potential suggested by the best episodes of the original series. *Star Trek* can thus be seen as a set of series that has been constantly defended, reclaimed and re-imagined by its fan base.

The phenomenon of the 'cult' TV series is one which has become prominent in the last two decades. This has been encouraged by the proliferation of new channels, and particularly by the spread of the VCR, which means that viewing of episodes is no longer tied to a particular weekly 'slot' and that fans can now build up collections of their favourite series. In the case of *Star Trek*, the development of a 'cult' audience was encouraged by the fact that the original series projected a positive vision of the future in an era dominated by distopian predictions. With the cold war at its height, and the possibility of nuclear war and the subsequent apocalyptic destruction of human culture as a constant threat, the original series provided its fans with a framework in which a positive future could be imagined, in comparison to which the political, social and medical systems of

today are seen as primitive and underdeveloped. The series also stim-
ulated its fans into debates over interpretations of many of its
pointedly 'symbolic' stories, and its emphasis on self-deprecating
humour also encouraged fans to 'play' with its textual elements. As
John Fiske points out:

> Essential to textual pleasure is an awareness, to whatever extent, of
> its textuality. The pleasure in playing with the boundary between
> the representation and the real involves a recognition of their
> differences as well as their similarities. Textual experience and
> social experience are different, but not totally unconnected. The
> discursive repertoires and competences that are involved in making
> sense of each overlap and inform each other ... (in Seiter *et al.*,
> 1991, p. 67)

If contemporary *Star Trek* 'fandom' with its network of conventions
and fan clubs, constitutes a 'cult' it must be stressed that it is not – as
the term perhaps implies – a small, self-contained group of 'fanatics'
but a global 'community'. There are many parallels between the rituals
of religion and those connected with modern mass media forms.
While the stars of popular music, TV and film are 'worshipped' as
modern 'icons', 'cult' TV series give their fans a sense of 'belonging' to
an exclusive group which is one way in which they define their identity. For 'devoted' fans of a series there is always much pleasure to be
drawn from the recognition of intertextual references and mutual
exchange of such information with like-minded others. The ever-
expanding nature of the overall *Star Trek* text naturally encourages
this. Many 'Trekkers' make their pleasure in *Star Trek* an active part of
their social lives. Some fans even dress up as Starfleet officers or aliens
to attend conventions or fan meetings. In any 'cult' there are likely to
be elements of ritualised drama, as if by imitating the figures in their
'sacred text' cult members can somehow experience the 'spiritual
dimensions' of that text. It must be emphasised, however, that the
vast majority of *Star Trek* fans participate in such activities with a self-
deprecatingly ironic approach and few would claim to be serious
'religious' devotees. This attitude is certainly reflected in episodes of
the new *Trek* series like *Trials And Tribble-ations*, which indulge in
ironic 'tributes' to the original series.

In the wake of their recreation in the *Star Trek* films and the new
Trek series, the most popular group to imitate has become the
Klingons. It might almost be true to say that 'Klingon fandom' has

become a 'cult within a cult'. In the new *Trek* series the Klingons are given an entire 'spiritual tradition' based on a complex and developed 'warrior culture' resting on notions of honour, service and intense family loyalty' in which ritual plays a highly significant part. In *TNG's Sins of the Father* the legendary warrior Kahless is revealed as the 'spiritual founder' of their entire culture. In *Lower Decks* we see Worf practising a form of Klingon martial arts, thus linking the Klingons 'traditions' to that of the Samurai. The Klingons hold many symbolic ceremonies in which the telling of heroic stories through bardic 'songs' is a prominent feature. These qualities are demonstrated strongly in stories such as *TNG's The Bonding*, in which Worf leads an orphaned boy through the Klingon Age of Ascension Rite; and *Firstborn*, in which the battles of the legendary warrior Kahless are re-enacted by warriors who sing traditional songs as they fight.

A number of 'Klingon' fan organisations have been formed, within which individuals are assigned 'military' ranks such as 'Commander' and 'Attack Co-Ordinator' and adopt Klingon names. Each individual fan club is called a 'ship', these are organised into regional 'Houses' and each House is part of an overall 'Quadrant'. The structures of fandom are deliberately set up on the basis of the social organisation of Klingons as depicted in *Star Trek*. One of the leading Klingon 'ships', the 'Klingon Assault Group' posts a regular newsletter, *Purple Haze*, on its Internet site. One posting informs the 'net browser' that:

> Terry, Commander K'Mak sutai Tadtha, is the Attack Co-Ordinator for the St. Louis/Metro East area. Trish's Purple Haze Wolfpack meets in West St. Louis County and is actually 3 ships in one and is actively recruiting for all three Wolfpack ships, including the all female Iron Butterfly. Purple Haze publishes a monthly newsletter. Phoenix is recruiting a command staff for a new ship in University City, the Phoenix Fire. Don's Blood Flame meets in Granite City and is recruiting additional crew too. Ray's Blood Cry meets in Alton. The St. Louis KAG ships are all one family of fandom, like a Klingon House. We have strong ties of loyalty to each other ... (Purple Haze, October/November 1995)

The Klingon language, which was originally devised by *Trek's* resident linguist, Marc Okrand, for the 1980s movies and was later adopted by the new *Trek* series, has become particularly popular with fans. In 1996 the Klingon Language Institute issued 1000 hard-bound copies of a Klingon translation of *Hamlet*. Its 'scribes' are reported to be working on a 'Klingon Bible'. As the *Guardian* reports, Klingon:

> is also, as *Newsweek* recently pointed out, 'the fastest-growing language in the universe (if you consider that it started with a base line of zero speakers in the mid-1980s). Since 1985 a dictionary of Klingon has sold more than 250,000 copies, a cassette course, Conversational Klingon, has sold over 50,000 in less than a year' and speakers read up on the finer points of syntactic evolution in a quarterly journal called HolQeD (which earthlings might translate as 'linguistics'. It's even being taught out of hours by quirkier academics at some American universities ... (14 July 1993)

'Klingon language camps' have been held, in which fans not only speak to each other in Klingon, but also adopt the clothing and mannerisms of *Star Trek*'s most well-known 'baddies'. Taking the role of a Klingon has even been seen by some fans as a 'therapeutic' exercise. As a Klingon, an individual can be domineering, rude and aggressive and still be accepted, thus allowing fans a 'safe outlet' for emotions that are normally repressed in 'polite society'.

It is surely no coincidence that, as the 'cult' nature of the *Star Trek* audience has grown, the respect for religious forms showcased in the narratives of the programmes has increased. The movement from the rather naïve humanism of the original series to the more culturally inclusive and even 'spiritual' viewpoint expressed in *DS9* and *Voyager* mirrors the growth of *Star Trek* fandom into a significant cultural phenomenon and reflects the considerable challenges to the philosophy of scientific rationalism and the belief in the inevitability of social 'progress' that have been made since the 1960s. In the original series, the scientific humanism of the Starfleet/Federation culture is invariably able to overcome the 'superstitious' beliefs of various 'primitive' races. Very often what appear to be 'gods' are merely more technologically advanced beings such as Apollo in *Who Mourns for Adonais?* or the computer Vaal in *The Apple*. The assumption appears to be that eventually, in any society, religious belief will be replaced by an enlightened and 'logical' view of the universe (as epitomised by the Vulcans). But in the new *Trek* series the religious beliefs of different cultures become increasingly identified as valuable elements of their heritage. In *TNG*'s *Sarek* the famous Vulcan 'mind control' is revealed as the product of an intense programme of meditation, thus linking the Vulcans to aspects of Buddhism and Hinduism, and by implication turning what appeared to be a purely rationalistic set of beliefs into a more 'spiritual' one. In *Voyager* Tuvok's Vulcan meditations and Chakotay's Native American spiritual practices are frequently featured. Chakotay's 'visions' are taken completely seriously by Captain Janeway, who sometimes participates in them herself. In *DS9* even the Ferengi are provided with their own 'spoof' religion with an afterlife in the 'Divine Treasury'.

It is in the searching examination of the Bajoran religion in *DS9* that *Star Trek* provides its most authentically 'spiritual' stories. The Bajoran religion is seen to have many 'cult' factions, and is something of a 'composite' of elements of contemporary religious belief. The main tenets of the religion are given considerable credibility, in that its 'prophets' are alien beings who actually do exist on a 'higher plane of consciousness'. After his encounter with the 'prophets' in *Emissary*, Sisko – who had become somewhat hard-bitten and cynical after the death of his wife – undergoes what can only be described as a 'spiritual renewal'. At times his actions appear to be motivated by mysterious, unexplainable forces which he cannot even identify himself.

The fifth season episode, *Rapture* (written by Hans Beimler and L. J. Strom), explores in detail Sisko's role as the 'Emissary'. Although he is initially extremely wary of being assigned to this role, in this episode he comes to realise that he really has been 'chosen' to be the conduit between the wormhole aliens and the Bajoran people. Having suffered a severe electric shock in a holosuite, he begins to experience a series of revelations relating to the future of Bajor which are given no obvious scientific explanation. To the bewilderment of other members of the crew, he begins to spend long hours in silent, ecstatic contemplation. Somehow 'possessed' by his visions, he locates the legendary ancient Bajoran city of B'hala, for which Bajorans have searched in vain for thousands of years. This discovery further enhances his semidivine status among the Bajorans and even convinces the normally devious Kai Winn that Sisko is indeed the prophets' 'chosen one'. Bashir informs Sisko that he is suffering from a condition that, if not treated soon, may kill him. But the treatment would stop the visions, and Sisko is determined to let them continue, despite the protests of his son Jake and his girlfriend, Kassidy Yates. In an attempt to explain this apparently self-destructive urge, a wild-eyed Sisko tells them the series of visions he is encountering are more important that his own life. Even when a tearful Kassidy protests that he risks leaving Jake as an orphan, Sisko will not relent, telling her that he feels as if he is 'holding the entire universe in his hands'.

Meanwhile, Starfleet Command announces that Bajor has finally been accepted into the Federation and a ceremonial meeting is set up to formalise arrangements for what has been the Federation's, and Sisko's, long-term goal since the beginning of the series. But at the last moment, just before Bajor signs the declaration, a wild-eyed Sisko bursts in and announces that he has seen a vision of a 'cloud of locusts' heading towards Cardassia. He tells the delegates that it is not yet time for Bajor to join the Federation, then collapses. The Bajorans interpret his visions as a series of messages from the 'prophets' and as a result the treaty is not signed. As Sisko's next of kin, Jake finally gives Bashir permission to operate, and the visions end. When Sisko wakes up, his initial feelings are of deep regret that his visionary journey was incomplete.

Starfleet's stuffy Admiral Whatley, who is supervising the process of Bajoran accession, represents the 'official' logically scientific Federation perspective in giving Sisko's visions little credence. Federation culture is now presented as somewhat narrow-minded, as the limitations of its scientific-humanist worldview are exposed. Although Sisko's visions are given a physiological explanation, the 'spiritual' nature of the visions themselves cannot be explained away by any convenient 'scientific' explanation. For the first time *Star Trek* acknowledges the 'reality' of spirituality and makes no attempt to explain it away scientifically or relegate it to the status of 'primitive' belief.

As the next chapter argues, the evolution of *Star Trek* has led to its adoption of many of the features of a 'mythical' system which has superseded and overtaken its original rationalist viewpoint. In doing so *Star Trek* is primarily responding to the demands of its fans, whose activities may seem 'illogical' but who see in *Star Trek* ways of confronting and working out many pressing modern dilemmas. Just as religious traditions in the past communicated their morality by means of 'sacred' stories, so *Star Trek* presents a distinctive worldview and a set of credible ethics with which its audience can become truly 'involved'. Just as devotees of the Bajoran religion stare into their 'sacred orbs' to receive 'visions', so many *Star Trek* fans treat viewing it as a kind of 'sacrament', caught up – like Sisko in the aforementioned episode – in a kind of 'rapture' which only the intimacy of the television medium can provide. As Gregor T. Goethals states:

> Through the ritual and iconic richness of its visual images, television answers ... sacramental needs. Its images offer the security of

real and imagined 'worlds', larger than the individual. And at the same time they hold out to the viewers, perhaps not the reality of heroism, but the excitement of vicarious human adventure. To live today in the awareness of a mystical, transcendent order of being and of unknown dimensions of time and human experience opens up fearful and undreamed-of worlds … (1981, p. 143)

Chapter **8**

Mythos and *logos*: *Star Trek* as mythic narrative

> Myths are ... revelations of the deepest hopes, desires and
> fears, potentialities and conflicts, of the human will ... every
> myth is psychologically symbolic. Its narratives and images
> are to be read, therefore, not literally, but as metaphors ...
>
> (Joseph Campbell, 1985, p. 55)

One of the apparent contradictions of *Star Trek* is that, while its audience insists on continually high levels of narrative consistency and scientific 'realism', it seems perfectly prepared to accept certain standardised dramatic conventions of action-adventure which violate such 'realist' principles. A good example of this is the way in which *Star Trek* characters may, in the course of a 'life or death' battle scene, pause to make 'significant', or even humorous philosophical observations to each other. In many traditional mythical tales there is similarly plenty of room for playful banter or philosophising, often featuring much use of irony and paradox, even if the heroes are in apparently mortal danger. The oral storytelling traditions depended on the audience's pre-knowledge of the narrative conventions of the form which allowed storytellers to 'play' in a self-referential manner with various contemporary and universal themes. The way in which postmodern TV narratives 'play' with the history of their own texts duplicates this process in the modern era. Many ancient storytelling forms have reasserted themselves through the medium of TV which, as argued in the Introduction, now assumes the cultural status once held by the traditional storyteller or 'bard'. Like traditional 'fireside' listeners, the TV audience must be prepared to suspend disbelief for the duration of the tale, knowing that the 'true meaning' of the story may well lie beneath its surface. As Roger Silverstone (1981, p. 1) points out:

television preserves forms of cultural expression that were previously thought of as being the peculiar prerogative of 'primitive' societies, and in doing so it anchors our historical, changing, uncertain experience into another which is relatively unchanging and more certain …

Claude Lévi-Strauss (1966, p. 6) argues that mythic narratives evolve through a process he calls *bricolage*, whereby a multiplicity of storytellers incorporate many apparently disparate cultural elements into their versions of traditional tales. Just as groups of mythical stories characteristically expand over time and absorb elements from a range of sources, so *Star Trek* has continued to 'soak up' many features of disparate mythical and generic systems. As *Star Trek* has evolved, it has taken on many of the qualities of a *saga*, a series of interconnected narratives based on the exploits of mythical heroes who 'seek their destinies' through heroic adventure. In an Icelandic saga such as the thirteenth-century *Prose Edda* there is – as in *Star Trek* – much violence, but the qualities of dignity and self-restraint of the legendary hero Baldr the Good are (rather like those of Worf, Odo or Picard) constantly emphasised.

The nature of both Kirk's 'five-year mission' and Picard's 'continuing mission' – to search the outer reaches of the galaxy for new life-forms – places both the original series and *TNG* in the mode of an *odyssey*: – a heroic journey into the unknown made constantly perilous by encounters with 'fantastical creatures'. In comparison *DS9*, set in a fortified space station surrounded by dangerous enemies, is more like *Star Trek*'s *Iliad*, but *Voyager*, like the wanderings of Homer's Odysseus, is centred on an attempt to return home from unknown territory. The presentation in *Star Trek*'s 'time-paradox' stories of a 'multiverse' with its shifting 'time dimensions' can be seen as an example of 'mythic time', which, according to Mircea Eliade, exists in a different framework from that of ordinary time (1961, p. 6). Eliade points out that traditional tales generally take place in a world in which conventional historical, linear chronological progression is generally denied. Such 'magical' figures as Q, the Traveler and the wormhole 'prophets' appear to exist permanently in such a setting, into which they frequently bring *Star Trek*'s main characters.

In terms of its overall narrative form, it is possible to compare *Star Trek* to mythical story cycles such the Arthurian legends, which grew to become probably the most popular and influential group of mythic stories of the medieval period in Western Europe. In this context, it is important to point out that the rapid development of both modern technology and the industrial conditions of modern film and television over the last three decades have accelerated the evolution of its *mythos* at a much faster rate than would ever have been possible for a saga or group of stories in the days of pre-literate cultures. Like *Star Trek*, the Arthurian legends were multi-authored texts which achieved mass popularity. Their authors created a particular 'universe' within which a literally infinite number of stories could be told. As these stories were embellished by oral transmission, they evolved into vehicles for the exploration of contemporary social and political concerns. Only the most popular and the most resonant storylines and characters survived. The main Arthurian characters grew, like those in *Star Trek*, into archetypal figures representing various universal psychological traits. There are many instances in the various *Star Trek* series that have parallels in the Arthurian legends. As the new *Trek* series develop their greater interest in, and emphasis on, spiritual matters these parallels increase. Like the Arthurian knights, *Star Trek*'s Klingon warriors are motivated primarily by the 'noble' concept of personal honour. In *DS9*'s *The Sword of Kahless* Worf and Kor engage in a search for the Klingon equivalent of the holy grail. Similarly, the orbs that the Bajorans stare into to receive their spiritual revelations are distinctively 'grail-shaped'.

Perhaps a more obvious comparison would be with the self-consciously mythic *Star Wars* saga, for which producer–director George Lucas, like Roddenberry, also created his own dramatic 'universe'. Lucas had become convinced through reading the work of the renowned expert on world mythology, Joseph Campbell, that a story which touched on strong mythological elements could be tremendously popular if mixed with modern high-tech gadgetry and cinematic technology. He even enlisted Campbell's help and advice in devising the entire *Star Wars* scenario. As a result the film trilogy, completed by *The Empire Strikes Back* (1980) and *Return of the Jedi* (1983) is very deliberately constructed around mythological themes. This is made quite explicit in the opening credits, which begin 'A LONG TIME AGO IN A GALAXY FAR FAR AWAY ...'.

Star Wars also contains prominent elements typical of mythic stories – a young hero in the 'Arthur' mould who is destined for greatness (Luke Skywalker); his more experienced helper (Han Solo); a princess in distress (Leia); a Merlin-like magician and 'spiritual adviser' (Obi-Wan-Kenobi); and a classical 'dark' villain (Darth Vader). The whole saga is given a quasi-mythic significance by constant references to 'The

Force', a kind of spiritual power perhaps more readily associated with Buddhist or Pagan concepts than the Christian monotheistic God. But the *Star Wars* movies, though often brilliantly cinematic to a degree that the *Star Trek* movies have rarely matched, are conceived basically as escapist entertainment. *Star Wars'* mythology has been deliberately – some would even say cynically – constructed. It makes no real attempt at setting the apparent evils of its Galactic Empire in any kind of social context. It is pure, if highly effective, mythological fantasy. Thus *Star Wars*, which has always been under the direct control of Lucas, can be said to be 'mythological' in a deliberately contrived way, whereas *Star Trek*, with its multiplicity of authorship, has grown more naturally into a mythological system. The development of *Star Trek's* storytelling techniques has evolved through its writers' perception of which elements its audience finds most likely to keep them 'tuned in'.

The term 'mythology' is an amalgam of what Ancient Greek philosophers called the *mythos* and the *logos*. *Mythos* refers to a group of connected narratives which – like the Greek myths, the Icelandic sagas or the Hindu *Mahabharata* – use a heroic mode of storytelling to reveal moral positions that attempt to define the place of humanity in the cosmos. Traditionally, a particular *mythos* is set in an indeterminate time before the present era and is frequently peopled by 'gods', 'demons' and 'angels', often with fantastical powers. The stories within such a *mythos* are often coded moral fables which reveal the key concerns of the society from which they originate. Some Greek philosophers such as Plato and Aristotle criticised *mythos* as a means of knowing reality and favoured the approach of *logos* – the rational, analytical mode of thought which has in more recent centuries become the foundation of the scientific and technological age. As Eric Dardel comments: 'In societies where, with the advent of the Logos, nature has come out of her darkness, the myth has been driven back into the shadows ... But even so it has not disappeared ...' (Dardel, 1954, pp. 33–51).

The tension between *mythos* and *logos* – between the myth and its interpretation, between faith and rationality, religion and science – gives *Star Trek* much of its dramatic focus and energy. In the original series *mythos* and *logos* are contrasted prominently, both in terms of characterisation and overall theme. As he constantly takes pains to remind us, the Vulcan Mr Spock clearly represents the logical mode of thought, which is frequently contrasted with the emotionalism and sentimentality of Dr McCoy. Captain Kirk stands in between the two and juggles advice from both Spock and McCoy to solve his problems.

In doing so his reasoning mirrors that of viewers caught between being absorbed into the fantasy world of *Star Trek* and judging its 'scientific' and 'dramatic' viability. This is illustrated in the original series episodes which frequently end in short light-hearted 'teasers' during which Spock, McCoy and Kirk's banter plays on their respectively logical, emotional and inclusive roles. McCoy frequently attempts to goad Spock into admitting that he has emotions, but Spock continually asserts his logicality. Yet in *The Galileo Seven*, the limitations of a purely logical approach are shown when Spock, stranded in a lost shuttlecraft with very little fuel left, decides at the last moment to jettison the fuel tanks. The resultant flare luckily alerts the *Enterprise* and Spock's 'highly illogical' risk saves himself and his crew. The half-human Spock is thus revealed as a living amalgam of *logos* and *mythos*. Though dominated by his logicality, even he at times has to admit the limitations of a purely rational approach.

Each of the succeeding *Star Trek* series builds on the *mythos–logos* conflict in different ways. In *TNG*, the same kind of rational–irrational discourse is assigned to the character of Data, who, as an android, is naturally 'logical' but whose greatest wish is to be 'more human'. In *Voyager* the Maquis officers are often presented as being more quick-thinking, spontaneous and 'streetwise' than those from the 'logical' but conventional Starfleet. The combination of the Federation and Maquis elements in the crew provides the *mythos–logos* balance once supplied by Kirk, Spock and McCoy. Thus *Star Trek* balances the conflict between rationality and emotion, and between science and the imagination. Through a process of trial and error, *Star Trek*'s writers have discovered that the presentation of this 'balancing act' has been the major factor in keeping its viewers 'hooked'.

Carl Jung's concept of 'archetypes' has a particular application to characters in TV shows. Jung theorised the existence of a 'collective unconscious' which all human beings share, within which can be identified universal or 'archetypal' figures such as the great mother, the child or the wise old man: 'The concept of the archetype, which is an indispensable correlate of the idea of the collective unconscious, indicates the existence of definite forms in the psyche which seem to be present always and everywhere … (1971, p. 160). The most successful TV characters are those which come closest to such archetypal images – like Alexis Carrington in *Dynasty* (the archetypal 'greedy bitch') or Bart Simpson (the archetypal 'naughty kid') – representations of the audience's most basic perceptions of human character. According to Martin Esslin: 'there has sprung up with TV a whole population of archetypal figures who appear daily or weekly and who can become familiar, intimately known, easily absorbed into the fantasy life and consciousness of millions of individuals ...' (1982, p. 72).

American 'psychedelic mystic' Robert Anton Wilson has identified the figure of Spock as one such collective archetype, a modern version of the figure of Pan or Mescalito, known to dozens of Shamanic Traditions:

> The greenish-skinned, pointy-eared man ... has appeared in the folklore of many cultures ... He has been seen most recently, in recent years, as a humanoid extraterrestrial in various flying saucer reports by alleged contactees. And, in the late 1960s, he began to appear regularly on TV, known as 'Mr. Spock' on the *'Star Trek'* show, and has remained on the tube ever since, despite frequent network attempts to cancel the show and get rid of him. The fans always want to bring him back ... him or his image, or as Jung would say, an 'archetype' that cannot be erased from the human mind ... (1978, p. 36)

Many of *Star Trek's* other leading characters can be said to have archetypal characteristics. While other Vulcans such as Tuvok and Sarek personify a logical approach, the android Data and the 'child-woman' Kes stand for 'innocent' and childlike perception. The series' captains are positioned to represent moral choice and control and the various doctors to embody compassionate viewpoints. 'Spiritual warriors' such as Worf, Kira and Chakotay can be said to represent the disciplined control of anger. All such characters are hero-figures with whom the audience can identify. Joseph Campbell (whose work is based on Jungian models) argues that under the surface all 'hero myths' have the same plot (which he refers to as 'the monomyth') and therefore carry the same meaning, which is ultimately a metaphysical 'rediscovery of the unconscious'. According to Campbell, the hero's physical adventures, be they the labours of Hercules or Theseus killing the Minotaur, are significant only as symbolic representations of the inner journey which every individual has to face: 'Anyone going on a journey, inward or outward, to find *values*, will be on a journey that has been described many times in the myths of mankind ...' (quoted in Segal, 1987, p. 21). Campbell describes this 'heroic journey' as being characterised by a pattern of 'separation', 'initiation' and 'return': 'separation' from his home and family, 'initiation' into the mysteries of a strange and fantastic world and 'return' to share the benefits among his fellows: 'A hero ventures forth from the world of common day into a region of supernatural wonder: fabulous forces are there encountered and decisive victory is won: the hero comes back from this mysterious adventure with the power to bestow boons on his fellow man ... (Campbell, 1949, p. 30). Campbell's archetypal hero 'boldly goes' into: 'a distant land, a forest, a kingdom underground, beneath the waves, or above the sky, a secret island, lofty mountain-top, or profound dream state' but it is always a place of strangely fluid and polymorphous beings, unimaginable torments, superhuman deeds and impossible delight ...' (ibid., p. 47).

Star Trek is certainly an arena for heroism, and its heroes are invari-ably incorruptible, steadfast figures whom the audience can rely on to triumph over their enemies. The characters are subjected to a number of 'unimaginable torments' including wrongful imprisonment, torture and a range of alien viruses and diseases and they frequently have to display 'superhuman' qualities to survive such traumas. They face a range of 'strangely fluid and polymorphous beings' in the many new life-forms they experience. These sometimes take the form of giant beings who live in space itself, such as the huge, living crystalline entity in *TNG's Datalore*, or the 'living spaceships' in *Encounter at Farpoint* and *Tin Man*.

The many 'heroic inner journeys' depicted in the new *Trek* series allow each of the major characters to take on the characteristics of Campbell's universal hero. In *TNG's The Inner Light* Picard is given a lifetime's experience in the space of just three minutes, and in *Tapestry* he is able to 'relive' part of his earlier life. In *Frame of Mind* Riker is subjected to a number of different 'realities', as are Worf in *Parallels* and Beverly Crusher in *Remember Me*. In *DS9's Emissary* Sisko's 'visions' in the wormhole help to prepare him psychologically for the 'heroic battles' that lie ahead. In *Voyager's Cathexis* Chakotay is trapped in an illusory world which resembles that of his spiritual explorations with a medicine wheel; and in *Projections* the Doctor comes to question the nature of his own holographic 'reality'. Each 'inner journey' tests the character to the limit and allows them 'heroic' revelations of self-discovery. In many ways these stories – like traditional tales – tell what is essentially the same story, that of the 'dismemberment' and subsequent 'reintegration' of the self.

A prominent mythic feature of *Star Trek* is its continual use of phys-ical transformations. Many traditional tales, most of which are fables which serve moral purposes, feature such transformations. The tradi-tional Germanic story of *The Frog Prince* – wherein a young girl is made to honour a promise made to a frog to share her bed in return for his finding her lost 'golden ball' – symbolises the mixture of repulsion and attraction towards sexuality often experienced by adolescent girls. Ovid's *Metamorphoses* recounts the many 'transformations' in Graeco-Roman mythology such as the turning of Narcissus into a flower, a story which warns of the dangers of too much self-love. Similar transformations abound in *Star Trek*: although they are frequently given 'scientific' explanations, they tend to fulfil the function of creating a framework for moral statements. In *The Enemy Within* and subsequent 'double' stories different facets of each character are counterposed and evaluated. These stories typically use the transformational device to suggest that individuals must accept their 'dark side' in order to be whole persons, thus providing another example of the *mythos–logos* equation. Over the years most of the major characters experience some form of physical or mental transformation – whether it be one of the many mental 'take-overs' such as that of Keiko O'Brien in *The Assignment* or Kes in *Warlord*, or such physical changes as the 'de-evolution' of crew members in *TNG*'s *Genesis* or *Voyager*'s *Threshold*.

The *Star Trek* universe is also inhabited by a number of 'cosmic tricksters' who resemble similar figures in traditional myths. For instance, both the Native American and West African mythological cycles involve stories in which a trickster – a playful, greedy, pretentious and deceitful figure – may confuse or lead mythical heroes astray. The archetypal trickster may appear in the guise of Coyote or Anansi the spider on the African Plains, Raven on the Northwest American coast or Eshu in West Africa. Tricksters are said to be responsible for all the quarrels between human beings and gods. They are crafty jokers with god-like powers, who are often ultimately undone by their own bungling, and 'trickster tales' are often told to illustrate moral rules and boundaries. *Who Mourns For Adonais?*, from the original series, features as its 'cosmic trickster' a powerful being who proclaims himself to be none other than the ancient Greek god, Apollo. He is the last member of a highly advanced race who, thousands of years ago, landed in ancient Greece where they were worshipped as gods. Apollo captures Kirk and his crew in an attempt to compel them to 'worship' him as the ancient Greek peasants did. But he underestimates both the scientific development that has taken place among the human race and the determination of Kirk and his crew not to succumb. Kirk breaks much of Apollo's power by preventing members of his crew from 'believing' in him and then 'humbles' him by using the *Enterprise*'s phasers to destroy his technological 'power source'.

Another trickster figure in the original series is Trelane, a being from
a higher civilisation who is apparently capable of creating an entire
planet out of his mind. In *The Squire of Gothos* Trelane captures Kirk
and his crew for his amusement, but the intervention of his incorpor-
eal 'parents' reveals him as a wilful and 'naughty' child.
Star Trek's supreme trickster, however, is undoubtedly Q (originally
modelled to some extent on Trelane), who makes guest appearances in
eight episodes of *TNG* and later makes occasional visits to *DS9* and
Voyager. Q's race, the Q Continuum, are virtually omnipotent by
human standards and he is capable of achieving almost anything
through the power of his thought. Q can take any appearance he
chooses, can change costumes and settings at will and can even divert
the paths of planets if he so wishes. As a recurring presence in *TNG* he
acts as a playful alter-ego to the rather stern and serious Picard. But he
is also, in the great tradition of the trickster, extremely vain, self-
obsessed and capable of acting entirely on a whim. *TNG*'s Q stories,
like the trickster tales, test the limitations of the morality that informs
them. In *Hide and Q*, Q plays the role of tempter, offering to make Data
human, make Geordi see and fulfil the rest of the crew's fantasies. But
they all reject his offers, feeling that to preserve their humanity they
must remain 'unsullied' by his meddling. Like the traditional trickster,
Q is fundamentally flawed and in his way he is far weaker than
humans. His 'god-like' status is offset by his insufferable pretentious-
ness, for which Picard has only scorn. In *Tapestry*, when Q tells Picard
that he is dead and that Q himself is God, Picard refuses to believe
him, angrily retorting that 'I refuse to believe that the afterlife is run
by you. The universe is not so badly designed'.
According to Theodore Gaster (1954, pp. 184–212), traditional
mythological stories evolve through four identifiable stages – *primitive, dramatic, liturgical* and *literary*. In the 'primitive' stage the story
is directly related to the ritual that accompanies it, usually a ritual
which is being performed for pragmatic purposes such as a plea for
rain to water crops. In the myth's 'dramatic' phase the ritual or cultic
performance may be transformed into a 'pantomimic' representation
such as that of St George slaying a dragon. By the much later 'liturgical' phase the key elements of the myth are already established as
a 'known quantity' by its audience, and contemporary writers can
begin to embellish it, a tendency which reaches its climax in the
'literary' phase. By the literary phase, the myth has become a tale, yet
it still carries within it the resonance of the original myth. As an
example, modern literary works based on the Arthurian legends, such

as T. H. White's *Once and Future King* (1958) and Marion Zimmer Bradley's *Mists of Avalon* (1982), have used the Arthurian legends as a base for building on and often reinterpreting the traditional characters and situations.

In Gaster's terms, *Star Trek's* original series could be said to represent its 'primitive' phase. In the 1960s a programme could only be watched at a certain time each week and the viewing of a particular show could become a regular weekly 'ritual' for the audience. Each episode of the original *Star Trek* is a self-contained story, thus allowing completely new viewers to take part in the 'ritual'. Every episode is focused on the three main heroes – Kirk, Spock and McCoy – who 'ritually' counterpose mythical and logical points of view. The 1980s film series can be said to embody the 'dramatic' phase in the evolution of *Star Trek*. Placing the familiar crew in a present-day setting in *The Voyage Home*, and making a 'diplomatic' Klingon–Starfleet dinner in *The Undiscovered Country* into a burlesque of bad manners, certainly created 'pantomimic' situations. The ironic distance between the 'naïvety' of the original 1960s series and its more self-aware big-screen equivalent is a constant source of reference. The early *TNG* stories (and the later, ironic 'tribute' shows such as *Relics*, *Crossover* or *Trials and Tribble-ations*) may be said to represent *Star Trek's* 'liturgical' phase, with their constant references to the 'legendary' stories of the original series, whereas the later *TNG* (after Berman and Piller gained authorial control), *DS9* and *Voyager* place *Star Trek* firmly in its 'literary' phase. The characters, and the relationships between them, such as the on–off attraction between Riker and Troi, are seen to develop and change over the course of the episodes. The passage of time is clearly acknowledged, and previous events are frequently referred to. With *Voyager* there is a conscious return to the 'heroic' mode of the original series, but the relationships between the characters are even more complex, owing to the Federation–Maquis split among the crew. Thus all three new *Trek* series can be seen as 'literary' embellishments of Roddenberry's original 'primitive' myth. This literary stage is one which has evolved naturally from the mythic nature of *Star Trek's* overall development.

Joseph Campbell identifies mythic stories as having four key functions for their audience – the sociological, the psychological, the cosmological and the mystical or metaphysical. As various chapters of this book demonstrate, *Star Trek* provides plentiful examples of each function. It has many stories which relate to contemporary social issues and it undertakes many psychological explorations of character.

Its own unique cosmology presents not only a complex 'future history', but a view of the entire past evolution of the universe. Finally it stimulates a sense of awe at the 'mystery of being' which – particularly in the *DS9* episodes relating to the 'prophets' – takes it into metaphysical realms. Ultimately it is as much about 'inner space' as 'outer space'.

Chapter **9**

Historicism, gothicism and paradox: *Star Trek* and genre

The main vehicle for the 'ritual' presentation of mythological stories in the various formats of modern media culture is that of genre. Throughout the twentieth century certain generic narrative forms have come to dominate popular culture, providing both familiar narrative environments for their consumers and reliable financial investments for their producers. The origins of genre stretch back to before the invention of cinema to the gothic horror novels of the late eighteenth century and the comic books and detective stories that achieved great popularity in the nineteenth century. In film's silent era various genres such as the historical epic and the slapstick comedy rose to prominence. Following the coming of sound in 1928, gangster films and musicals were in vogue and in the post-war era 'film noir' detective stories and westerns dominated. As TV was established, much of its programming was 'slotted' into various genres, such as soap operas, police stories and hospital dramas. In the modern era, science fiction has emerged as perhaps the dominant genre in both film and TV. As the technologies of computers, space travel, genetic engineering and mass media grow in influence, so SF stories have increasingly become the most appropriate 'language' for dealing with contemporary anxieties about their potential effects upon society.

Generic fictions have increasingly been found to be a rich source of interaction between creators and audiences. Audiences become progressively more attuned to the conventions of a particular genre, to the extent that they can come to 'read' those conventions as a series of symbolic signs. Thus a modern piece of generic pastiche such as Quentin Tarantino's *Pulp Fiction* (1994), which features extremely graphic portrayals of violence, has nevertheless quite correctly been understood by its modern audience as a comedy based on upsetting expectations of generic cause-and-effect chains. As Bennett and Woolacott argue:

> periods of generic change and innovation in popular fiction often coincide with those in which the ideological articulations through which hegemony was previously secured are no longer working to produce popular consent ... the refraction of history in which genre engages acts as a catalyst enables other ideological forms to be rearticulated in a new configuration ... (in Tulloch, 1990, p. 74)

This could in itself be taken as a description of the changes which *Star Trek* underwent in the 1990s as the 'next generation' of series writers began to challenge Gene Roddenberry's liberal-humanist ideology. The shift in the third season of *TNG* from closure-orientated stories to those with less resolved endings which gravitate towards the serial mode marks the transition of *Star Trek* from a series of what Umberto Eco (1979, ch. 2) calls 'closed texts' to the status of an interconnected 'open text' – one in which 'readers' are called upon to interpret the message of a story themselves', and for which no single 'explanation' suffices. The stories themselves may leap from serious juxtapositions of ethical or diplomatic problems to mocking self-parody, sometimes within the course of a single episode. Although *Star Trek* relies on a 'surface' level of realism and 'scientific' credibility to make its stories seem acceptable, its creators are fully aware that its audience – knowing the conventions of the series as it does – will accept the most fantastical stories if they are presented as being consistent with those conventions. Thus *Star Trek* becomes a 'forum' for generic storytelling which can encompass a vast range of storytelling modes from 'family dramas' to 'detective stories' to ecological thrillers and stories of spiritual 'possession'. Its established narrative conventions – which are formulated against the backdrop of a relativistic Einsteinian universe – allow for the most extreme manipulation of storylines and character development. A *Star Trek* episode may take us back to the beginning of time, show regular characters 'de-evolving' into 'monsters' or 'returning from the dead' or create any number of duplicates of those characters. The notion that 'anything can happen in *Star Trek*' allows *Star Trek*'s writers to present a unique range of perspectives and to make use of a number of contrasting storytelling modes.

It must be stressed here that as well as having its own 'alternative history' *Star Trek* has an entire system of 'alternative science'. The series takes place mainly within one 'quadrant' of our galaxy and, though it invents the 'warp drive' as a means of travelling between star systems, it generally maintains a realistic perspective on the size of the galaxy itself. Of course our galaxy is one among billions, but *Star Trek* rarely attempts to stretch the bounds of credibility too far by travelling to other galaxies. One of Roddenberry's most important early conceptions was that of 'M' class planets – worlds whose environmental conditions are similar enough to Earth to make contact with the inhabitants feasible. Although a considerable number of non-humanoid beings are encountered, *Star Trek*'s 'political universe' is confined to humanoid creatures who inhabit 'M'-class worlds. This is both a practical – and within the parameters of scientific credibility *Star Trek* sets for itself – feasible scenario. In *TNG*'s 'archaeological thriller', *The Chase*, it is revealed that all the humanoid races in the galaxy have a common genetic origin. Thus the Klingons, Romulans, Ferengi, Cardassians and the vast majority of species encountered can be seen as part of a 'human family'. Dramatically this works well, because it allows different humanoid species to embody particular human characteristics and for the political alignments and social and religious differences within the *Star Trek* universe to reflect on the complexity of present-day Earth cultures.

Lawrence M. Krauss, in *The Physics Of Star Trek*, reveals that much of its technology, including the computer systems of the ship, the 'virtual reality' holodeck and such devices as the 'tricorder' have a clear basis in established scientific theory. Using Einsteinian notions of 'curved space', Krauss also theorises that the 'warp' drive that makes faster-than-light travel possible might even become a realisable possibility, and would in itself involve the notion of time travel, another regular *Star Trek* narrative device. But he concludes that other elements, such as the transporter beam and food replicators, are pure fantasy. *Star Trek* is, like all science fiction, necessarily a marriage of science and the imagination. We are left in no doubt of the crucial role that technology has played in the creation of Earth's utopian society. Woven into virtually every script is what *Star Trek* fans rather lovingly call 'technobabble': sets of instructions or explanations passed between the crew to explain particular phenomena with 'twenty-fourth-century' science. As Geordi says to Reg Barclay in *TNG*'s *Realm Of Fear*: 'The residual energy from the plasma streamer must have amplified the charge in the buffer enough to keep your patterns from degrading ...'. Of course, this is pseudo-science, but *Star Trek*'s team of scientific and technical advisers have to ensure that it is *consistent* pseudo-science. Many prominent features of *Star Trek* technology – such as the 'universal translator' (which by the time of *TNG* becomes explained as an implanted technological device) that allows (almost) all humanoid species to communicate with each other – may have little basis in any real 'science' but work well as dramatic devices to keep the action moving. In order to maintain credibility with the fans, *Star Trek*'s designers have published intricately detailed 'plans' of the various *Enterprises*, accompanied by 'scientific' schematics as to how the ships work. A significant section of the *Star Trek* production team is employed in the perfection of the tiniest details of what becomes a complex, if imaginary, scientific construct. Such is the 'cultic' nature of *Star Trek* fandom that any anomaly will be instantly picked up. In his *Nitpicker's Guide for Next Generation Trekkers*, Phil Farrand devotes an entire 400-page volume to such technicalities. To 'outsiders' such apparent 'fanaticism' may seem to indicate the obsession for trivia which denotes the rather disparaging term 'Trekkie', but the rigorous scrutiny of such an audience group has had the effect of forcing *Star Trek*'s creators to create a scientific environment that is – in its own terms – consistent and credible, as well as ensuring a high degree of continuity between episodes.

The transporter is perhaps the best known of all *Star Trek*'s scientific 'inventions'. Originally a cost-cutting 'special effect' devised by Roddenberry to avoid the constant necessity of shooting expensive 'landing' scenes, the transporter was the most visually distinctive feature of the original series, making imaginative use of rudimentary special-effects technology. It also became possibly the most well-known element of *Star Trek* to be recognised by the wider public. Kirk's (apocryphal) phrase 'Beam me up Scotty' has become an almost universally understood shorthand phrase for anyone who wishes to be 'magically transported' from a particular situation. The idea of the transporter fulfils a very common human fantasy – that of magical escape – which features in a great many traditional stories and myths. Its operation may be, as Spock would say, 'illogical', but it touches a universal, perhaps even archetypal, nerve.

Star Trek has absorbed a wide range of influences from the whole gamut of different traditions within the science fiction genre. As a genre science fiction characteristically deals with social anxiety about technological change, and is thus a distinctive product of the industrial revolution. Mary Shelley's *Frankenstein* (1818), in which an inventor creates an 'artificial man' that both threatens and parodies humanity itself, is often seen as the first SF story. As a character, Frankenstein's monster is certainly a precursor of Spock, Data, Odo and *Voyager*'s Doctor, characters whose 'outsider' status focuses attention on the nature of 'humanity'. *TNG*'s *Thine Own Self* provides an echo of the Frankenstein story when an amnesiac Data unwittingly infects a whole village with radiation poisoning. As a result the villagers 'kill' and bury him. Edgar Allan Poe, another writer normally associated with 'horror', is often seen as the inventor of the SF short story. His haunting psychological study, *William Wilson* (1840), in which the main character encounters and is plagued by his *doppelgänger*, has no 'technological' justification but is the model for many SF stories, including the numerous *Star Trek* 'double' episodes. Both *Frankenstein* and *William Wilson* are products of 'gothic' romanticism, betraying the origins of SF in the gothic tradition. As Aldiss asserts: 'Science fiction is the search for a definition of man and his status in the universe which will stand in our advanced but confused state of knowledge, and is characteristically cast in the gothic or post-gothic mode ...' (1973, p. 8).

Thus while much SF may be based around the application of the theoretical limits of technologies, in terms of characterisation and narrative it has its roots in the fantastical. SF has always been a very inclusive genre, and the exact point at which it 'merges' into horror has always been hard to define. Much low-budget 1950s SF relied on 'monster stories', and the *Alien* film series, though nominally SF, is actually dominated by the visual and narrative conventions of horror. Three episodes written by Brannon Braga from *TNG*'s final season include strong elements of the horror genre: *Sub Rosa* features Beverly Crusher returning to the house of her recently deceased grandmother and beginning a passionate affair with a 'spirit' who has been the lover of several previous generations of women in her family; in the extraordinary *Genesis*, various members of the crew 'de-evolve' – Riker into a primitive man, Troi into a reptile and Worf into a pre-Klingon 'wild beast'; and in the surreal *Phantasms*, Data begins to have strange dreams, one of which features Deanna Troi as a living cake. Each story, however, has a 'scientific' explanation, whereas 'pure' horror stories would rely on the magical.

Science fiction movies, which follow a very different historical trajectory from SF literature, also provide a number of reference points that have been used in *Star Trek*. For many years SF was a 'low-budget' film genre which appealed mainly to teenage audiences. In the 1950s this led to the making of hundreds of SF movies, mostly tailor-made for the 'hamburgers and drive-in' American movie culture of the time. Many were sensationalist and highly exploitative, generally featuring a horrific 'monster' which is revealed in the closing scenes. Roddenberry tried hard to steer *Star Trek* away from such a 'juvenile' framework, which had also dominated TV SF up to the mid-1960s. Yet a number of 1950s SF films can be clearly seen to have influenced *Star Trek* over the years. *It Came from Outer Space* (1953) and *Invasion of the Body Snatchers* (1956) featured the narrative device of 'alien possession' (obviously a cheap practical alternative for film-makers, because it avoided the need for alien make-up). This device has been used on numerous occasions throughout the entire run of *Star Trek*, allowing members of the cast to show 'hidden' dark sides to their personalities. The 'look' of the space-ship and the space battles depicted in *This Island Earth* (1955) have a remarkable resemblance to those of the original series. The scenario of *Forbidden Planet* (1956), where a Prospero-like scientist controls a whole planet with his thoughts but eventually begins to go mad, has a striking resemblance to the story of *Requiem for Methuselah*.

Other more contemporary SF films have also had a pronounced influence on the new *Trek* series. *Star Wars* (1977) set a new standard for the use of special-effects technology and for the 'realistic' depiction of alien environments. Perhaps its most striking sequence was the celebrated (and much imitated) 'bar scene' featuring an assortment of intermingling alien 'lowlifes'. In many ways, Quark's bar in *DS9* is a tribute to this scene, which gives the alien environment a reassuring kind of sleaziness that, rather ironically, 'humanises' it. Many individual episodes also pay tribute to particular SF films. *DS9's Whispers*, with its 'film noir'-styled voiceover narrative and its plot involving 'replicants', is directly influenced by Ridley Scott's *Blade Runner* (1982). Aaron Lipstadt's *Android* (1982) develops its lead character as a humanised android who has to fight for his rights as a sentient being and who is certainly a precursor of Data. The scenario of the spaceship as a dark, threatening environment as developed in the *Alien films* (1979–97) is duplicated throughout *DS9*. The new *Trek* series' 'time-paradox' episodes also develop many of the themes of Robert Zemeckis's *Back to the Future* trilogy of 1985–90.

Over the course of its existence, various strands of SF literature have also had a considerable effect on *Star Trek*. In *The Billion Year Spree: The History of Science Fiction* Brian Aldiss identifies two main strains of SF that have historically been influential – the Burroughsian and the Wellsian. The Burroughsian tradition takes its name from the writings of Edgar Rice Burroughs, whose *Mars Trilogy* (1912–19) brought him huge commercial success. Burroughs' writings, which display little literary merit or intention, are not 'science' stories but fantastical adventure tales which merely use an 'SF' setting'. They inspired the 'sword and sorcery' subgenre of SF epitomised by Michael Moorcock's 'Eternal Champion' novels, which can be said to have influenced *Star Trek*'s portrayal of the Klingon 'warrior culture'. H. G. Wells, along with his near-contemporary, Jules Verne, achieved a similar level of success with stories based on genuinely 'scientific' premises – such as time travel in *The Time Machine* (1895), space travel in *The First Men in the Moon* (1901), interplanetary war in *War of the Worlds* (1898) and genetic engineering in *The Island of Dr Moreau* (1896) – which are the precursors of most serious twentieth-century science fiction. These stories characteristically stressed a pessimistic view of the future which anticipated the works of Kafka, Huxley and Orwell. *Star Trek*'s dedication to 'scientific credibility' and its concern with the 'cosmic destiny' of humanity, link it directly to Wells's conception of SF.

The original series was much influenced by contemporary 'mainstream' SF and employed a number of well-known SF novelists, such as Theodore Sturgeon, Harlan Ellison and Robert Bloch, among its scriptwriters. *Star Trek*'s subsequent creation of an entire social and political 'universe' recalls the work of 'mainstream' SF authors who – working within the Wellsian tradition – took on the 'epic' form with a distinctly liberal-humanist approach. Olaf Stapledon's *Last and First Men* (1930) is an evolutionary fantasy on a grand scale, moving the history of humanity millions of years into the future. Isaac Asimov's *Foundation* trilogy (1951–2) posits the notion of 'psychohistory' as a science of predicting the future, and unfolds into an epic depiction of the destiny of an entire future galactic society. Asimov's benevolent notions of robotics, first presented in *I-Robot* (1950), which stress that all robots should be programmed never to harm human beings, are also clearly influential on the creation of characters such as Data. Ray Bradbury, who – in works such as *The Martian Chronicles* (1950) – used SF narrative devices to tell humorous or 'gothic' character-based stories, is another writer who had a strong effect on Roddenberry's original conception of *Star Trek*. Bradbury's stories are full of ironically humorous touches and are often satirical comments on contemporary life in a SF setting, a style which is found in many early *Star Trek* stories. Bradbury and Asimov were both personal friends of Roddenberry and members of the 'committee' of SF writers whose intervention helped save *Star Trek* from being cancelled at the end of its first season. In *Star Trek Creator*, his biography of Gene Roddenberry, David Alexander details Roddenberry's friendship with both authors, who in fact acted as unofficial 'advisers' to Roddenberry at the time of the creation of the original series. The fiction of Arthur C. Clarke, whose best-known works *Childhood's End* (1953) and *2001: A Space Odyssey* (1968) present an optimistic Wellsian view of the future which views technology as the 'saviour' of mankind and sees humans as having an 'evolutionary destiny', were another prominent influence on the early *Star Trek*. The ending of *Star Trek: The Motion Picture*, where Decker and Ilia merge consciousness with the space probe to form a newer 'higher consciousness' is a distinctly Clarkeian notion that to some extent recalls the last scenes of *2001*, in which the astronaut evolves into a 'starchild'.

Such 'evolutionary' notions of the human condition are grounded in notions of historicism, an outlook first proposed by the Italian philosopher, Giambattista Vico (1668–1744), who argued that history is the expression of human will and that all great cultures, such as the Roman Empire, experience cycles of growth and decline. Vico saw human nature as something which changes in different historical periods. As a genre, science fiction often takes a historicist approach. But whereas the great majority of science fiction scenarios, from *Brave New World* and *1984* to *Blade Runner* and *Brazil*, postulate a distopian future, in *Star Trek* we are frequently told that, on Earth in the twenty-third and twenty-fourth centuries, war, poverty and inequality are 'things of the past', because greed and prejudice are no longer the motivating forces in human society. According to Roddenberry's original formulation, the United Federation of Planets has expanded by *consent*, not by conquest. Factional religions have been replaced by a universal scientific humanism, which has triumphed over the 'barbarism' of previous centuries. Technology itself has been 'humanised'. The present historical era has been superseded by one in which human beings have fundamentally *changed*. As Captain Picard states in *The Neutral Zone*: 'A lot has changed in the last 300 years. People are no longer obsessed with the accumulation of things. We have eliminated hunger ... want ... the need for possessions ... we've grown out of our infancy ...'.

As Alexander (1994, p. 538) recalls, Roddenberry had strong objections to those scenes in *The Undiscovered Country* where Kirk, Scotty and other Starfleet officers display racially bigoted attitudes towards the Klingons. His conception of Starfleet was of a highly idealistic organisation which demanded the highest personal standards of its officers. Roddenberry's utopian view of the future is summarised by his insistence that, by the twenty-third century, 'intolerance' itself will be a thing of the past:

Intolerance in the 23rd Century? Improbable! If man survives that long, he will have learned to take a delight in the essential differences between men and between cultures. He will learn that differences in ideas and attitudes are a delight, part of life's exciting variety, not something to fear. It's a manifestation of the greatness that God, or whatever it is, gave us. This infinite variation and delight, this is part of the optimism we built into *Star Trek* ... (Whitfield and Roddenberry, 1968, p. 36)

By the time Berman and Piller had assumed control of *TNG*, Roddenberry's rather naïve historicist notions were being challenged. While the 'utopian' nature of life on Earth is taken as 'given', the sarcastic comments of characters like Q and Quark, which infer that humans' lives are generally rather dull, very strongly suggest that this not a utopia in which *everyone* would like to live. The most successful character-based episodes in the new *Trek* series clearly propose that, despite the technological, social and political advances that have been made, the fundamental nature of 'humanity' has not changed. In *Chain of Command* (written by Frank Abatemarco and Ronald D. Moore) Picard is lured into a trap by the Cardassians, who capture him and subject him to torture. His sadistic torturer, Gul Madred, is determined to use whatever means possible to break his will. Madred insists that Picard must admit that there are five lights overhead, when in reality there are four. This becomes the 'sticking point' which Picard, despite the physical and psychological pain he is in, will not go beyond. Finally Picard's release is secured by Starfleet Admiral Jellico, who is in temporary command of the *Enterprise*, but Picard is very badly shaken. He finally admits to Riker that by the end of the torture he really did see five lights. Patrick Stewart supplies a gripping, thoroughly convincing performance in a story which emphasises that everyone – even a Starfleet captain – has a breaking point. At one point Picard appears naked, visually symbolising that he has been stripped of the dignity which is his most distinguishing characteristic.

An equally harrowing experience is suffered by Miles O'Brien in *DS9*'s *Hard Time* (written by Robert Hewitt Wolfe). After being falsely accused and convicted of being a spy by a race known as the Argrathi, he is subjected to a mind implant which provides him with the experiences and memories of a 20-year prison sentence, although this 'correctional treatment' itself takes only a few hours. A series of flashbacks reveal that the prison 'regime' O'Brien remembers was brutal, with beatings being administered for any transgression and the prisoners being fed only sporadically. When he comes back to consciousness he really believes that 20 years have passed. Publicly he maintains that he was alone in the cell, but this is contradicted by the flashbacks, which reveal that he had a 'cellmate', Ee'char, whose efforts kept him sane during the long 'confinement'. On his return to the station he is moody and disturbed, becoming verbally aggressive towards Quark, his friend Bashir and his daughter Molly. He also refuses to attend a course of counselling that Bashir recommends. Tormented by guilt, he is on the point of committing suicide when Bashir intervenes. The truth is then revealed that, crazed by hunger, he killed Ee'char for a tiny piece of bread. Only when he can admit his 'crime' does his road to psychological recovery begin. As well as being an absorbing study of guilt and despair, *Hard Time* is perhaps the most searching examination of the central psychological theme of *Star Trek* – the nature of 'humanity' itself. Bashir tells O'Brien that the Argrathi tried to strip him of every shred of his humanity, but that only in the moment of the 'murder' did they succeed. O'Brien realises that, despite the 'historicism' he had been taught in school about human nature having 'evolved' past selfishness and greed, he had been 'reduced' to the primal aggressive emotions which still lurk beneath humanity's civilised surface.

The new *Trek* series reflect the influence of the many new developments in contemporary SF literature. Since the 1960s the utopianism of 'mainstream' writers like Clarke has become deeply unfashionable among those at the 'cutting edge' of the genre. The self-consciously 'literary' 'New Wave' school of SF – dominated by British writers like J. G. Ballard – stresses a distopian view of technology combined with a psychologically-based 'exploration of inner space'. *TNG* episodes like *The Inner Light*, *Tapestry*, *Frame Of Mind*, *Phantasms* and *All Good Things* all place a similar focus on the psychological 'inner lives' of the characters, which are often presented as being indistinguishable from 'reality'. In *DS9*'s *Distant Voices*, Bashir – who in reality is in a coma – comes to realise that the figures of all the other main series characters are projections of various conflicting feelings within his own mind. In a 'twist' which could have come out of one of Ballard's complex 'environmental psychology' stories, Bashir discovers that the 'ailing' ship itself – which the other characters are attempting to repair – represents his own body.

Another modern variant on SF is the 'cyberpunk' genre, first popularised by William Gibson in novels such as *Neuromancer* (1984), which features a highly distopian view of corrupt and 'seedy' future where humans live much of the time in computer-generated 'virtual realities' (which Gibson prophetically named 'cyberspace') and are increasingly dependent on artificial body parts. *Star Trek* episodes focusing on the problems of 'holodiction', and of crew members such as La Forge and Kim becoming sexually attracted to holodeck characters, reveal a similarly 'seedy' side to *Star Trek* technology, which is taken to its logical extreme by Quark offering pornographic holodeck programs. The creation of *Star Trek*'s most threatening race of 'villains', the Borg, is directly influenced by cyberpunk's narrative concepts and visual imagery. The 'Borg stories' focus attention on current anxieties about the 'loss of humanity' which the use of new technologies of computerisation and genetic engineering may imply. Though the Klingons, Romulans or Cardassians may be ruthless conquerors, their mode of existence (and, as we have seen, their genetic origin) is basically the same as that of humans. Each race has dissident groups intent on reforming their totalitarian governments, and the presentation of individual members of these races emphasises that they are as capable of acts of compassion or love as humans. The same does not appear to be true of the Borg, who are a soulless technological collective, rather like an ant colony, and who conquer by 'assimilating' other races. Subjugated races are given the Borg implants which turn individuals into members of the 'hive'. The Borg have one mind, and appear to be incapable of individuality.

In Michael Piller's *The Best of Both Worlds* we glimpse the nature of the Borg threat for the first time, when a Federation colony is found to be completely wiped out. The Borg then kidnap Picard, assimilate him and turn him into their mouthpiece, 'Locutus of Borg'. The image of the half-mechanised, 'assimilated' Picard at the end of the first part of the story announcing 'I am Locutus of Borg. Resistance is futile', is one of the defining moments of the new *Trek* series. As the Borg, in their huge cube-shaped spacecraft, head for Earth in order to assimilate the Federation's home planet, Riker turns the tables by recapturing Picard and using the knowledge Picard now has of the Borg to deactivate them. The communalised nature of the Borg, which is their strength, thus also appears to be their weakness. This is emphasised in the later *I, Borg* where an individual Borg is rescued by the *Enterprise* crew, begins to become aware of his individuality and even attains a name, 'Hugh'. Picard has the chance to implant Hugh with a virus that could wipe out the entire Borg collective, but he balks at this genocidal act and returns him to the Borg, unharmed but newly aware of his individuality. *I, Borg* underlines the essentially compassionate nature of

Star Trek ethics, which imply that no race is intrinsically evil, and individuals are only made so by social and political systems. However, when the Borg attack Earth in the movie *First Contact*, Picard has many regrets over his decision. *Star Trek*'s cyberpunk-influenced 'Borg stories' touch upon fundamental modern fears about the potential of technology to destroy the individuality of humanity. Whereas in the original series the 'unemotional' Spock was constantly being 'humanised', to the Borg dispensing with emotions is not a struggle. They are merely seen as 'irrelevant'.

While much of *Star Trek* merely uses SF settings as symbolic scenarios for dealing with particular ethical issues, it could be argued that *Star Trek*'s main contribution to the genre itself has been its many 'time-paradox' stories. In the *Back to the Future* films the inbuilt contradictions of idea of 'time paradox' had been the source of much humour, but in *Star Trek* the device is used for more serious ends, as a means to explore the nature of human destiny. Kurt Vonnegut's satirical and tragicomic SF novel *Slaughterhouse 5* (1969) directly anticipates *Star Trek*'s 'time-paradox' stories by having his main character, Billy Pilgrim, jolted between different moments in time and space ranging from the present day to a future setting on the planet Tralfalmadore. While there is a great deal of dry humour in the story, *Slaughterhouse 5* also provides a sombre reflection on 'human barbarism', in the scenes where Pilgrim is sent back to experience the bombing of Dresden in the Second World War.

Four of *Star Trek*'s most successful episodes feature variants on the 'time-paradox' theme. In *City on the Edge of Forever* (written by Harlan Ellison and rewritten by Roddenberry) Kirk and Spock time travel to the Depression era of the early 1930s, where they have to prevent the 'pollution of the time line'. The story concerns their meeting with Edith Keeler, a young social worker who Kirk falls in love with. Spock discovers that, in the time line they have entered, the well-intentioned Keeler will lead a peace movement that will keep the USA out of the Second World War. As a result, Hitler will be triumphant and the future of humanity will be a barbarous and violent one in which Starfleet will never come into existence.

Despite his feelings for her, Kirk has to allow Keeler to be killed in the road accident which 'Federation history' says will seal her fate. The episode ends not with the customary banter between Kirk, McCoy and Spock but with Kirk's terse 'let's get the hell out of here', one of the series most poignant moments, made all the more powerful by its divergence from a familiar *Star Trek* pattern. *City on the Edge* is often cited by fans as the best episode of the original series. By using the notion of 'time paradox' it is the only original series episode in which the whole existence of Roddenberry's *Star Trek* universe is threatened. Although the episode achieves a definite sense of closure, it certainly does not supply the kind of 'feelgood' ending that characterised the resolution of so many 1960s TV episodes.

TNG's *Yesterday's Enterprise* (written by Ira Steven Behr, Ronald D. Moore, Hans Beimler and Richard Manning) suddenly plunges the viewer, without warning, into a scenario in which Picard's *Enterprise-D* is a ship of war engaged in a losing battle with the Klingons in a time line in which the Federation–Klingon peace treaty has never occurred. Only the super-sensitive Guinan notices that things are somehow 'wrong'. Meanwhile the crew discovers that the *Enterprise-C* – the present ship's predecessor – has emerged from the past from a nearby time rift. In the familiar time line of the series, the *Enterprise-C* was the ship which, in answering a distress call from the Klingons, set off the process that led to the current Federation–Klingon treaty. Guinan explains her uncertainties to Picard, who deduces correctly that the sudden appearance of the *Enterprise-C* in the future has changed the time line, preventing the peace accords from being made. The *Enterprise-C* crew volunteers to re-enter the rift, so restoring 'normal' time, and only Guinan is aware that anything has changed. But it is later revealed that the events of *Yesterday's Enterprise* have in fact altered the time line in which the series exists. Tasha Yar is still alive in the parallel time line but, after being made aware of her demise in the time line that the crew are attempting to restore, she opts to go back through the rift with the *Enterprise-C*, even though that course of action is almost certain to involve the eventual destruction of the ship by the Romulans. At this point we assume that she must have died a more fitting and heroic death in the 'past', but in the two-part *Redemption* (which closes season four and opens season five) we are introduced to Tasha's fully grown daughter Sela, the result of a forced union between Tasha and the commander of the Romulan ship. But Tasha died attempting to escape when Sela was four and the embittered Sela is now a vicious and dedicated officer of the Tal Shiar, the Romulan 'secret police'. Thus any change in the time line, however 'justified' it may seem, can have unforeseen and dangerous consequences.

In *DS9*'s *Past Tense* (written by Ira Steven Behr, Robert Hewitt Wolfe and René Echevarria), following a transporter accident, Sisko, Bashir and Dax appear in the USA in the twenty-first century. The social policy of the time involves the relocation of the homeless and the jobless in so-called 'Sanctuary' districts. As in the movie *First Contact* (made some three years later), we are relocated in *Star Trek*'s distopian 'past', and the plot centres around Sisko's and his crew's efforts to preserve the time line that leads to the formation of the Federation. Sisko has to take the place of a rebel leader involved in a hostage-taking crisis, whose death (as their century's history tells them) played a vital part in ensuring that the Sanctuary system was abolished, so leading to a new USA where social justice prevailed and progress towards a utopian future was possible. *Star Trek*'s promise of an eventual utopia had always been tempered by the idea of the twenty-first century as an era of confusion and disaster, out of which came the seeds of a new society and way of life. When *Star Trek* began, the twenty-first century was three and a half decades away, still very much the stuff of science fiction itself. But the society depicted in *Past Tense* is deliberately shown to be uncomfortably close to our present one, with the 'Sanctuary' policy merely an extension of certain current right-wing attempts at population control. Contemporary audiences could also hardly fail to notice the similarity between this scenario and the riots which shook Los Angeles in 1993. While *Star Trek*'s political messages had generally been concealed behind futuristic and alien environments, it now delivered a scathing attack on the contemporary US social system, with its social exclusion of a disaffected 'underclass'.

DS9's *Children of Time* (written by Echevarria) presents perhaps *Star Trek*'s most intense 'time-paradox' dilemma. While exploring the Delta Quadrant, the *Defiant* is caught in an energy field which sends it 200 years into the future and into orbit of a planet peopled by a community of 8000 people, all but one descendants of the *Defiant*'s crew. The only one still alive is Odo, who (as a shape-shifter) has a very long lifespan. The leader of the colony is Yedrin Dax, the current host for the Dax symbiont. Yedrin explains to Sisko that, according to their history, in two days' time the ship will be drawn into a temporal anomaly which will send it back 200 years and which will cause it to crash on the planet, so beginning the time line that leads to the present situation. In the process, Kira will die. Sisko is faced with an agonising moral choice. Now that he knows what is 'supposed to happen' he would be able to avoid the crash. But if he does not allow the crash to take place, the entire time line (and thus all 8000 colonists) will never have existed. Yet if he goes ahead with the fulfilment of the past history of this time line, he will not only cause Kira's death but also strand his crew permanently in a previous era. As the tension mounts, Kira discovers her own grave and the members of the crew, who are divided as to which course should be taken, begin to get to know many of their descendants. Finally Sisko decides that they have no option but to allow the crash to happen, and Kira prepares to die. But the 'alternative' Odo, who has 'evolved' into a much warmer and more communicative individual, reprograms their flightpath so that the crash is avoided. Instantly, the colony ceases to exist. In something of a reversal of the resolution of *The City on the Edge of Forever*, Odo had decided to wipe out the entire time line to save Kira, with whom he is in love.

In its 'time-paradox' stories *Star Trek* presents a series of dramatic dilemmas that use the imaginative space that science fiction allows for sophisticated philosophical reflections on questions of the nature of reality and the mutability of destiny. If Kirk *had* saved Edith Keeler in *City on the Edge*, could his presence on Earth not have prevented Hitler's victory in the Second World War which would supposedly have ensued? If Sisko had not taken a key role in the rebellion in *Past Tense*, might not somebody else have done so? Are the 'alternative' Tasha Yar in *Yesterday's Enterprise* or the crew's descendants in *Children of Time* 'real' or not? The answers to these questions are firmly left for the audience to ponder. The presentation of a multiplicity of time lines or parallel universes suggests that the utopian future of the twenty-fourth century we see in the programmes is itself one such possible 'reality', one to which in future the human race could aspire.

While *Star Trek* primarily inhabits the SF genre, in its lighter moments it has frequently indulged in various forms of generic pastiche. The narrative circumstances that surround the entry of the familiar characters into a new generic setting in the first such story, *A Piece of the Action*, are somewhat contrived. Here an entire planet has supposedly based its culture on a book which a visiting Federation starship left behind some 100 years before, *Chicago Mobs of the Twenties*. This gives the principals the chance to take part in a full-dress parody of early Hollywood gangster films. In a typical piece of bluster, Kirk unites the warring gangs on the planet by depicting the Federation as another 'gang' which will demand an annual 'piece of the action' from the planet's government. *Patterns of Force* deals similarly with a planet on which the Nazi political culture has been revived; and *Spectre of the Gun* puts Kirk and his crew into an imaginary western setting.

The holodecks of the new *Trek* series provide a more credible setting for generic adventures. Thus Data can 'play' at being Sherlock Holmes in *Elementary, Dear Data,* Picard can imitate the Chandleresque Dixon Hill in *The Big Goodbye* and Worf and Alexander can indulge in the western fantasy of *A Fistful of Datas*. All these stories work as effective comic pastiche, but the fantasy world of the holodeck is obviously lacking in narrative tension, as the events shown within it are mere simulations. In each case an element of danger is provided by some shipboard breakdown of computer systems which allows the fantasy world of the holodeck to provide real dangers (when, as *Star Trek* jargon puts it, 'the safeties are off'). In *Elementary, Dear Data* a holodeck character (Holmes' arch-opponent, Professor Moriarty) becomes self-aware and takes over the ship; in *The Big Goodbye* an alien scan disables the 'safeties'; and in *A Fistful of Datas* Data's memory circuits are crossed with the *Enterprise*'s holodeck database, putting Worf and his son in real danger.

A Fistful of Datas is, however, the only holodeck-genre story of the last five seasons of *TNG*. The need to have 'safeties off' had made such stories rather obvious and predictable. However, this narrative technique has never been fully abandoned. Rather than trying to make such stories more 'scientifically' credible, the writers have often chosen to exaggerate the pastiche even further. This tendency reaches a climax in *DS9*'s *Our Man Bashir* (written by *Star Trek*'s master of comic pastiche, Ronald D. Moore), which places Bashir in a James Bond-type 1960s spy spoof holoprogram, complete with submissive female spies and power-crazed villains. The episode features that most well-worn *Star Trek* plot device, a transporter accident, which results in the 'transporter patterns' of Sisko, Kira and Dax being stored in the holodeck. This allows Brooks, Visitor and Farrell to play outrageously against type as 'Bond villains' and 'Bond girls'. The 'virtual Sisko' takes the role of Dr Noah, who plans to destroy the world with a series of earthquakes. As in the previous stories, naturally the 'safeties' are off and Bashir must see the program through to its conclusion to avoid disaster – in this case the deaths of the three command officers. Eventually Bashir, in an ironic reversal of the typical Bond plot, allows Dr Noah to 'win' by pressing the button which will destroy the world. Thus *Our Man Bashir* parodies not only Bond movies but *Star Trek*'s own holodeck stories. Like *Trials and Tribble-ations*, it deliberately stretches credibility to its limits and relies for much of its comic effect on the audience's knowledge of the conventions of *Star Trek* itself.

Generic fictions fulfil much of the traditional function of myths, providing audiences with a series of dramatic models which – over time and with constant repetition – evolve into symbolic patterns that are used to help rationalise and structure a universe which sometimes appears to be governed by random chaos. As we have seen in this chapter, *Star Trek* has evolved into a generic and mythical system which is inclusive of many of the main strands of the SF genre, and which makes frequent allusions to other generic forms. At the same time it has developed a multidimensional view of the nature of time and human destiny which has provided it with a uniquely malleable set of storytelling conventions. *Star Trek* presents a vision of existence in which ultimately there are no 'fixed' realities – only a series of 'points of view' or relative perceptions. This is an accurate reflection of the condition of postmodern culture, in which the cultural certainties of the past have been replaced by an infinite number of interchangeable cultural models. Yet at the same time *Star Trek* harks back to the oldest forms of storytelling and uses its generic form to present stories which touch upon truly universal themes.

Part III

Psychological, political and social themes in *Star Trek*

We hold these truths to be self-evident, that all men are created equal, that they are endowed by their Creator with certain inalienable Rights, that amongst these are Life, Liberty and the Pursuit of Happiness. That to secure these rights, Governments are instituted among Men, deriving their just powers from the consent of the governed. – That whenever any Form of Government becomes destructive of these ends, it is the Right of the People to alter or abolish it, and to institute new Government, laying its foundation on such principles and organising its powers in such form, as to them shall seem most likely to effect their Safety and Happiness ...

(US Declaration of Rights, 1776)

I come from an ideal culture.

(Beverly Crusher in *The High Ground* [*TNG*])

Chapter 10

Humanism, self-actualisation and holodiction: psychological themes in *Star Trek*

Star Trek's stories typically reflect a humanistic psychological perspective. Whereas behaviourist or Freudian approaches are primarily concerned with the pathological or problematic aspects of the psyche, the goal of humanistic forms of psychology is to develop ways in which individuals can 'extend themselves' in order to become 'self-actualised' and fulfil their individual potential. Abraham Maslow argues that such fulfilment can only be achieved if a series of basic human 'meta-needs' have already been attained. Maslow organises these into his famous 'hierarchy of needs', which is structured as a kind of 'pyramid' (at the summit of which is the state of 'self-actualisation') where lower needs have to be fulfilled before an individual can step up to the next 'level'. At the bottom of the hierarchy Maslow places physiological needs such as air, food, water, sleep and sex. Further up come feelings of safety and security, then love and belonging, then social and self-esteem. The implication of this is that a society can only become self-actualised if this series of meta-needs has been fulfilled among the general population. Maslow's description of his theoretical ideal society 'Eupsychia' has many resemblances to the model which *Star Trek* has adopted:

> this would almost surely be a (philosophically) anarchistic group, a Taoistic but loving culture, in which people (young people too) would have more free choice than we are used to, and in which basic needs and meta needs would be respected much more than they are in our society. People would not bother each other so much as we do, would be much less prone to press opinions or religions or philosophies or tastes in clothes or food or art or women on their neighbours. In a word, the inhabitants of Eupsychia would

tend to be more Taoistic, nonintrusive, and basic need-gratifying (whenever possible), would frustrate only under certain conditions that I have not attempted to describe, would be more honest with each other than we are, and would permit people to make free choices wherever possible. They would be far less controlling, violent, contemptuous, or overbearing than we are. Under such conditions, the deepest layers of human nature could show themselves with greater ease ... (Maslow, 1970, pp. 277–8)

In *Star Trek* the utopian society on Earth is portrayed as an 'ideal culture' in which every individual can become 'self-actualised'. In the new *Trek* series it is emphasised that Starfleet officers are virtual 'Renaissance' men and women, skilled and educated in many disparate areas. Regular workouts using advanced fitness training techniques and technologies ensure physical 'perfection', while many members of the crew of *TNG* indulge in various artistic and scientific pursuits. Following Spock's prowess on the Vulcan harp, Riker and Data are both musical virtuosos – Riker on the jazz clarinet and Data on the violin. In *All Good Things* the 'future' version of engineer Geordi La Forge becomes a successful novelist. In *TNG's Frame of Mind* Beverly Crusher plays theatrical director to Riker's stage actor; and in *The Defector*'s 'teaser' Picard gives Data a 'master class' in Shakespeare as Data takes the role of the king in a scene from *Henry V*. Picard is also a respected amateur archaeologist. Throughout *Star Trek* there is an emphasis on the highly 'cultured' nature of Federation life. Starfleet officers often know the works of the great writers, dramatists and composers intimately, and the names of many present and past artistic and scientific figures are frequently evoked. It appears that what today is regarded as 'high culture' is now the culture of all, and the links between the science, music, literature and drama of the twenty-fourth century and those of today form a cultural continuity. Just as the society of *Star Trek* represents the triumph of humanistic liberalism, so its 'self-actualised' characters embody that triumph in their personal accomplishments.

In this context, it is no surprise that *Star Trek*'s main characters are idealised figures whose primary function is to embody the ethical themes of the drama. Science fiction is first and foremost a literature of *ideas* and a great many SF stories tend to sublimate character development to their conceptual framework. A good example of this is Stanley Kubrick's movie of Arthur C. Clarke's *2001: A Space Odyssey* (1968) which develops a grand metaphysical theme concerning human evolution but features largely 'anonymous' and underdeveloped characters. Although many critics of the movie have seen this as a failing, it can be argued that Kubrick deliberately chose to de-emphasise character in order to place his ideas in the foreground. But while such a strategy towards characterisation may be possible for a single movie, it is very unlikely to be a feasible option for the makers of a TV series. Though *Star Trek*'s characters must always be 'functional' in the development of ideas in its stories, they also need to be appealing enough to keep an audience tuning in regularly.

In *Star Trek* the question of 'what it is to be human' is frequently asked. According to Stuart Holroyd, one of the primary concerns of humanistic forms of psychology is to: 'specify what constitutes full human-ness, to define the conditions and psycho-dynamics that on the one hand enable people to attain it and that on the other hand prevent them doing so ... (1989, p. 129). Over the years *Star Trek* has evolved a structure of characterisation that epitomises its search for the 'nature of humanity'. In the original series the many dangerous situations and ethical dilemmas that are encountered are invariably resolved by the psychological 'triumvirate' of Kirk, Spock and McCoy, who fulfil basic 'functions' within the stories themselves. The majority of episodes are resolved by Kirk finding a balance between the often opposing 'logical advice' of Spock and the 'emotional advice' of McCoy. In the new *Trek* series with their 'ensemble' casts these functions tend to be split between different characters. In *TNG* the 'Kirk' function is duplicated by both Picard and Riker, with the extremely cerebral Picard having to exercise finely balanced judgements, while Riker performs an 'action' and 'romance' orientated role. In *DS9* this function is again divided between captain – Sisko – and first officer – Kira. In *Voyager* there is a similar use of Janeway and Chakotay, though in this case chief pilot Tom Paris tends to be the most romantically inclined member of the crew. The 'McCoy' function, representing the more emotional, caring side of humanity, is represented in *TNG* by Deanna Troi and Beverly Crusher, in *DS9* by Bashir and O'Brien, and in *Voyager* by Kes and Neelix – all characters who can always be relied upon to provide 'humanitarian' advice.

Spock's function as 'logical outsider' caught between human and alien values is replicated in *TNG*'s expanded cast by both Data – whose lack of emotion is programmed rather than learned – and Worf, whose human upbringing sets him apart from other Klingons just as Spock's mixed-race origins distinguish him from other Vulcans. Whereas Spock attempts to suppress his emotional qualities, Data longs to experience human emotion. In *Encounter at Farpoint* Riker dubs him 'Pinocchio'. As the series develops, he learns to write poetry, act and play the violin. He also keeps a pet cat and comes to regard the other Starfleet officers as his friends. In the second episode of the first season, *The Naked Now*, when a shipboard disease (previously experienced by the original cast in *The Naked Time*) drives the crew into extreme emotional states, he is seduced by Security Officer Tasha Yar, whom he (hilariously) informs that he is 'fully functional' and 'programmed in multiple pleasuring techniques'. Later, in the fourth season's *In Theory*, he attempts to conduct a romance with a female crew member, Jenna D'Sora, by means of a special 'love program' he has devised. But his attempts at being romantic are, not surprisingly, too contrived and his 'dates' do not last long. He remains incapable of experiencing emotions until the first *Next Generation* movie, *Generations* (1994), but when he inserts an 'emotions chip' into himself he is almost over-whelmed by the resultant flood of feelings.

With his human upbringing, Worf is another 'divided' character. If, in the *Star Trek* 'universe', the Vulcans represent the extremes of logic, the Klingons represent the opposite emotional and mythological pole. This is further intensified when Worf later joins the cast of *DS9* in *The Way of the Warrior*, where his loyalty to Starfleet leads him to fight his own people. Another 'logical alien outsider' in *DS9* is the station's 'detective' Odo, who specialises in logical deduction to solve crimes and who (like both Worf and Odo) is estranged from his own people. Odo certainly experiences emotions, but he maintains an emotional distance from the humanoid races on the space station. Like Spock, Data and Worf he remains divided inside, with his emotions in a constant battle against his logic. In *Voyager* there are several 'divided' characters: Tuvok is detached from the rest of the crew by his charac-teristically Vulcan aloofness; in contrast, the half-Klingon B'Elanna Torres constantly has to suppress her fiery, expressive side to stay within Starfleet disciplines; and the holographic Doctor, like Data, gradually becomes more 'human' as the series progresses.

The psychological intimacy between the three original principals is undoubtedly what inspired female fans to write 'unofficial' *Star Trek* stories in which their 'love' is actually consummated. In the 1980s films, Kirk and the rest of the crew are prepared to go to any lengths – even including, in *The Search for Spock*, 'stealing' the *Enterprise* itself – to save Spock. There is a strong sense that Kirk and McCoy are 'incomplete' without him. Indeed, as a result of the mind meld attained shortly before Spock's 'death', McCoy carries Spock's consciousness within him throughout the film. On many occasions it is emphasised that all three have no conventional family ties – Kirk in particular (in the classic naval mode) being 'married to his ship'. In *The Wrath of Khan* David Marcus – who is later revealed to be Kirk's 'long lost' son – joins the crew, but loses his life in a battle with the Klingons in *The Search for Spock*. The narrative logic seems to insist that Kirk must lose his 'biological family' to be reunited with his 'psychological family' (Spock and McCoy).

The tendency for the *Star Trek* crews to become 'psychological families' is a natural product of the format of a TV series, in which characters must constantly return to their 'functional' roles in relation to each other. Yet the conventions of the two major forms of TV series drama – the episodic series and the continuing serial – are quite different in this respect. Whereas in serials the main focus is on the characters' continuing relationships, the characters in episodic series tend to remain unattached, so that each new adventure may present the dramatic possibility of a new romantic story. In an episodic series, even if major characters are romantically inclined towards each other, they rarely consummate their relationship, and are more inclined to 'tease' the audience (and each other) with a constant flirtatiousness. A typical example from the 1960s was the pairing of Steed and his glamorous female assistants in *The Avengers*. The 'professional' relationship between Mulder and Scully in the *X Files* is a 1990s equivalent.

Under Roddenberry's control, *TNG* was conceived of as such an episodic series, but as a result of change of narrative approach that took place in the third and fourth seasons under the influence of Michael Piller's new writing team, it began to absorb considerable elements of the continuous serial. As we saw in Chapter 4, the later seasons explore the family backgrounds of its characters, which are frequently 'dysfunctional', in some detail. The most fully developed cycle of 'family stories' in *Star Trek* (which are almost all written or co-written by Ronald D. Moore) is that involving Worf, who is subject to the intense pressures of a culture in which family loyalties are paramount. Yet even Worf's first loyalty appears to be to his 'psychological family' on board the *Enterprise*. In *Sins of the Father* his late father, Mogh, has been accused of treason and, according to Klingon tradition, the sons of a particular house must bear responsibility for their father's actions. On pain of death, Worf and his Klingon brother, Kurn, confront the Klingon High Council to attempt to clear the family name. Although Worf learns that his father was innocent, he nobly accepts 'discommendation', which makes him an outcast from

Klingon society, in order to prevent a civil war on his homeworld. Thus he chooses the Federation's liberal political values over his 'family honour'.

In *Reunion* Worf's former lover, K'Ehleyr, is killed, leaving him in charge of his son, Alexander. At first Alexander goes to live with Worf's adoptive human parents but in *New Ground* they return the boy to him. The role of single parent is one he struggles with, often to much comic effect. Alexander, who has been largely brought up by humans, has at first little interest in Klingon traditions, despite Worf's insistence on their importance. In *First Born* Worf attempts to persuade Alexander to take part in the Klingon 'Rite of Ascension', with little success. A 'family friend', K'Mtar, arrives and tries very hard to persuade Alexander of the importance of following 'the way of the warrior', but Alexander still shows little interest. In an extraordinary plot twist, K'Mtar turns out to be a guilt-wracked version of Alexander from the future, who has returned to ensure that Alexander learns fighting skills. It seems that at some point in the future Worf was attacked and killed in the presence of Alexander, who did not have the skills to defend him. Yet despite this dire warning, Worf still allows Alexander to make his own decision, knowing that the future time line from which K'Mtar/Alexander comes is just one possible outcome of the situation. Again Worf conforms to the liberal-humanist values of his 'psychological family'.

Both *DS9* and *Voyager* can be said to be series–serial hybrids, as both develop a number of long-term sexual and family relationships while retaining some 'single romance' stories and strong elements of the 'repressed love' that characterised relationships within *TNG*. In *DS9*'s *Looking for Par'mach in All the Wrong Places* Worf and Dax begin an ongoing relationship which continues throughout the fifth season's episodes. Miles and Keiko O'Brien (who were married shortly before their departure from *TNG* in *Data's Day*) live on the station with their daughter Molly. Kira has romantic involvements with the Bajoran first minister, Vedek Bareil, and later with her former resistance cell leader, Shakaar, although neither seem fully satisfying for her. Meanwhile Odo 'carries a torch' for her throughout the series, in a way that is painfully exposed when he is stranded alone in a cave with the 'false Kira' in *Heart of Stone*. Only the doomed 'future Odo' in *Children of Time* is fully capable of expressing his love. *Voyager* features another apparently 'stable couple' in Neelix and Kes, although in *Parturition* their relationship is threatened when Neelix reacts with extreme jealousy to Kes's friendship with Paris. In the later *Time and Again* Kes rather undramatically ends the relationship, before 'jumping' into a future time line where – in an echo of *All Good Things* – she is married to Paris.

In *Voyager* the crew are all separated from their families, a fact which is perhaps the main motivating factor for their attempts to return. Any family connections tend to be seen in the form of flashbacks, as in *Tattoo*, where Chakotay's early rejection of the values of his father and his tribe is shown. Yet Janeway frequently refers to her crew as a 'family'. Jeri Taylor's tragi-comic *Real Life* features a story in which the Doctor, in an attempt to find out more about being human, programs himself with a holographic 'family' consisting of 'sensible', intelligent children and a dutiful, obedient wife. B'Elanna Torres is rather nauseated by these sycophantic characters and protests that real family life can never be that 'perfect'. She persuades the Doctor to let her reprogram the simulation, forcing him to cope with an independent wife and a disaffected teenage son who (in a witty positioning of *Star Trek*'s cultural mores) rebels against his parents by 'hanging out' with Klingon youths and claims to reject Federation values as 'weak'. However, when the Doctor's holographic 'daughter' dies, the family is drawn together in genuinely moving scenes of grief. As a result the Doctor learns to value the other members of the crew more highly and thus becomes a more functional member of Voyager's 'psychological family'.

Despite the incorporation of permanent or semi-permanent sexual relationships in the later *Trek* series, the ways in which command positions restrain the emotional life of leading characters is still emphasised strongly. Perhaps the most powerful presentation of this theme is *Voyager*'s *Resolutions* (written by Jeff Taylor) where Janeway and Chakotay are stranded together on a deserted planet. Having contracted an infectious virus they are unable to return to the ship and the always-logical Tuvok decides that there is no option but to abandon them there after they have been provided with more-than-adequate Federation survival technology. Soon the psychological barriers between the two begin to dissolve. As a first step, Janeway tells Chakotay to drop the military formality of addressing her as 'Captain'. As the months pass and Janeway's attempts to cure the virus lead nowhere, they grow increasingly intimate. But it is clear that Janeway will only 'surrender' to Chakotay when she finally accepts that all hope of escape is gone. She has almost reached that point when the ship returns to enact a rescue. As soon as she and Chakotay are restored to *Voyager* their relationship snaps instantly (and rather shockingly) back into a formal mode. The episode illustrates the conflict between the responsibilities of command and the 'dictates of the heart' – thus counterposing the classic *Star Trek* extremities of *mythos* and *logos*. Despite the greater psychological realism of the new series, the theme of repressed love – a key convention of the adventure series – is preserved as a dramatic possibility.

The great majority of such *Star Trek* stories depict the eventual reintegration of characters into the 'psychological family' of the crew, but *DS9's The Visitor* (written by Michael Taylor) points in the opposite direction, with a cautionary tale about the potentially stifling effects of family relationships. Benjamin Sisko's son Jake originally wants to follow in his father's footsteps into Starfleet, but he later decides to map out an entirely different course for himself as a writer. *The Visitor* begins with Jake as an old man being sought out by a young aspiring writer who reveres him for his two books of fiction but is puzzled as to why he gave up writing before the age of 40. The story is told mostly in flashbacks, which establish a new 'alternative time line'. We first go back to our recognisable 'present day' DS9, where Benjamin Sisko is involved in an accident with the warp coils which transports him into sub-space. Some months later Benjamin reappears in front of Jake, but the efforts of Bashir and Dax are not enough to prevent him slipping back into apparent oblivion. Following Benjamin's 'death', the Bajorans lose confidence in the Federation and make an alliance with the Cardassians. This eventually results in DS9 being abandoned to the Klingons, shortly before which Benjamin makes another short 'appearance'.

Over the next two decades Jake manages to overcome his grief and build a new life for himself. By the age of 40 he has had two books published, and is newly married. Then his father (to whom virtually no time at all has passed) reappears briefly to him. Jake becomes obsessed with finding a way to bring his father back. As a result he abandons writing and enters full-time study in the field of sub-space mechanics. He works so hard at this that he neglects his wife, who eventually leaves him. At the age of nearly 70 he reconvenes the old *Defiant* crew (with an aged Dax, Bashir and Nog on board) and travels to the wormhole, where 50 years after the original incident very similar 'sub-space' conditions will occur. He succeeds in locating his father's 'time signature' and the two make contact in sub-space, where Benjamin expresses great regret that Jake has wasted so much of his life trying to save him. But still Jake is unable to 'pull' his father out of the timeless void. The final visitation occurs in the 'present' of the story. Jake explains that he and his father's sub-space time signatures are linked and that when he dies his father will go back to the moment in time just before the accident occurred, giving them both a 'second chance'. As Jake dies, what he predicted occurs. Benjamin swerves to avoid the accident, and the normal *DS9* time line continues. The alternative timeline has apparently now never existed.

The Visitor uses *Star Trek*'s established 'time-paradox' scenario to recount a kind of Oedipal story of a son's need to escape from the influence of his father. It combines the approach of a story like *First Born* (where another son confronts a father who is younger than him) with that of *Star Trek*'s more straightforward 'family stories'. In the time line from which the story is told, Jake's potential has been largely unfulfilled because he has devoted so much of it to searching for his father. The knowledge that Benjamin is still alive somewhere is agonising for him, and he can never fully unload his grief. The moral of the story – that people need to 'move on' despite whatever emotional traumas they may suffer – is clear, but it is painfully realised. Yet the use of the 'time-paradox' plot device allows Jake to 'begin again', so giving himself another chance to lead a more 'self-actualised' life. Thus *Star Trek* turns even tragedy on its head in continuing to stress optimistic possibilities for the future. In again emphasising that destiny is in the hands of individuals, it takes a characteristically humanistic stance.

Many of the scenarios that *Star Trek*'s characters face – such as meeting their own 'doubles', experiencing shifts into parallel universes, being subject to illusions created by aliens or encountering telepathic or 'superhuman' beings – serve to explore the 'humanity' of its characters by challenging their sense of 'reality'. Almost every major character in *Star Trek* from Captain Pike in *The Cage* undergoes some kind of 'reality shift' in the course of their duties. Sometimes these are caused by temporal or spatial anomalies that may slow down, speed up or 'rewind' time. Others are created by benevolent or malign alien influences. Often an episode will be seen from the point of view of a character whose perceptions – which are reflected in what we see on the screen – may be unreliable. The audience is frequently given the task of deciding which viewpoint being presented is real. Such episodes, by presenting reality as essentially a subjective concept, often ironically expose the ritualised suspension of disbelief that the act of watching a TV 'adventure show' requires. Just as the positioning of alien characteristics and the 'family stories' explore the nature of 'humanness', so the 'reality shift stories' focus on ways in which the characters who have been affected by such phenomena discover more about their essential nature through the experience. Three episodes contributed by Brannon Braga, all containing such a sly vein of ironic humour, show his fondness for playing psychological 'games' with an audience that has become familiar with the multidimensional nature of the *Star Trek* universe. Braga succeeds in placing viewers 'inside' the stories by leaving until the end the revelation as to which reality is 'correct'. The characters engage in a psychological struggle to establish their own integrity which reflects the 'work' the viewer is called upon to do in 'seeing through' the false realities. In *TNG*'s *Frame of Mind*, the action continually shifts between Riker's performance as a mental patient in a play on board the *Enterprise* and what is apparently a real asylum on the planet Tilonus IV. At the end of the episode it is revealed that he is being held prisoner by the Tilonians and that the scenes we have been watching have occurred largely in his mind. But Riker has consciously to 'break through' several layers of 'false reality' before he can escape from this illusion. The events are seen entirely from Riker's point of view, which allows viewers to share in his confusion as they try to stay 'one step ahead' of the plot. In *Phantasms* Data – having provided himself with a program to simulate the human experience of dreaming – has a series of disturbing 'dreams', in one of which he encounters Deanna Troi as a 'living cake'. Thinking he is developing human neuroses, Data consults a holographic Sigmund Freud, who explains the dreams as being projections of incidents that must have happened when he was a young child. But in a sequence that gently mocks Freudian sensibilities, Data informs Freud that as he never was a child, this prognosis cannot apply. In fact, what appear to be 'dream images' are actually warnings of invisible parasites which are attaching themselves to members of the crew. Data's dreams thus have a rational explanation, but not one to which even the most famous human psychoanalyst can point him.

An even more complex 'reality conundrum' is seen in a third Braga story, *Voyager*'s *Projections*, in which the Doctor's instruments tell him that he is the only 'human' on the ship, while the rest of the crew register as holograms. A hologram of *TNG*'s Reg Barclay appears and tries to persuade him that in reality he is Dr Lewis Zimmerman (his creator and physical model) in a holodeck on a space station and that all the events of the last few months since *Voyager* was lost in the Delta Quadrant have been part of a simulation that he has been running. Barclay explains that the simulation has gone wrong due to an unexpected power surge and that in order to escape from the program the Doctor must end it by destroying the ship. At this point the audience is likely to share the Doctor's suspicion that 'Barclay' is some kind of disguised alien entity who is manipulating him. But when the Doctor finds that he is bleeding after a fight with an invading Kazon warrior, he becomes convinced that what Barclay is telling him is true. Just as he is about to fire a phaser into the warp core, a projection of Chakotay appears and informs him that if he does so he will wipe out his own holographic matrix. Minutes later he comes to consciousness in sick bay, and 'normal reality' appears to be restored; but when Barclay reappears he realises he is in another simulation. Finally the 'real' crew helps him escape, but in the last moments of the episode he is seen cautiously 'checking reality' again. Braga 'tricks' the audience into the expectation that this will be another story where the ship is threatened, but ultimately it appears that the only threat was to the Doctor himself. Most of the characters in the story have in fact merely been 'voices' inside the Doctor's head.

The character of the Doctor is the most fully-realised extension of the idea of the 'sentient hologram' which, like any other species, must under Federation morality be granted certain individual rights. In *TNG* various incidences of 'breakdowns' or unexpected properties of holo-technology sometimes allow holodeck characters to 'cross over' from their existence in virtual reality to develop self-awareness of their holographic status. In *Elementary, Dear Data* Conan Doyle's villain, Professor Moriarty, temporarily takes over the ship by manipulating the holodeck controls. In *Ship in a Bottle* Moriarty convinces Picard and Data that he has found it possible to have a life outside the holodeck, but Picard comes to realise that this has been done by Moriarty creating a simulation of the entire ship inside the holodeck itself. Barclay's ingenious final solution is to design a miniature holo-program in which Moriarty and his holographic 'wife' can live out their lives in a perpetual illusion that they are travelling through the galaxy.

Other holodeck excursions introduce the element of the psychology – and the decidedly dubious morality – of 'human–hologram relations'. In *11001001* we meet Riker's fantasy holodeck woman, Minuet, but Riker is confident enough in his own sexuality not to take his 'relationship' with her too seriously. In contrast, the sexually insecure Geordi La Forge (in *TNG*'s *Booby Trap*) and Harry Kim (in *Voyager*'s *Alter Ego*) both find themselves 'falling for' holodeck characters and suffering a considerable degree of guilt as a result. The holodeck can be a site which can amplify an individual's personal inadequacies. Reference is made to 'holodiction', a condition in which an individual becomes too embroiled in virtual worlds. In *TNG's Nth Degree* the nervous and bumbling Reg Barclay enacts a fantasy holodeck program in which he orders around the ship's senior officers. The holodeck stories thus cast a wary eye on the potential psychological dangers of such virtual technology.

Many psychologically-based *Star Trek* stories explore notions of telepathy. In the original series Spock is provided with the ability to 'mind meld' with other beings. The Vulcan mind meld creates a telepathic link between those who have experienced it, so that each shares elements of the other's consciousness. The ability to 'meld' is only achieved through years of intense mental training, and gives its user a way of communicating with all kinds of species. In *The Devil in the Dark* Spock melds with the 'rock beast' the Horta, and in *The Changeling* he melds with a rogue space probe. In the movie *The Voyage Home* he melds with Gracie the whale. In each case the intervention is the only way in which these creatures can be understood. In *TNG's Unification*, Picard shares with Spock a mind meld he had previously undertaken with Spock's father, Sarek, who has since died. In *Voyager's Meld* Tuvok mind melds with the deranged murderer, Suder, in order to try to understand why Suder has apparently killed for no reason. But the meld has a psychologically disturbing effect on Tuvok, as he has 'taken in' the murderer's emotions. In all these cases, the effort of the meld is seen to be particularly draining on the Vulcans' mental energy, often releasing their normally suppressed emotions. The Vulcan personality presents a certain type of logical ideal to which many humans may aspire, but it is always made clear that the Vulcans' suppression of emotion involves considerable suffering for them.

The exploration of telepathy is made more explicit in *TNG*, which introduces the Betazoids as a telepathic race. Whereas the Vulcans only achieve their telepathic powers through intense mental concentration, to Betazoids telepathy is a natural part of their existence. But like Vulcans, Betazoids can also experience considerable suffering if their telepathic powers are disturbed or enhanced. Thus, whereas 'Vulcan stories' explore the logical side of human nature, 'Betazoid stories' focus on the dangers of emotional excess and over-sensitivity. Ship's counsellor Deanna Troi is half-Betazoid, which gives her useful, if not always totally effective, telepathic or empathic powers. When she temporarily loses these powers in *The Loss*, she becomes extremely insecure, loses her usual calm self-confidence and begins to behave erratically. She is forced to resign her position until the powers return. In *Violations*, Jev, a member of another telepathic race, the Ullians (who normally exercise considerable restraint over their telepathic powers), implants memories into Troi, Riker and Beverly Crusher. Troi has a flashback of a past sexual encounter with Riker during which Riker suddenly turns into Jev, and the shock sends her into a coma. The episode uses the theme of telepathy to explore the psychological effects of rape on its victims.

Deanna's mother Lwaxana is a full Betazoid and as such has even stronger telepathic powers than her daughter. The two are often seen 'conversing' on a telepathic level. Although Lwaxana is normally portrayed as a comic character, *Dark Page* is a sometimes harrowing exploration of the effects of grief, in which Deanna manages to penetrate the telepathic block that Lwaxana has erected for years to prevent her knowing about the death in childhood of her older sister. It seems that much of Lwaxana's 'blustery' character has been adopted to cover up the deep pain she still feels about this, which as a Betazoid she feels all the more keenly. In *Tin Man* Tam Elbrun, a Betazoid whose telepathic powers are so hypersensitive that the confusion of 'voices' he can hear is driving him insane, can finally only find peace by leaving humanoid society behind for ever by merging with a strange 'organic spaceship'. In these episodes it is made clear that telepathy can be as much a 'burden' as a 'blessing'. Both the Vulcan and Betazoid stories emphasise the importance of emotional control in achieving a state of 'self-actualisation'.

In *Voyager*'s powerful *Remember* the theme of mental 'invasion' is used for a different purpose. The crew is engaged in making contact with the Enarans (an apparently friendly and 'democratic' telepathic race) when Torres begins experiencing vivid and highly disturbing 'dreams' in which she is transported back to the scene of an Enaran 'holocaust' that occurred around 50 years before. To Torres, these 'dreams' have the qualities of experienced reality. She finds herself sympathising with the social outcasts who are being persecuted, but under the influence of her father she eventually betrays them. Eventually it transpires that a dying Enaran woman, still guilt-ridden at her inaction during the repression on her planet, is determined to transfer her memories to someone for posterity. Here the theme of telepathy is used to emphasise the point that such examples of genocide should never be forgotten.

Another well-established *Star Trek* plot convention with psychological connotations is that of the 'takeover' or 'possession' of characters by alien entities, first seen in original series episodes such as *Whom Gods Destroy* and *The Lights of Zetar*. These episodes tend to gravitate towards melodramatic extremes, as in *TNG*'s *Power Play*, where O'Brien, Troi and Data are 'possessed' by alien entities who hold a group of crew members hostage; *DS9*'s *The Assignment*, in which an alien entity takes over Keiko O'Brien and forces Miles to sabotage the station; or *Voyager*'s *Warlord*, where Kes is taken over by the consciousness of a power-crazed military dictator. More powerful and convincing examples of 'alien possession' include Picard's co-option into the Borg collective in *The Best of Both Worlds* and O'Brien's 'mental incarceration' in *Hard Time*, both experiences which are shown to have long-term psychological repercussions.

Picard is arguably the most fully-realised character in all of *Star Trek*. Two episodes from the later seasons of *TNG* feature stories which explore his 'inner life' in considerable depth. Both episodes feature Picard living an alternative life, but this is engineered in a more subtle manner than in the more direct *doppelgänger* episodes. In *The Inner Light* (written by Peter Lauritson, Morgan Gendel and Peter Allan Fields) he is 'attacked' by an unknown and apparently innocuous probe which transmits a 'nulceonic beam' that locks directly onto him. After less than half an hour he reawakens, convinced he has experienced an entire lifetime on a doomed planet. The memories have been implanted by a long-extinct race who designed the probe as a way of keeping the memory of their civilisation alive. In this existence he has led a simple family life in which he achieves the kind of happiness and contentment that he can never attain in his somewhat austere and detached life as captain of the *Enterprise*. The fact that Picard's entire 'lifetime' in the episode is an 'illusion' induced by an alien probe does not matter in psychological terms. The episode effectively makes up for the lack of family love in Picard's life, but also points somewhat painfully to that lack. As with his takeover by the Borg, the effects of Picard's experiences in *The Inner Light* are explored in a number of succeeding episodes. Despite the grief it eventually entails, the 'life' he is given in *The Inner Light* helps him to heal the psychological scars with which his experience with the Borg had left him.

The story which perhaps best epitomises *Star Trek*'s humanistic psychological perspective is Moore's *Tapestry*, which balances a certain degree of philosophical humour with wry reflections on individual destiny. The episode begins with Picard critically injured and his artificial heart apparently about to fail. Suddenly we are transported inside Picard's consciousness, where he meets Q, who claims that this is the afterlife and that he is God, a suggestion for which Picard (as a good humanist and sceptic) displays only contempt. But Picard does allow Q to act as his 'confessor' and his conscience. Q asks Picard if he has any regrets in his life and asks whether, given the chance, he would have lived his life differently. Picard replies in the affirmative. Q then gives him the chance to relive a crucial episode in his youth as a Starfleet trainee, in which, in a fight with three aggressive Nausicaans, he is stabbed in the heart and only survives through being given a heart transplant. When Picard – given his second chance – avoids the injury, Q 'fast-forwards' Picard into the resultant 'present-day' scenario in which he (although he still has his real heart) is a mere junior lieutenant on the *Enterprise*. It appears that after avoiding the fight, Picard then 'played it safe' for the rest of his life and thus never rose from a low rank to any kind of command position. Unable to bear this, Picard chooses to relive the incident again, and this time voluntarily suffers the blow in order to bring about the restoration of the original timeline. Q, with his superhuman powers, then restores the artificial heart to working order and brings him 'back to life'. Later, Picard realises that the whole experience has been extremely therapeutic. He is now able to put the regrets about his past life which have haunted him for many years into perspective. He also realises that Q has given him an important insight into the way human destiny unfolds. *Tapestry*'s psychological message – that a personality is made up of a 'patchwork' of both 'good' and 'bad' decisions and that individuals develop by learning vital lessons from their mistakes which can later prove to be key sources of strength – demonstrates again the humanistic ethos of *Star Trek*, which places the destiny of individuals firmly in their own hands.

Chapter 11

Liberalism, the new frontier and the American Dream: political themes in *Star Trek*

[Liberalism's] aim is to create a nation, not of humble though kindly treated workers dependent upon a small rich class who alone can enjoy the full benefits of a civilised life; and not of proletarians regimented, controlled, and provided with standardised comforts by a group of dictators or bureaucrats acting in the name of the State; but a nation of free, responsible, law-abiding and self-reliant men and women – free from the grinding servitude of poverty and ... from the tyranny of circumstance; with healthy bodies and alert and trained minds; enjoying a real equality of opportunity to make the most and best of their powers for their own advantage and that of the community; and to choose the way of life for which they are best fitted; having a real share of responsibility for regulating the management of their common affairs and the conditions of their own life and work; and secure of sufficient leisure to live a full life and to enjoy the delights of Nature, letters and the arts.

(Ramsay Muir, *The Liberal Way*, 1934, pp. 221–2)

As its political discourse gradually broadens and develops, *Star Trek* evolves into a detailed investigation of the limitations of the liberal–humanist ethos. The stark moralism of the original series, in which the Federation represents an unequivocal force for good, eventually gives way to situations in which the supposed superiority of liberal human values is continually being challenged. Although the new *Trek* series certainly persist in their espousal of liberal values, these are filtered through a multiculturalist perspective which is represented by the various alien cultures – particularly the Klingons,

Vulcans, Romulans, Ferengi, Bajorans and Cardassians. At the same time the encounters with highly developed alien beings such as Q, the wormhole 'prophets' and the Caretaker all test the limitations of human concepts. These developments represent a series of attempts by the new *Trek* writers to resolve the many political contradictions that are built into the original *Star Trek* scenario, the roots of which can be found in the ideological conflicts within the philosophy of liberalism itself. As Robert Eccleshall argues:

> in some respects, modern liberals appear to sit uncomfortably astride the ideological worlds of conservatism and socialism. With conservatives they wish to define freedom as the right of individuals to strive for inequalities of wealth, and yet, like socialists, they want to argue that liberty is diminished unless everyone is given access to the resources necessary for a decent life … (in Eccleshall *et al.*, 1984, p. 36)

The original series of *Star Trek* displays elements of both types of liberalism. The series' constant references to Earth in the twenty-third century as a planet without social class divisions, racism, sexism, poverty, war or organised religion can be seen as representing the future human society as a kind of 'socialist paradise' which might even be characterised as 'pure communism'. The multiracial nature of the crew, and the lack of any ideological conflict between them, expresses both the tolerance and solidarity of this society. It is said that humans have 'evolved' beyond greed or the need to accumulate material possessions, which might be taken to imply that money (and with it capitalism) has been abolished. Yet Roddenberry's future-utopia remains an ideal rather than a specific political construct, as the series never actually takes us back to Earth in the twenty-third century. The economics of the future society are also somewhat ill-defined. However, the culturally expansionist nature of the Federation – and even the very name of the ship, the *Enterprise* – strongly suggests that, even if its motivation for wishing to share technology and to trade with newly discovered races is as entirely benevolent as it appears to be, the Federation represents the spread of an extended (if enlightened) form of capitalism.

The military ethos of *Star Trek* also tends to emphasise a more conservative perspective. Starfleet is unarguably a military organisation: although its officers may be highly trained scientists, they are also soldiers. Whatever equality may exist on Earth, the military remains rather rigidly hierarchical. The *Enterprise* may be a ship of peace but it carries highly advanced weapons capable of destroying entire planetary systems. Indeed, the military set-up in *Star Trek* is rather 'lovingly' created, with the hierarchy of ranks within Starfleet being based closely on that of the US Navy. Pride in a 'military bearing' seems to be thoroughly built into the original series and many opportunities are taken to liken the *Enterprise* to a naval vessel. Roddenberry, who had a strong military background himself as a wartime pilot for the USAF and had also been a policeman, partially modelled Kirk on sea captain Horatio Hornblower from C. S. Forester's adventure stories. The Federation's apparent willingness to make treaties with 'fascistic' regimes also suggests a certain conservatism in foreign policy matters. In many ways the positioning of Federation 'foreign policy' reflects that of John F. Kennedy (another role-model for Kirk), who instituted many liberal domestic reforms whilst simultaneously pursuing a foreign policy that was essentially conservative and often inflammatory – dramatically confronting Kruschev in the 1962 Cuban Missile Crisis and supporting military intervention in Cuba and Vietnam.

It was perhaps inevitable that the 'military balance of power' Starfleet encounters in the original series would be likened to that of the cold war and that the Klingons in particular might be seen as the equivalent of the Soviet Union. In the movie *The Undiscovered Country* this theme is brought to the fore as Kirk and Spock are imprisoned in the Klingon 'gulag' and the conciliatory Chancellor Gorkon (a rather obvious Gorbachev-surrogate) is murdered by Klingon 'hard-liners'. We are also told that the Klingons, like the Soviet Union, have destroyed their economy by concentrating too much of their economic resources on a military build-up. The events of the film are presented as a clear parallel with the ending of the cold war and the fall of the Soviet Union. Many of those who saw the film concluded that *Star Trek* had always been a symbolic representation of the Cold War era in which it was born. Such a notion implies, however, that the original series is essentially a politically conservative 'tract' in which the Federation represents a 'supercharged' USA in space with the Klingons cast as the 'communist threat'.

This broad view is fairly widely held, but it is rather simplistic and inaccurate. The Klingons are hardly an 'ever-present threat'. In fact they make appearances in only six of the 79 episodes, and rarely does any fighting break out. There is no attempt to portray them as in any way communistic: indeed, if either side's social organisation could be called 'communistic', it is the Federation's. Although any 'ideology' the Klingons might possess is clearly opposed to that of the Federation, they are in fact old-style imperialists whose mentality is in many ways more medieval than modern. Rather than being truly threatening or 'driven' by any political creed, they are frequently portrayed as rather pathetic, comical figures – as in *The Trouble with Tribbles*, where they display an embarrassed loathing against the 'harmless' furry creatures. In *Errand of Mercy* they invade the planet Organia, intending to subdue it brutally but are prevented from doing so by the apparently defenceless Organians – beings who have evolved well beyond the need for conventional military protection. The emphasis of the story falls on Kirk's realisation that he, like the Klingon leader, Kor, is a 'warrior' who actually savours a fight. This theme is heavily echoed in *Day of the Dove*, in which an alien entity manipulates Starfleet and the Klingons into vicious hand-to-hand combat. In *Friday's Child* Kirk succeeds in preventing the Klingons forming an alliance with the planet Capella, and in *Elaan of Troyius* he wins a skirmish with a Klingon battle cruiser, but there is little indication that the Klingons might have either the military power or the inclination to attempt to destroy or take over the Federation. Also, unlike like the communist-surrogate aliens of pulp 1950s SF movies, the Klingons are never shown to be 'infiltrating' Federation society.

The other main 'baddies', the Romulans, make only three appearances in the original series. Some commentators have likened them to the Chinese communists, but there is precious little evidence for such an assertion, beyond their slightly 'Asiatic' appearance. Their main characteristic appears to be a certain deviousness, symbolised in their possession of the cloaking device first mentioned in *Balance of Terror*, which a surgically-altered Kirk later steals in *The Enterprise Incident*. The overwhelming emphasis in the original series is on various forms of first contact with *new* species and entities, most of which make only a solitary appearance. There are in fact more stories about meetings with highly evolved 'superbeings' than there are about encounters with Klingons or Romulans. Most of the galaxy is still a 'wide open' uncharted region, and space is not yet – as it will be by the time of *TNG* – mostly divided up into zones of influence. Although the original series may sometimes stray into allegorical 'cold war' territory, it is mainly positioned as a drama which stresses human compassion and open-mindedness in a series of 'one-off' encounters with newly discovered civilisations.

In fact, the original series' main political dimension is that of the 'rediscovery' of America's lost 'frontier' and of the consequent reinvention of a newly defined 'American Dream'. In this respect the contradictions of American liberalism are again displayed prominently. The myth of the frontier has been tremendously influential on American national culture and politics. Through the late nineteenth century, as the frontier gradually moved west, American 'civilisation' poured into 'new' territory, provoking the 'American Dream' of a utopia-on-Earth which had been fundamental to the hopes of many of the groups of religious settlers (such as the Pilgrim Fathers) who first colonised the continent and whose descendants eventually founded the USA itself. In popular American mythology the frontier symbolises both freedom and this imagined utopia. As Goethals asserts:

> The frontier provided a mythological space in which forces of good and evil, of order and disorder, engaged in mortal combat. From this struggle for right and order emerged a special kind of hero who had a public obligation to establish order, resorting to violence only when there was no alternative ... (1981, p. 66)

American politicians have often traded on the symbolism of the frontier. In his election addresses of 1960 John F. Kennedy spoke of a 'New Frontier' of progressive health, housing, and civil rights programmes. At the same time Kennedy committed the USA to the exploration of the 'new frontier' of space. The New Frontier, he said:

> sums up not what I intend to offer the American people but what I intend to ask of them. It appeals to their pride, not to their pocketbook; it holds out the promise of more sacrifice instead of more security ... But I tell you that the New Frontier is here whether we seek it or not ... uncharted areas of science and space, unsolved problems of peace and war, unconquered pockets of ignorance and prejudice, unanswered questions of poverty and surplus ... (quoted in Sorensen, 1965, p. 167)

Kennedy rose to power while the USA was in the throes of the 'space race' with the Soviet Union, and he promised that the Americans would put a man on the moon by the end of the decade, a prediction which was realised by the Apollo 11 flight in 1969. In this context, the very first words of William Shatner's famous voiceover 'Space, the final frontier ...' may imply that the Federation's utopian culture is (as

Spock would say) a 'logical' historical extension of Kennedy's 'New Frontier'.

The frontier myth is also the foundation of that quintessential American genre, the western, which is a largely mythologised account of frontier life in the American West in the late nineteenth century. At the time *Star Trek* began the western was still the most popular genre in TV and film. Gene Roddenberry had worked on a number of the western series that dominated the schedules, including *Have Gun, Will Travel*, for which he was head of the writing team. It is hardly surprising, given the ubiquity of the western and *Star Trek*'s status as a 'frontier drama', that certain aspects of the western manifested themselves in the original series. Indeed, Roddenberry himself originally floated the idea of the series to the networks as a 'wagon train to the stars' (Whitfield and Roddenberry, 1991, p. 21). Yet whereas the western represented a worldview that was nostalgic and conservative, demonstrating a violently male-orientated and often racist perspective, *Star Trek* is expressly a liberal reinterpretation of the frontier myth. It is scrupulous in insisting that the bloody and genocidal history of the American frontier will not be repeated, that human beings have learned their lessons and will no longer presume superiority over any racial group. Whereas most westerns characteristically present their 'Indians' as 'savages', and thus implicitly justify the process of cultural imperialism, *Star Trek* emphatically distances itself from this 'dark side of the American Dream' by the Federation insistence on the principle of the Prime Directive, the philosophy behind which is explained by Kirk to a 'tribesman' in *A Private Little War*:

> We once were as you were ... spears ... arrows ... There came a time when our weapons grew faster than our wisdom and we almost destroyed ourselves. We learned from this to make a rule for all our travels – never to cause the same to happen to other worlds ...

The episodes based around the Prime Directive give the clearest indication of the often contradictory liberal philosophy of the original series. *A Private Little War*, in which Kirk provides the natives of a primitive planet with arms to counterbalance those the Klingons have been supplying, has been interpreted by some commentators as a defence of US policy in Vietnam. Despite much agonising over the Prime Directive – with McCoy arguing against arming the natives – Kirk is quite prepared to create a 'balance of terror' on the planet, even though he is deliberately flaunting Starfleet's non-interventionist ethos. *The Omega Glory*, one of the original series' rather dubious 'parallel development' stories, features a tribe called the 'Yangs' who are being suppressed by an Asiatic race known as the 'Kohms' with the assistance of a crazed former Starfleet captain who wrongly thinks the planet's atmosphere may contain an 'elixir of youth'. The Yangs, whose 'holy text' is actually the US Declaration of Rights, are presented as a 'freedom-loving' race. On one level the story can be read as a parallel to the US wars in Korea and Vietnam. In the final, unashamedly patriotic, shot of the episode, Kirk – who had earlier proudly recited the Declaration – is seen gazing up admiringly at a US flag while *The Star-Spangled Banner* plays in the background. Both episodes were scripted by Roddenberry himself, and both display clear notions of 'patriotic duty' which perhaps reflect his own military background as well as the inherent contradictions in his liberal world-view. Roddenberry was a professed opponent of the Vietnam War, yet like many liberals he remained a 'patriotic American'. It is significant, however, that *A Private Little War* is one of the few episodes of the series where the morality of Kirk's actions is presented as being open to question.

It is certainly true that whenever the *Enterprise* is confronted with an unequal society, Kirk is likely to pursue an interventionist policy which may arguably involve breaking the Prime Directive. But the Prime Directive does not imply a complete policy of non-interventionism. If it did, Starfleet could hardly exist at all. In fact the Prime Directive stresses non-interference with the 'natural evolution' of developing cultures. It therefore only really applies to civilisations with a lower level of technology than the Federation. In *A Private Little War* Kirk defends his actions by claiming that the only way to preserve the planet's 'natural evolution' is to arm both sides equally. On other occasions the intervention is said to be justified by the fact that the 'pollution' of developing cultures has already taken place. Sometimes – as in *The Omega Glory* and the 'Nazi planet' of *Patterns of Force* – this has been caused by other Starfleet captains. In both *Return of the Archons* and *The Apple* Kirk frees societies held in thrall to a computer. In *The Cloudminders* he forces the hierarchical rulers of the planet to recognise the rights of the suppressed underground miners, so radically rearranging the planet's social structure. In *A Taste of Armageddon* he encounters a planet which has agreed to conduct a continual state of computerised war with its enemies – an arrangement with involves both sides sending large numbers of civilians to voluntary deaths in 'disintegration chambers'. By destroying the Ekotians' disintegrators

Kirk forces them to choose between continual war and the chance of peace. Such lapses from the Federation's 'non-interventionist' ethos can be seen to reflect the paradoxical nature of US foreign policy, with its twin planks of the traditional US 'isolationist' doctrine and the post-war 'world policeman/defender of democracy' role. American liberals were often confused as to which position to take on such issues, and *Star Trek*'s original series in many ways reflects this confusion. It is clear that the Prime Directive, like the Declaration Of Rights, is very much open to interpretation.

In *The American Monomyth* (published in 1977 and thus only referring to the original series), Robert Jewett and John Shelton Lawrence argue that the hero-based classical monomyth as espoused by Joseph Campbell is being replaced in the mass media era by an 'American monomyth', of which they cite *Star Trek* as a prime example. They view this monomyth as an 'escapist fantasy' and a secularisation of Christian redemption dramas, in which the hero is a surrogate Christ-figure. Typically, such a hero is described as sexually 'segmented'; that is, unlike the hero of the classical monomyth, he can never form a permanent relationship. In what Jewett and Lawrence see as the archetypal plot pattern of their monomyth, the hero is a selfless 'outsider' who saves a 'frontier' community from a great threat and then retreats into his solitude. This description, as well as fitting many John Wayne-type western heroes, may to some extent be applied to Kirk on those occasions when he does break the Prime Directive. But Jewett and Lawrence's analysis concentrates only on a selected number of *Star Trek* episodes that happen to fit their theory. Kirk's intervention in various planetary societies is ultimately intended to draw them towards union with the Federation, rather than support their isolation. And Kirk himself is certainly no 'loner', having a completely interdependent relationship with Spock and McCoy. As outlined in the previous chapter, his 'sexual segmentation' is the product of the conventions of 1960s TV series, which demanded that the hero should always be able to have new romances. In their attempt to identify *Star Trek* as an essentially conservative text, Jewett and Lawrence fail to understand the contradictions in the political ethos of the series. Their 'monomyth' is a response to popular disillusionment with the myth of the American Eden, but Roddenberry's mythic vision of a Utopian 'ideal culture' of *Star Trek* can more accurately be seen as a triumphant *fulfilment* of that Edenic American Dream.

By the time *The Next Generation* was launched, the world's political landscape had changed as radically as the broadcasting environment in which it appeared. With the end of the Cold War already in sight, the moral and ideological simplicities of that era had been superseded by a world of more complex political alignments. The USA, though it had become clearly the dominant military power in the world, now found itself confronted by a series of often intractable political situations which it often did not have the power to resolve. A good example was the Iranian hostage crisis of 1979–80, the lack of resolution of which had much to do with the fall of Jimmy Carter's Democratic administration and the rise of Ronald Reagan's new conservatism with its attendant militarist posturing. In many other situations around the world, particularly when terrorist groups exploited the power of the mass media, the USA found itself unable to intervene militarily in any effective way. The humiliating US defeat by a 'peasant army' in Vietnam had brought home the realisation that, despite its overwhelming military power, the USA was limited in its ability to impose its political values on other nations. In the 1970s the Watergate scandal and the emerging revelations about the conspiracy to kill Kennedy also shook the faith of more conservative liberals. Meanwhile, Kennedy's 'New Frontier' of space exploration – which had symbolised the idealism of the 1960s – remained virtually uncharted. Due to public apathy (expressed in declining TV ratings) the moon landings had ended in 1973 and the projected trips to Mars and other planets (which NASA had been planning for the 1980s) had never taken place. Thus much of the idealism – and the naïvety – of the 1960s had been replaced by a more cynical and less morally defined political culture.

As we have seen, the original series' relationship to the cold war was in fact a very tentative one, but the tone of greater political realism in the new *Trek* series allows for many stories which quite explicitly mirror the role of the USA in world affairs in the post-Cold War era. In particular, *TNG* presents several situations where the Federation encounters terrorist groups and a number of scenarios where hostages are being held: in *Starship Mine*, the *Enterprise* is commandeered by a terrorist gang who intend to steal the warp engines' toxic waste, which can be used as a dangerous weapon; in both *Too Short a Season* and *Legacy*, Picard has to bargain for the return of Federation hostages; in *Power Play*, the alien entities who take over the bodies of O'Brien, Data and Deanna Troi hold a number of *Enterprise* personnel; and in *The High Ground*, ideologically motivated terrorist rebels capture Beverly Crusher. Such stories reflect the problems of resurgent nationalism and religious and cultural factionalism which have emerged in

the wake of the end of the Cold War. They also represent a more realistic view of the effects of interventionism. Although Picard is
invariably able to recover the hostages, there is little he can do to
resolve the internal political conflicts of the strife-torn planets themselves. Whereas Kirk would have forced warring factions to find a way
to resolve their differences, Picard's hands are usually tied. Although
the Federation – like the USA in the 'Third World' – possesses overwhelming military capacity, this apparent superiority does not mean
it can always solve local conflicts. In fact, its intervention may well
make things worse. In *TNG* Starfleet has to 'tread carefully', trying to
balance respect for local laws and customs with the safety of the crew
and the strategic interests of the Federation.

As a result of this, in *TNG* the Prime Directive is adhered to far more
scrupulously than in the original series. This is particularly stressed in
a number of early *TNG* episodes. In *Pen Pals* a young girl from a
'primitive' world is brought aboard the *Enterprise* while the crew
corrects the volcanic stresses that are threatening the planet. But
before she can be returned her memory has to be wiped so that her
knowledge of a 'higher civilisation' will not 'pollute' the 'natural
development' of her race. In *Too Short a Season* we see the after-effects
of an earlier Prime Directive violation on the planet Mordan 4 by
Starfleet's Admiral Jameson who, like Kirk in *A Private Little War*, had
many years before ensured that both sides on the planet were equally
armed. But this has led to nearly half a century of bloody conflict and
Jameson (who has taken a dangerous, unlicensed 'youth drug' in
order to be able to conduct the negotiations) attempts to return to
undo the damage he has done. Jameson's argument – that by arming
both sides equally he was attempting to preserve the spirit of the
Prime Directive – exactly mirrors Kirk's earlier justification for doing
so. The wisdom of the Prime Directive – and Kirk's earlier foolhardi-
ness in breaking it – are heavily underlined here. Yet the ethical
difficulties encountered in upholding the Prime Directive are still
particularly stressed. In *Justice* the Edo, who practise the ultimate in
a 'zero tolerance' crime prevention policy, sentence Wesley Crusher
to death for a minor transgression. In a situation where Kirk would
have barely hesitated at all before acting, Picard agonises over
whether to intervene, but eventually decides to take back Wesley by
force. When he does so the Edo capitulate, but not without taunting
Picard for breaking his own 'laws'. Similarly, on the matriarchal
planet of *Angel One* a group of dissident former Federation crewmen
are sentenced to death before Riker persuades the planet's leader,

Beata, to commute the sentence to exile. Although these situations are resolved, the ethics of the Prime Directive are already being questioned.

From the third season onwards, *TNG* stories are much less likely to end in the neatly resolved ways displayed in earlier episodes. Federation actions are often taken 'regretfully', as in *The Ensigns of Command*, where a planet's colonists have to be forcibly evacuated. In *Who Watches the Watchers* the Federation is engaged in 'scientific observation' of the Mintakans, a still-primitive culture, by using disguised observation stations. But once the Federation accidentally exposes itself to the natives of the planet, a whole series of disastrous consequences ensue. Beverly Crusher insists on beaming up a wounded Mintakan to save his life, but this time the 'memory wipe' does not work. Soon Picard and his crew are being revered as 'gods' and Picard has to allow himself to be injured to convince the natives that he is mortal. However, the potential future effects of the incident on the society are deemed uncertain and the long-term effects of the Prime Directive violation on the development of the culture remain unanswered. In fact, Picard is deeply worried about how his appearance will be interpreted by future generations. Here the morality and limitations of the Prime Directive are questioned, throwing into focus the issue of the impact of technologically advanced cultures on 'primitive' races. The shortcomings of the Federation practice of 'spying' on developing cultures are exposed here, in a story which reflects on the dangers of anthropological intervention in the lives of 'primitive' societies.

In *First Contact* the Federation again uses subterfuge – in the form of a surgically-altered Riker – to observe a less-developed race. Here, however, the Malcorian society is highly technological and on the verge of developing space travel. Riker is captured and local scientists quickly establish that his physiognomy is alien. But the discovery causes a political crisis on the planet, as the orthodox priests of the Malcorian religion insist that they are the only sentient race in the universe. The prime minister of Malcor is more rational, and accepts Riker's alien nature. But eventually he decides that the time is not yet ripe for revealing the existence of other races in the universe to the Malcorian population. The Federation mission is ultimately fruitless in a way that one of Kirk's missions would never have been. Again the potential dangers of Federation interventionism – however well-intentioned – are made clear.

TNG's final 'Prime Directive' story, Naren Shankar's *Homeward*, provides perhaps the most searching critique yet seen of both the Prime Directive and the political and cultural policies of the Federation. The culture of the planet Boral 2 consists, like that of the Mintakans in *Who Watches the Watchers*, of 'primitive' tribal groups. Worf's adoptive brother, Nikolai Rozhenko, has been stationed by the Federation as a 'cultural observer' on the planet, whose atmosphere is growing increasingly unable to support life. The *Enterprise*'s sensors indicate that soon the entire atmosphere on the planet will be destroyed, killing all the inhabitants. The Federation's policy, which here adheres strictly to the Prime Directive, is to allow this natural disaster to occur. Nikolai, who (like Kirk in *The Paradise Syndrome*) has 'gone native' by 'marrying' a native woman, has little time for such Starfleet ideology. While much of the population has already been killed by the atmospheric storms, Nikolai has in effect already broken the Prime Directive by sheltering the entire village he lives in down in some caves below the planet's surface. His pleas to Picard to save the planet's inhabitants go unheard. Picard is determined to stick to the letter of the Prime Directive. In an astonishing scene, Picard and his crew solemnly watch the storms destroy the planet's atmosphere while Picard delivers a sober speech in which the Prime Directive is raised to new heights as a 'moral guide'. Here we see how the philosophy of the Prime Directive, while embodying sound liberal principles, can become as much a 'sacred cow' as any of the fundamentalist religious beliefs which the Federation's logical humanism specifically denies. The original purpose of the Prime Directive was to prevent the 'cultural pollution' of developing races, but the implication here seems to be that this belief has become an unbending orthodoxy. As Nikolai quite logically tells them, they prefer to watch an entire race be wiped out than allow it to become 'polluted'. The narrowness of the Prime Directive as a doctrine, and the unbending logic of certain forms of liberalism, is thus clearly exposed.

However, Nikolai, who had 'dropped out' of Starfleet because of what he saw as its over-rigid ideology, has taken matters into his own hands. Having created a replica of the Baralian caves on the *Enterprise*'s holodeck, he has beamed the entire population of his village onboard. Of course, the villagers believe they are still underground. Nikolai demands that they be taken to a new planet and resettled. Picard is furious at this deception, but short of murdering the entire tribe he has little option but to agree. Finally a new home is found and the villagers (together with Nikolai) are resettled there without ever having known they had been on a spaceship. But one individual tragedy in the story indicates exactly why the Prime Directive was formulated in the first place. One young villager manages to find a way off the holodeck and onto the Starship. Having seen the reality of his situation he agrees that he cannot be allowed to return to the tribe. But he cannot cope with the cultural differences in his 'new life' and he commits suicide. Thus *Homeward* is *TNG*'s most complete and balanced dissection of the Prime Directive, showing both its limitations and its *raison d'être*.

There is relatively little reference to the Prime Directive in *DS9*, which features few 'first contact' situations with 'primitive' races, but in *Voyager* it is often re-emphasised. Even though the ship has been transported into a far-distant part of the galaxy, as far as Janeway and the Starfleet officers onboard are concerned the Prime Directive still applies. In *Caretaker* Janeway uses the Prime Directive as her rationale for destroying the array which represented the crew's chance of returning to their own sector of space, although how staying to protect the threatened Ocampa race constitutes obeying the Prime Directive is rather puzzling. In *Prime Factors*, *Voyager* encounters the Sikarians, a civilisation which possesses the technology for them to get home. But ironically the Sikarians have their own version of the Prime Directive and do not wish to share this technology. Generally, however, the newer *Trek* series are much less concerned with the Prime Directive than their earlier counterparts, perhaps because by now the theme has been so thoroughly mined, or perhaps because the writers have become increasingly uncomfortable with the contradictions in *Star Trek*'s liberal humanitarian ethos that Prime Directive stories had frequently exposed.

After the assertion of new controlling authorial voices in the later seasons of *TNG*, *Star Trek* increasingly distances itself from Roddenberry's naïve and often contradictory liberalism. In particular, Roddenberry's romanticised view of military life is challenged. The military and scientific ethics of Starfleet had already come under considerable scrutiny in early episodes like *Coming of Age* and *Conspiracy*, in which Picard uncovers the existence of a conspiracy among the top echelons of Starfleet. At this point, with *Star Trek* still under the strong influence of Roddenberryesque liberalism, the conspiracy turns out to be the work of a parasitic alien race. Thus Starfleet itself is exonerated of any moral blame. But by the time of the second season's *The Measure of a Man*, in which a Federation scientist almost succeeds in having Data declared the 'property' of Starfleet, attention is already being turned to the questionable ethics of Starfleet itself. Increasingly the personal morality of Picard and his crew –

which is generally impeccable – is set against the 'impersonal' bureaucracy of Starfleet's command structure. In *The Drumhead* Picard expresses his disgust at the way Starfleet Admiral Nora Satie is conducting a 'witch hunt' against a crew member guilty of nothing more than a minor deception. Meanwhile the stresses upon individual characters of the military lifestyle are examined in the many 'family'-orientated episodes of the fourth and fifth seasons.

Perhaps *Star Trek*'s major achievement in political terms is its depiction in *DS9* of the after-effects of the Cardassian occupation of Bajor. Without doubt this occupation resulted in a holocaust on a huge scale, and Starfleet are positioned as 'peace-makers' between the warring parties, assuming a role that parallels that of the US in many contemporary political situations. In many ways the situation on Bajor, with its theocratic traditions and its factionalised groups, is a mirror for a number of very 'messy' modern political wars, such as those in Yugoslavia, Lebanon, Afghanistan or various Gulf states. The fundamentalist 'Bajor for the Bajorans' groups who – in *The Circle* and *The Siege* – temporarily succeed in dislodging the Federation from DS9 have a particular resonance with militant Islamic and anti-American terrorist factions such as Lebanon's Hezbollah. The control of Bajor's priesthood over its temporal affairs mirrors that of the political clerics in Iran and pre-Chinese invasion Tibet, whereas the issues that emerge in the post-occupation era mirror those in post-war Yugoslavia or post-apartheid South Africa. Like the leaders of many post-revolutionary states such as Cuba, Kenya or South Africa, Major Kira is herself a former terrorist, who carries some not inconsiderable guilt about some of her more violent actions as a resistance fighter. The complex morality of post-war reconciliation is thus one of *DS9*'s major political themes.

Many of the episodes which deal with these themes involve the former Cardassian controller of DS9, Gul Dukat. Dukat is a wily and apparently unprincipled figure, a political survivor who is presented as having a complex psychological profile. In *Indiscretion* (where he temporarily sacrifices his political credibility to save his half-Bajoran daughter, Ziyal) and *Return to Grace* (where, with Kira's help, he regains his credibility by hunting down a Klingon ship that has destroyed a Cardassian outpost) he develops an intriguing relationship with Kira. Pointing out to her that they both did things during the war which they may now regret, he tries to persuade her that, despite being former mortal enemies, they are in fact natural 'soulmates'. But Kira, while recognising that they both share a will for

survival and a passionate sense of patriotism, refuses to be taken in by
Dukat's attempt to instigate what would be simultaneously a sexual
and a political 'seduction'. Her revulsion at Dukat's crimes remains,
but she develops a definite respect for him, which causes her to re-
examine her own prejudices against Cardassians. Having been born
and brought up in a refugee camp and been engaged as a resistance
fighter since her early teens, Kira naturally has a well-developed
hatred of her former oppressors. But here, in a development that
symbolises *Star Trek*'s rejection of the simplistic morality of its earlier
years, she has to acknowledge their 'humanity'. *DS9* displays a
profound recognition that, in situations where post-war reconciliation
is being attempted, the attitudes which have framed *both* sides' positions must change for real peace to ensue. In this way it closely reflects
the political realities of today's world, where – in such locations
as Northern Ireland, South Africa, Yugoslavia or Lebanon – former
enemies must find mutual ground to maintain and extend the peace.
So the series moves decisively beyond the idealistic but simplistic
liberalism of the Roddenberry era and redefines *Star Trek* as a drama
with a sophisticated awareness of contemporary political realities.

Perhaps the most powerful 'political' episode of *DS9* is *Duet* (written
by Peter Allan Fields from a story by Lisa Rich and Jeanne Carrigan-
Fauci), in which *Star Trek* develops its 'darkest' political theme, the
examination of the Bajoran holocaust in which 10 million are said to
have died. A Cardassian who appears on the station claims to be
Marritza, a lowly clerk who worked for Gul Darhe'el, a notorious
Cardassian mass murderer responsible for the massacre at Gallitep,
where mothers were raped and killed in front of their children and old
people who could not work were buried alive. A number of Bajorans
claim that the man is actually Darhe'el himself, and photographic
records confirm this. When confronted with this revelation, the man
freely confesses to be Darhe'el, and begins to taunt Kira with excessive
boasting about the number of Bajoran 'scum' he had 'eliminated'. All
Kira's rage against her former oppressors surfaces and she vows to have
him executed. But Gul Dukat informs Sisko that Darhe'el died some
years ago, and Bashir's medical examination reveals that the
Cardassian's body contains massive quantities of a dermal implant.
Kira realises that the prisoner really is Marritza.

Haunted for years by guilt at being present – and, as far as he is
concerned, morally implicated – in the scene of the war crimes,
Marritza has had himself surgically altered, hoping that his trial and
execution would cause his own people to examine their conscience

and offering his own death in atonement for his guilt. The fact that Marritza's attempt was so clumsily executed only adds pathos to his situation. Kira is visibly moved by this example of a Cardassian prepared to sacrifice himself for the 'greater good', and tries to persuade Marritza that he was not to blame for the massacres. He shows signs of accepting this, but as Kira escorts him across the Promenade, he is suddenly assassinated by an angry Bajoran. When Kira protests that the man was not Darhe'el, the murderer snarls 'He's a Cardassian ... that's reason enough ...'. This provides a suitably tragic ending for Marritza's noble attempt to assuage his people's guilt, but shows that the situation that remains on Bajor is one in which prejudice is still very strong. Thus the kind of reconciliation that Kira and Marritza are attempting cannot be brought about merely by wishful thinking – there is still a great deal of work to be done.

In the creation of the 'Maquis situation' the writers shift towards a more ambivalent presentation of Federation political ethics which echoes that already established in early *DS9* stories. The background to this scenario is outlined in *Journey's End*, where we hear that the Federation has signed a treaty with the Cardassians, under the terms of which a number of Federation colonies need to be evacuated so that the Cardassians can take them over. The story, in which Picard has to attempt to resettle a group of stubborn Native Americans, touches on the heart of *Star Trek*'s 'rewriting' of the history of the US frontier. Yet its resolution, with the Native Americans being left to the mercies of the Cardassians, is somewhat unconvincing in the light of what follows. In *Pre-Emptive Strike* we meet the Maquis for the first time, and their fight to prevent their colonies being taken over by the Cardassians is presented in a very sympathetic light. The rebellious Ensign Ro, who defects from Starfleet when she sees the morality of the Maquis' cause, is a new kind of *Star Trek* character who does not fit into Roddenberry's model of ideal military discipline. In making the Maquis its enemies, the Federation is shown to be playing the role of a potential oppressor.

In *DS9* the Maquis are portrayed somewhat differently. Whereas in *Pre-Emptive Strike* Picard is moved by the colonists' plight and has some sympathy for Ro's defection, Sisko is far more hard-headed. In *The Maquis, Parts 1 and 2* Sisko's old Starfleet colleague, Cal Hudson, defects to the Maquis and tries to persuade him to join their 'struggle', but he refuses. With the 'prophetic' awareness of the future that he has been provided with by his encounter with the wormhole aliens, he fervently believes that they are a dangerous organisation which offers only 'false hope' to the colonists and whose existence is likely to dangerously destabilise the entire political environment. Sisko is appalled when Eddington, one of his senior officers, defects to the Maquis, and in *For the Uniform* he mercilessly hunts him down. Sisko's predictions are finally proved correct when the growing threat of the Maquis drives the Cardassians into an Alliance with the Dominion. This results in the Maquis – and many of the colonists they represent – being wiped out. As Sisko feared, the galactic balance of power consequently undergoes a considerable shift, leaving the entire Federation at risk. Thus, while the Maquis stories begin with a cross-examination of *Star Trek*'s liberal conscience, they grow into a depiction of how liberal principles can offer illusory hopes which may lead to disaster.

In *Voyager* the Maquis element in the crew provides a constant presence on the ship which redefines the way Starfleet itself is presented. Commander Chakotay is himself from the Native American planet depicted in *Journey's End*, which suggests that the Cardassians had been hoodwinking Picard in their assurance that they would leave these colonists alone. Captain Janeway has to weld together a crew composed of Federation and Maquis elements. In the new situation in which *Voyager* finds itself, Janeway frequently finds that the ability of the ex-Maquis crew to improvise in difficult situations exceeds that of Starfleet. The old emphasis on smooth, military precision which dominated *TNG* is thus subverted. This is particularly emphasised in the presentation of the character of B'Elanna Torres, who may be somewhat impulsive and undisciplined, but whose brilliant improvisational skills as an engineer save the ship on a number of occasions. In comparison to the Maquis, the Starfleet crew sometimes appear rather staid and unbending.

The main political themes of the new *Trek* series tend to centre around the interrelationships between the major players in galactic politics – the Federation, the Klingons, the Cardassians and the Romulans. These groups all have roughly equal levels of technology. In the original series the idea of a galactic 'balance of power' is hinted at in episodes such as *Errand of Mercy*, *Balance of Terror* and *The Enterprise Incident*. It is established that the Romulans operate from behind a 'Neutral Zone' and remain mysterious, desiring little contact with other races. By the time of the film series it is clear that the Federation and the Klingons have made peace. But until several seasons into *TNG* the presentation of galactic politics is still rather sketchy. In fact, with the major players at peace there is little galactic conflict.

Starfleet's major 'enemies' in *TNG* are undoubtedly the Romulans, who are constantly scheming to gain some kind of strategic advantage. They have a totalitarian, militaristic society, and a powerful and very resourceful secret service in the Tal Shiar. In *Future Imperfect* Riker is kidnapped and tricked by the Tal Shiar (who are attempting to obtain military secrets) into believing that 16 years have passed and that he has had a family. In *The Mind's Eye* they kidnap Geordi as part of an elaborate plan to destabilise the Federation–Klingon Alliance. *Unification* features the reappearance of Spock, whose ambition is to bring about the reunification of the ancient split between the Vulcan and Romulan peoples, to which end he is working with the anti-totalitarian Romulan Underground. In *Face of the Enemy* Deanna Troi is forced to impersonate a Tal Shiar officer as part of a Romulan Underground plot.

Although full-scale war never breaks out between the Federation and the Romulans, it is made clear that this is a constant possibility which Picard's crew must make all efforts to avoid. In *The Defector* the Romulan admiral, Jarok, defects to the Federation. He is convinced that the Romulan government is going to attempt to retake the Neutral Zone, which has preserved what has sometimes been an uneasy peace for over two centuries. He leads the *Enterprise* into the zone, but it transpires that he had deliberately been fed disinformation so as to lure the ship into a trap. The Romulans demand the *Enterprise*'s surrender, using its 'aggressive' entry into the Neutral Zone as an excuse, but at the last moment the *Enterprise* is saved by the arrival of three Klingon Birds of Prey.

The Pegasus (written by Ronald D. Moore) avoids such an easy resolution. When Riker's former captain, now Admiral Pressman, appears on the ship, he gives Riker specific instructions not to let Picard know the real nature of their 'top-secret' mission to recover the *Pegasus*, a ship on which Riker, as a young ensign, had served under him years before. The situation grows tense as a Romulan ship appears in search of the same vessel. When the *Pegasus* is finally found, trapped in a deep rift inside an asteroid, Pressman orders the *Enterprise* to undertake a perilous journey into the asteroid itself. When Picard uncovers details of a 'cover-up' of a mutiny which took place on the *Pegasus*, he is suspicious and demands to know why so much importance is being placed on finding the ship. Riker's initial refusal to disobey the admiral causes tremendous friction between them. When Riker beams over to the *Pegasus* with Pressman they discover that the 'secret' – a Federation prototype for a cloaking device – has been preserved intact.

It is also revealed that during the mutiny Riker was the only officer to remain loyal to the arrogant and obsessive Pressman, and that after they had escaped in a runabout the rest of the crew were killed in a subsequent exchange of fire. For years Riker – who was then a young ensign just out of Starfleet Academy – has been tormented by guilt over the incident and has deeply regretted his actions. To make matters even more difficult, the cloaking device itself is illegal, having been banned in a treaty with the Romulans.

Caught between the ethics of loyalty and conscience, Riker finally rebels by informing Picard about the true nature of the mission. Meanwhile the Romulans have sealed the entrance to the asteroid. The cloaking device, a new variant that can penetrate solid matter, is engaged so that the *Enterprise* can make its escape. But Picard makes a point of decloaking in front of the Romulans, so destroying Pressman's plan to use the new weapon to change the balance of power in the quadrant. He then arrests Pressman for violating the Federation treaty, but it seems highly unlikely that the Federation will give up the technology. (Indeed, when *DS9* acquires the *Defiant* in its third season, the ship is equipped with a cloak.) Thus the resolution of the story is double-edged – although Riker's guilt is somewhat assuaged, it may be that the breaking of the treaty will lead to future wars.

The Klingons – who are never slow to show their loathing of the Romulans – obviously have a considerable part to play in the galactic balance of power. *TNG*'s 'Klingon stories' represent the Klingon 'warrior culture' as a one which is becoming increasingly outmoded in present conditions, whilst the Klingon Empire itself is clearly in a state of considerable decay. Several episodes focus on the internal politics of the Empire, which is depicted as being riven by corruption and full of competing factions. In *Reunion* Worf supports Gowron in his campaign to lead the Empire, and in *Redemption* he is called upon to defend this position as Picard oversees Gowron's installation. In *Rightful Heir* Worf again saves the day by suggesting that the Kahless clone become the Klingons' 'constitutional monarch', leaving Gowron, as head of the High Council, to retain real power. By the time that Worf joins the cast of *DS9*, the Klingons have again become major players in the galactic 'power game'. In *The Way of the Warrior* their attack on Cardassia prompts Worf to be sent to *DS9* as an envoy to attempt to bridge the gap between the Klingons and the Federation. But despite now being regarded by most Klingons as a traitor, he decisively sides with the Federation. In *Apocalypse Rising* it finally transpires that the Klingons are being manipulated by the Dominion, who have replaced Gowron's military leader, General Martok, with a shape-shifter. By the time of *Soldiers of the Empire* the Klingons are again allied to the Federation, and Worf temporarily acts as a member of the Klingon forces. At the end of the fifth season, the Klingons stand together with the Federation against the combined Cardassian–Dominion threat.

The Klingon political stories form *Star Trek*'s most detailed and searching examination of an alien political culture. The changes in Klingon political culture that are enacted provide another example of the movement away from the simplistic political positioning of alien races in the original series. In general, the Klingons are portrayed with remarkable sympathy through much of the later *Trek* series. They are increasingly shown as a highly cultured race, with Klingon opera, literature and cuisine apparently becoming highly popular on many other planets. As the Federation becomes portrayed as less-than-perfect, so the Klingons' virtues are emphasised. Indeed, at times the Federation appears to be rather 'spiritually bankrupt' in contrast to the faith by which the Klingons live. Federation citizens brought up in a liberal utopian culture might flinch at the Klingons' apparently brutish ways, but as understanding grows between the two cultures the distinctive Klingon perspective achieves increasing respect.

If the Klingons are seen to represent an outmoded political culture which nevertheless has a valuable contribution to make to its alliance with the liberal Federation, the initially mysterious Dominion is something more insidious. The Dominion is controlled by the Founders, the powerful shape-shifting race which for centuries had been hounded and victimised by its neighbours, whose response has been to use its powers to create a new Empire of its own. With the discovery of the wormhole, the Dominion now threatens the entire Alpha Quadrant. Whereas Klingon leaders are willing to fight and die with their troops, the Founders control their armies from a distance. The Dominion's soldiers are the Jem' Hadar, a genetically-engineered race which the Founders have created to serve them. The Founders have built into the Jem'Hadar an addiction to the drug ketracel-white, which only they can supply. This dependence keeps the Jem'Hadar loyal and makes them merciless and emotionless killers. The picture of distant 'politicians' manipulating chemically-controlled cannon fodder is a disturbing one which has particular resonances with US control over its soldiers in Vietnam and the Gulf War. Generally *DS9* makes no bones about showing that war is a very 'messy business' in which even the liberal humanist morality of the Federation sometimes has to be sacrificed.

Thus, though the original series largely avoids the human issues related to real military conflict, the new *Trek* series confront them directly. Despite their conflicts with militaristic 'warrior races' such as the Klingons, Romulans and Cardassians, ultimately the Borg and the Dominion are Starfleet's most terrifying enemies, in that both appear to have no notion of fairness or 'honour'. Essentially the Klingons and Romulans in particular are 'old-fashioned' villains, whereas the Borg and the Dominion represent detached and unemotional attitudes to conquest and political control. In the stories which feature these new enemies, the new *Trek* series confront hard political realities in a way that the romanticised original series could never really attempt.

Chapter 12

Multiculturalism, gender and eugenics: social themes in *Star Trek*

> I say to you my friends ... even though we face difficulties of
> today and tomorrow ... I STILL have a dream ... Free at last ...
> Great God Almighty we are free at last ... I've got some diffi-
> cult days ahead, but it really doesn't matter to me now,
> because I've been to the mountaintop ... and I've looked over
> and I've seen the Promised Land. I may not get there with
> you, but I want you to know tonight that we as a people will
> get to the Promised Land.
>
> (Martin Luther King, speech made to the Civil Rights march
> on Washington, 28 August 1963)

From its earliest days, *Star Trek* has been informed by a multiculturalist vision in which Martin Luther King's famous 'dream' of
complete racial integration has become a reality. In his original
outline for the series, Gene Roddenberry insisted that, by the twenty-
third century, racial discrimination would be seen as a regrettable
relic of the past. The presence of Uhura, Sulu and Chekov on the
bridge, as well as a number of black actors who appeared as senior
Starfleet officials in the original series, clearly established *Star Trek's*
anti-racist standpoint, even if all these characters played relatively
minor roles. Roddenberry regarded the presence of a leading alien
character on the deck of the *Enterprise* as essential, and fought hard
against initial network resistance to keep Spock in the series. Such a
presence was for him crucial in demonstrating that the Federation
was a multicultural organisation. But the Vulcans were only the first
of the many different alien races to be created, each with their own
cultural and ethical viewpoints. With racial prejudice extinct on its
'future-Earth', *Star Trek* has always used conflict between the various

alien races to present stories that reflect on contemporary racial conflicts.

The theme of racial prejudice is one that a number of *Star Trek* episodes explore. In *The Undiscovered Country* the anti-Klingon prejudice displayed by Kirk and other members of his crew was heavily criticised by Roddenberry (who had little control over the movie) as being untrue to the 'real' spirit of *Star Trek* in which racism only exists between *alien* races. Yet even in the original series anti-alien prejudice does not appear to be completely unknown in Starfleet. In *Balance of Terror* Lieutenant Stiles, who has fought the Romulans in battle, displays a decidedly racist attitude towards Mr Spock because of the close physical resemblance between the Vulcan and Romulan races. But, in a plot resolution typical of the original series, Spock's heroic actions finally persuade Stiles to trust him. Any hint of a lack of 'perfection' among Starfleet officers is thus swiftly quashed. This is in sharp contrast to a new *Trek* episode like *TNG*'s *The Enemy*, in which Worf refuses to give a blood transfusion to a dying Romulan on grounds of racial hatred, or the many *DS9* episodes in which O'Brien (who, like the earlier Stiles, is a battle veteran) has to fight hard to control an inbuilt prejudice against Cardassians. In *TNG*'s *The Drumhead* a Starfleet officer who claims to be part-Vulcan has chosen to hide the fact that in fact he has a Romulan grandparent. This tends to suggest that even in the highly tolerant society of the Federation, recent enemies tend to be regarded with a suspicion that may even tend towards racism. Yet such manifestations of prejudice are clearly labelled as aberrations from the Federation's moral code.

Much of *Star Trek* focuses on how Starfleet deals with conflicts between various warring alien races. The original series' *Let This Be Your Last Battlefield*, with its rather crude portrayal of a futile life-and-death struggle between the last members of two 'reversed' half-black/half-white races, has an obvious anti-racist subtext. But the most memorable 'multiculturalist' episodes of the original series tend to be those in which the crew is presented with new life forms which may at first appear to be different from human beings but are soon shown to have surprisingly similar characteristics. Such episodes did much to redefine *Star Trek* in its early days as a new kind of popular science fiction. Many of the low-budget, teen-orientated SF thrillers of the 1950s – such as *The Creature from the Black Lagoon* or *The Beast with a Thousand Eyes* – ended with the 'terrifying' presentation of a 'monster' which the heroes had to eliminate. In one of the earliest *Star Trek* stories, *The Man Trap*, Kirk kills such a 'scary monster'. *The Devil in the Dark*, where Spock refuses to kill the rock-creature, the Horta, establishes the *Star Trek* principle that creatures which may appear to be 'different' or 'threatening' to us have, if enough time is taken to understand them properly, perfectly recognisable motivations. Such a story is, beneath its SF surface, a far more subtle and effective plea for racial tolerance than the obvious allegory of *Let This Be Your Last Battlefield*. In *Metamorphosis*, an alien cloud-creature reveals itself to be in love with fabled Federation scientist Zephram Cochrane and eventually gives up its immortality to merge with a human woman to be with him. In *Star Trek*, being from another species – no matter how different – is no barrier to peaceful co-existence or even love.

In the new *Trek* series a number of episodes feature encounters with creatures which, even if they may be potentially dangerous, must be accorded fundamental respect. This attitude of tolerance towards all sentient life forms is as important a principle to Starfleet as the Prime Directive itself. Many of these stories centre around Data, who (as an android) has a unique perspective on such matters, and often find him having to overcome the prejudices of human scientists in order to play advocate for the rights of 'non-organic' life forms. In *Home Soil* an apparently uninhabited planet on which the *Enterprise* is planning to perform terraforming operations turns out to be the home of a 'microbrain' whose existence may be threatened by the process. On Data's insistence the terraforming is abandoned. In *Evolution* an accident in Wesley Crusher's typically ambitious genetics project results in the creation of rapidly multiplying microscopic life forms known as 'nanites'. Dr Paul Stubbs, a Federation scientist engaged in an important astronomical project, discovers that the nanites are 'eating' the *Enterprise*'s warp core and – considering them a threat to his work – proceeds to irradiate a large proportion of them. The nanites respond to this attack by closing down the ship's life-support systems. Data is convinced that the creatures are intelligent and links himself directly into the ship's systems so as to communicate with them. After Stubbs is persuaded to apologise personally to them and the Federation promises them a planet to colonise, the nanites relent and restore the ship to full working order. In *Voyager*'s *The Cloud*, the crew attempts to draw energy from a passing nebula, but when this turns out to be an intelligent living entity an apologetic Janeway abandons the plan.

Many new *Trek* episodes explore the nuances of alien cultures. In *TNG*'s *A Matter of Honor* (written by Burton Armus) Riker is assigned to a command position on board a Klingon ship as part of an exchange programme between the Federation and the Klingons. This turns out to be a rather dangerous exercise. On Klingon ships, authority over subordinates is maintained by physical force. Subordinates may legitimately challenge their superiors and fight them for positions of power. Conditions are spartan, and the Klingons scoff at Federation 'comforts'. Riker has to work particularly hard to become accepted by the Klingons. He joins in their hearty banter and asserts himself physically over lower ranks. But when the Klingons discover dangerous bacteria on board, Captain Klag accuses Riker of being sent to destroy the ship and orders an attack on the *Enterprise*. Using an emergency transponder Worf has provided, Riker beams the Klingon captain onto the *Enterprise* and stages with Picard a Federation 'surrender' to assuage the Klingons' sense of 'honour'. When Klag returns, Riker lets himself be struck down in front of the crew so that Klag's authority can be restored. The experience has taught Riker much about the 'unwritten rules' of Klingon conduct and in order to survive among them he knows that he cannot act by his usual Starfleet principles. In doing so he learns much respect for the 'Klingon way'.

Jeri Taylor's *The Wounded*, the *TNG* story that first introduces the Cardassians, does so against the background of considerable interspecies tension. It demonstrates clearly that, for Starfleet officers who have been involved in wars, overcoming prejudice may not be easy. Much background information is given here on the recent Cardassian–Federation war, which has now ended in a peace treaty. But when Federation Captain Ben Maxwell begins attacking Cardassian ships, Picard – who has been given express orders by Starfleet to preserve the peace at all costs – is forced to join with the Cardassians in pursuit of him. After Maxwell eliminates a vessel with over 600 Cardassians on board, Picard prepares to destroy his ship, an action which would be an unprecedented attack by one Starfleet ship on another. Only a last-minute appeal by O'Brien, who had served under Maxwell during the Cardassian wars, brings the 'rogue captain' to his senses. In one scene in Ten Forward, O'Brien tells a visiting Cardassian engineer a moving story about his experiences in the wars, relating an incident in which he was forced to kill for the first time. The episode focuses particularly on the different reactions to the Cardassians displayed by Maxwell – who suspects (perhaps rightly) that the Cardassians are preparing for another attack, and is quite prepared to spark off a new war – and O'Brien, who – despite the personal pain of his encounters with the Cardassians – is finally prepared to 'give peace a chance'.

The Wounded is an episode that sets up much of the scenario for

DS9, throughout which both Bajorans and humans have to work hard to overcome their prejudices against the Cardassians. Much of this is focused through the characters of O'Brien and Kira, who have both fought them in battle. Kira in particular has to combat the prejudices of an entire lifetime as a resistance fighter. In *Second Skin* she is kidnapped and surgically altered by the Cardassians in an elaborate ruse to make her believe that she is really a 'double agent' whose memories have been implanted. She never gives in to these suggestions, but the relationship she develops with Ghemor (a leading Cardassian politician, who thinks she is his daughter) provides her with some psychological compensation for the death of her own father during the occupation. In fact Ghemor turns out to have considerable sympathy for the Cardassian dissident movement. By the time of the fifth season's *Ties of Blood and Water* he has defected to the Federation, and Kira again plays the role of his 'daughter' at his deathbed.

Just as many of the above stories can be 'read' by the audience as dramas that reflect on contemporary inter-racial situations, many other episodes have been seen as comments on the ethics of sexual politics. In the original series, such issues are rarely touched upon in anything but a superficial way. In *Elaan of Troyius* (written by John Meredyth Lucas) the *Enterprise* is engaged in 'delivering' Elaan (a 'princess' from the planet Elas) to Troyius, which has been at war with Elas for centuries. Her arranged marriage to the Troyian leader is expected to bring peace between the two planets. Yet the reluctant Elaan has to be 'educated' by Kirk to see the significance of what she has been assigned to do. In the process she cries tears which contain a chemical intoxicant that causes Kirk to fall in love with her. Finally the marriage goes ahead, and Elaan has no advocate on board to advance her rights as an individual. In many ways she is regarded primarily as just another 'alien problem' which has to be solved. Kirk characteristically finds a 'cure' for the 'lovesickness' by reminding himself of his 'love' for the *Enterprise*.

In contrast, *TNG*'s *The Perfect Mate* (written by Michael Piller, Rene Echevarria and Gary Percante) – which follows a virtually parallel storyline – is a far more searching examination of the ethics of arranged marriages. Again the story features two races that have long been at war, the peoples of Kriosia and Valt Minor. The Kriosian ambassador, Briam, brings aboard the *Enterprise* a 'gift' for Alrik, the ruler of Valt Minor. The intervention of two mischievous Ferengi reveals the gift to be Kamala, a stunningly beautiful young woman who is to be 'given' in marriage to Valt's leader. When Picard discovers this he displays considerable indignation at the notion that the *Enterprise* is carrying human 'cargo' and Beverly Crusher protests, vigorously presenting the 'feminist' point of view by asserting that the Federation should not condone what amounts to little more than prostitution. But Picard insists that he is bound by the Prime Directive not to interfere.

Whereas Elaan had been unhappy at first to be assigned the role of consort, Kamala has been specially 'selected' at birth and carefully prepared from an early age to fulfil this role. But like Elaan, she has a 'magical' power over men, despite her apparent subjection. She is an empathic metamorph, a genetic rarity with the ability to adopt whatever personality or interests a man may want her to. As she coolly explains to a clearly flustered Riker, she has an extremely high pheromone-production rate, which makes her sexually almost irresistible. Riker quickly realises that she may be a 'danger' to the whole crew. She voluntarily confines herself to her quarters, but Picard's visits, during which he argues that she should value herself as an individual, see his resistance to her gradually breaking down. To add further irony, Alrik turns out to be a rather effete character who is far more interested in the trading deals that the new arrangements will bring than in Kamala herself. As in *Elaan of Troyius* the marriage eventually goes ahead. But Picard's well meaning-intervention turns out to be both a tragic mistake and a kind of 'emotional Prime Directive' violation. He succeeds in showing Kamala that she has a value in herself beyond being available to please others. But just before the marriage ceremony she shocks him with the revelation that she has committed herself emotionally to him and can thus never bond with Alrik. She is therefore doomed to a loveless marriage.

The Perfect Mate is an episode which appears to 'rewrite' the story of *Elaan of Troyius* – itself based on Homer's Iliad – in the context of a 1990s view of sexual politics. Earlier, when Picard told Beverly Crusher that Kamala's participation in the arranged marriage was voluntary, Crusher had protested that Kamala had been brainwashed all her life into thinking of her main function as being an object of desire for men. By attempting to apply his liberal Federation values to the situation, Picard has arguably made it far worse. If he had not intervened, Kamala would have genuinely been able to love Alrik, whatever his disposition to her. But now her 'brief encounter' with Picard is set to dominate her life. Yet Kamala's potential 'happiness' has been sacrificed for a greater self-awareness. *The Perfect Mate* thus works as a kind of 'feminist fable', with Kamala representing the way in which modern advertising and media culture 'prepares' women by presenting them with essentially unreal images of physical perfection in the form of 'supermodels'. At the same time its tragic outcome explicitly attacks the traditional practice of arranged marriage itself. We are left in little doubt that such a practice certainly does not exist on Earth in the twenty-fourth century.

TNG's *The Outcast* (written by Jeri Taylor) was the first *Star Trek* episode to touch upon the themes of sexual ambiguity that would later become more prominent in *DS9*. Riker begins a working relationship with Soren, a member of the androgynous J'naii race who have enlisted the *Enterprise*'s help in a search for a missing shuttle craft. They have many discussions in which they compare their different cultures, and a strong bond begins to develop between them. Eventually Soren reveals that 'she' is one of a minority of her race who tend towards a particular sex, but that in her society this must be kept a secret. If her feelings are exposed, she will be subject to 'reprogramming'. Yet she is bold enough to declare her attraction to Riker, who has fallen in love with her. But one of the J'naii crew has been spying on them and Soren is immediately arrested. Riker appears at her trial and attempts to defend her, but – despite her eloquent speech in self-defence concerning her right to determine her own sexuality – the sentence is a foregone conclusion. In desperation, and with scant regard for the Prime Directive, Riker enlists Worf's help to rescue Soren from prison. But although they succeed, Soren refuses to beam up with Riker. The conditioning has already taken effect, and 'she' now firmly rejects her old 'female' tendencies, claiming to be much happier in her new, adjusted, state. A crestfallen and embittered Riker departs. As in *The Perfect Mate*, the Federation's 'emotional intervention' into another culture is well-intentioned but ultimately futile and destructive. However much Riker or Picard were acting from liberal-humanist principles, these principles did not prove adequate in either situation. *Star Trek* thus confronts one of the main dilemmas of multiculturalism – that it is necessary to understand and respect the practices of other cultures even if their values contradict one's own. This, of course, is the main dynamic that drives the many 'Prime Directive stories'. In the original series such restrictions would never prevent Kirk from 'solving' whatever problem he came up against, but in the new *Trek* series the situations that are encountered characteristically remain unresolved.

The Outcast is also the first *Star Trek* episode to touch upon gay themes. The harsh sexual monoculture of the J'naii is a deliberate parallel with the repression of gays that has characterised much of modern history. The reaction of the authorities is a reminder of the once-common 'experiments' in 'reconditioning' homosexuals by means of electric shock and other behaviourist techniques. It would certainly have been virtually impossible to include gay issues in the original series, and even in 1992 they are only introduced by means of subtle undercoding. Critics of *Star Trek* have often asserted that it has tended to 'dodge' gay issues, and gay fans have lobbied for the inclusion of openly gay characters in the series, but by presenting such issues in the context of episodes like *The Outcast* it arguably becomes possible to give such matters greater 'weight'.

Another episode of *TNG*, Michael Horvat's *The Host*, sets the precedent for the rather sexually ambiguous character of Dax in *DS9* by introducing the Trill race, selected members of which host a worm-like symbiont which carries the experience of several lifetimes. Beverly Crusher falls in love with a Trill, Odan, and they are enjoying a passionate affair – Crusher's first for many years – when Odan's host body becomes ill and dies. The symbiont is temporarily transferred into Riker's body so that Odan can continue the crucial peace negotiations in which he is involved. Crusher eventually accepts that Odan really 'lives' in Riker and Odan even makes love with her in Riker's body. But after the new host arrives and Beverly waits expectedly to meet 'him', the host turns out to be female. While able to accept Odan as another man – even in her friend Riker's body – she cannot accept Odan as a woman. There is no suggestion that such a relationship would be frowned on in Federation circles, and the new Odan herself seems very keen to continue it, but Beverly's heterosexual orientation asserts itself strongly. Again, the subject of homosexuality is dealt with by means of subtle analogy, but some still felt that *Star Trek* was failing to deal effectively with the issue by presenting Beverly's avoidance of the relationship.

In *DS9* the presentation of the character of Jadzia Dax involved the 'filling in' of much detail about the Trill race's customs. It becomes established that only a few Trills qualify for the privilege of becoming a host to a symbiont and that they have to undergo a rigorous training procedure (rather analogous to Starfleet training) in order to be judged worthy of this. Dax herself is something of a sexually ambiguous figure. Though she has the body of a very attractive young woman, she carries within her the life experience of many previous male and female hosts. Her friend Sisko still jokingly calls her 'old man'. In a number of early *DS9* episodes she rejects the advances of the brash young Dr Bashir, and when she finally does choose a mate it will be Worf, with his 'dangerous' Klingon sexuality. In *Rejoined* (written by Moore and Echevarria), it is also made clear that there is a taboo among Trills against sexual relationships with the partners of previous hosts. If discovered, such a relationship could lead to exile and thus the host's symbiont would be condemned to die with them. But when a Trill woman who in a previous 'life' had been Dax's wife arrives on the station, Jadzia finds that she is immediately drawn to her. It seems that the two had a successful and loving marriage before a tragic incident led to the death of one of their hosts. Dax herself is prepared to go into exile, which means she would surrender her 'immortality' for love. But although eventually the dictates of Trill society determine that they cannot be together, it is made quite explicit that this is not because they are both female. The episode features *Star Trek*'s first 'lesbian kiss', some 25 years after the famous Kirk–Uhura kiss in *Plato's Stepchildren*. Although it again suggests an open tolerance for same-sex relationships in the Federation's 'ideal culture' the episode is – like *The Outcast* and *The Host* – another powerful 'love that dare not speak its name' story.

A number of *Star Trek* episodes reflect on contemporary anxieties surrounding the development of genetic engineering. SF stories had speculated about this theme for many years, but only recently (with controversial new developments in cloning) has the technology itself begun to seem feasible. The use of clones has always been a good 'cheap option' for producers of filmed and TV SF, and *Star Trek* is no exception. But it is made clear from the series' earliest days that the Federation regards genetic engineering as dangerous and unethical. In the original series' *Miri* Kirk and McCoy are confronted with a planet which is inhabited by 'children' who are in fact hundreds of years old and the result of a genetic experiment gone wrong. But a disease is spreading across the planet that will cause the children to die when they reach puberty, and only McCoy's discovery of an antidote saves the situation. The way in which the children have become 'corrupted' again outlines clearly a distrust of genetic manipulation.

In *Space Seed* we hear of the Eugenics Wars of the 1990s, in which a group of genetically engineered humans embroiled the world in bloody conflict. Khan Noonian Singh, who has been recovered from a state of cryogenic suspension, once ruled nearly half the Earth. After he attempts to commandeer the *Enterprise* for new conquests, Kirk exiles him to a harsh virgin planet from which he eventually emerges as the highly embittered villain of the *Wrath of Khan* movie. The eugenics movement, which began in the late nineteenth century as an offshoot of Darwinism, centred on the idea that a 'better grade' of human being could be created by some form of 'selective breeding'. Followers of eugenics believed that the poor, the educationally subnormal or 'mentally deficient' should be discouraged from breeding in order to promote a 'better' human race. One of the leading proponents of eugenics was the 'father' of SF, H. G. Wells, whose *The Time Machine* had postulated a distopian future in which the human race had split into the intelligent, cultured Eloi and the bestial Morlocks. But the theories of eugenics, which were satirised most memorably by Aldous Huxley in *Brave New World* (1932), were also adopted by Hitler and the Nazis, who used them to justify their ideal of the 'master race' and the extermination of millions of members of what they considered 'inferior races'. *Star Trek*, with its impeccable anti-racist credentials, has always distanced itself from the eugenic perspective. Both *Space Seed* and *The Wrath of Khan* illustrate the dangers of creating genetically enhanced 'supermen'.

In *TNG*'s *The Masterpiece Society* (written by Michael Piller, Adam Belanoff and James Kahn) the problems of creating even a well-intentioned genetically engineered society are shown. The *Enterprise* successfully intervenes to save the human inhabitants of Moab IV when their planet is threatened by a fragment of a star, but their presence produces a considerable dilemma. Moab IV is a very peaceful and prosperous genetically-engineered society which has been isolated from the rest of the galaxy since its inception, and a number of its inhabitants react to the Federation presence by wishing to leave the planet to experience life on other worlds. Picard is in something of a 'Prime Directive' dilemma but his Federation ethics – which include the fundamental rights of individuals to freedom of movement – mean that he has to grant these people's wishes. However, on Moab IV every individual has been programmed to fulfil a particular part in that society, and it is feared that the departure of even a handful could disastrously 'unbalance' the society. Despite this difficult predicament for Starfleet, the main focus of the story is on the fragility of the society itself, which really cannot cope with any outside influences and can only exist in isolation, again warning of the potential dangers of genetic engineering and of the futility of trying to 'perfect' humanity.

DS9's *Dr Bashir, I Presume* (written by Ronald D. Moore and Jimmy Diggs) is a more ambiguous treatment of the same theme. Julian Bashir is always an 'awkward' character socially, as evidenced by his ineffectual attempts to romance Jadzia Dax in a number of first season episodes. He is also something of a 'scientific prodigy' whose work puts him at the forefront of current medical research. In *Dr Bashir, I Presume*, when his parents are called to the station, it is revealed that his advanced mental capacities originate from a programme of genetic enhancement, which his parents insisted on him undergoing as a child. This procedure was illegal under Federation law, and its revelation threatens Bashir's continued career in Starfleet, as under these conditions of general prohibition genetically advanced humans are not allowed to join Starfleet. Bashir's father negotiates with Starfleet Admiral Bennett and accepts a two-year prison term on condition that Julian is allowed to continue in his post. Though the dangers of such genetic enhancement are represented by Julian's resentment against his own parents for making him 'live a lie' all his adult life, it is also made clear that the mental capacity that allows him to make developments that will save many lives has been beneficial both for him and for the advancement of Starfleet science. The logic of the Starfleet prohibition is clear, but the human dilemma of Julian's parents – who originally had the procedure carried out in order to save him from the effects of being a 'slow child' – is also highlighted. The father's self-sacrifice helps to redeem him in his son's eyes, but Bashir is certainly a very ambiguous 'victim'. The episode also raises interesting questions about the potential competitiveness within such a highly educated and developed society as Federation Earth. Even in this utopian society there are 'children who fall behind at school'. Whatever its merits, it must be a society, like any, of winners and losers.

Perhaps the most extreme projection of the potential effects of genetic engineering is the portrayal in *DS9* of the Jem'Hadar, who are genetically engineered to be addicted to a drug, ketracel-white, and to have absolute loyalty to the Founders, The Jem'Hadar are the perfect soldiers – completely ruthless killers bred to be totally obedient. In *The Abandoned* Odo attempts to coax an abandoned Jem'Hadar child away from his violent instincts, but discovers that the tendency to violence also appears to be inbred. Unlike the Klingons, Romulans, Cardassians or even the Borg, the Jem'Hadar appear to be unredeemable. As such they are a distinctive product of the post-Roddenberry *Star Trek* universe, a projection of the most negative aspects of militarism and social control in a set of series which has always been anchored in a military context.

In twenty-fourth century Federation society drug taking appears to have gone the way of racism and sexism. The 'enlightened' members of this society have apparently little need for stimulants, although in *TNG* the *Enterprise*'s bar does sell synthehol, a form of alcohol whose effects can be instantly shaken off. Yet drug addiction problems certainly do exist in the less utopian corners of the *Star Trek* universe, as we see in *Symbiosis*, where Picard discovers that the Brekka have for centuries been controlling and exploiting their neighbours the Ornara by keeping them in a state of addiction to a drug grown only on Brekka. By refusing to allow transport of the drug, Picard forces the Ornarans to withdraw from its effects. In *DS9*'s *Hippocratic Oath*, Bashir's attempts to find a 'cure' for the Jem' Hadar's addiction to ketracel-white turn out to be just as futile as Odo's attempts to 'humanise them', because the addiction is genetically programmed into their systems. Such stories reflect a recognition that the 'drug problem' is not one that can ever be neatly 'solved'.

Medical ethics play a considerable part in many *Star Trek* episodes. A number of these focus on the issue of euthanasia. In *TNG*'s moving *Half A Life* (written by Peter Allan Fields and Ted Roberts) the scientist Dr Timicin, to whom Lwaxana Troi has taken a characteristic shine, works aboard the *Enterprise* to try to test theories which may save his planet's dying star. But the experiments fail and Timicin is crushed. Lwaxana tells him that he has plenty of time to try to solve the problem, but he informs her that he is nearing 60, at which age his society's custom is for everyone to accept voluntary euthanasia. This is carried out at an emotional ceremony with the individual's friends and family attending. Lwaxana is appalled at this custom, and appeals to Picard for help. But Picard, in deference to the Prime Directive, can do nothing. Lwaxana then tries to persuade Timicin that he must continue with his work in order to save his own planet, and argues a forceful case for this. Timicin eventually agrees to seek asylum on the *Enterprise*, but this provokes an angry response from his government, which sends armed ships to retrieve him. Finally his daughter, who is angry at his rejection of their culture, beams aboard and tells him that his actions contravene everything she was taught. He is shamed into accepting his fate, but Lwaxana agrees to accompany him during the ceremony. The episode works as an eloquent statement of the rights of the ageing, but again the Federation has to accord respect to a society with whose ethics it may not agree.

Voyager's *Emanations* (written by Brannon Braga) takes a different stance on the same issue. In the Uhnori culture, the dead are transported to one of the planet's moons, where they believe that they enter a real physical afterlife. When Harry Kim, who has seen thousands of rotting bodies on the moon, is accidentally transported onto the planet, what he reveals has serious implications for the Uhnori belief system. It now appears that individuals are regularly pressured by their families to accept voluntary euthanasia, in the belief that a 'better life' is waiting for them. While Dr Timicin's society's beliefs are built on a form of social rationalisation which perhaps is seen to have some justification, the Uhnori's belief system is more corrupt. The use of euthanasia is here more of a mechanism for removing 'unwanted' members of society. The episode also explores the difference between belief in a literal and a spiritual afterlife, and here the arrival of the Federation shatters the faith that binds the community. Harry realises that the only way he can return to *Voyager* and restore this faith is to die himself, be transported to the moon and hope that the Doctor can revive him in time. His plan succeeds, but the episode again illustrates that although certain societies may practice what appear to be immoral actions the Federation must preserve its respect for their cultures.

DS9's *Melora* (written by Evan Carlos Summers, Steven Baum, Michael Piller and James Crocker) focuses on the ethics of disability. Melora is a woman from the low-gravity planet Elaysia who comes to work on DS9. In this environment she is confined to a wheelchair, the like of which Bashir says has not been seen on Earth for hundreds of years. Only in rest periods can she relax in a zero-gravity environment. On her arrival at the station she is extremely 'touchy' with all the crew, refuses to allow any concessions to be made to her and rejects outright any sympathy she may be offered. But when Bashir offers her the possibility of a 'cure' for her disability she is certainly interested, even though this would mean a return to her home would be impossible. A romance develops between them, which is consummated rather dramatically in zero-gravity conditions. However, when she and Bashir take a shuttle through the wormhole and are taken prisoner by hostile aliens, she manages to switch off the gravity in the cabin and use her experience of zero-gravity conditions to win the day. This convinces her that her 'disability' is not such a disadvantage and she elects to remain in a wheelchair.

Melora examines a number of aspects of the 'politics' of disability. The woman herself notes that the Cardassians (who as we have already learned kill off 'defective' children at birth) have designed the station without any wheelchair access, which reflects the situation the disabled find themselves in within many public buildings today. Her uncompromising and somewhat bitter attitude when she first arrives appears to be a defensive reaction against being patronised by the able-bodied. But ultimately her disability is only relative and the episode emphasises that she has her own special nature. Above all, the story places crucial importance on the primacy of individual choice in such situations. In typical new *Trek* fashion the problem has no 'magical' solution but Melora must come to terms with both positive and negative aspects of her position. Again the liberal morality of Roddenberry's concept of *Star Trek* is tested rigorously.

Although the new *Trek* series characteristically present many social problems as unresolvable, their approach to social issues rarely departs from the liberal–humanist perspective developed in Roddenberry's time. It is true, however, that they admit more openly that even if Starfleet possesses the 'right' way to live, any attempt to impose this on other races will inevitably lead to social catastrophe. Above all, *Star Trek* preaches respect for other cultures and argues that mutual tolerance is the only way forward. This approach is epitomised in *Darmok* (written by Joe Menosky and Philip Lazenbik), one of the most unusual and evocative episodes of *TNG*. Although, like many other episodes, it centres on a 'first contact' situation that becomes rather dangerous, here the entire focus is on the problem of communication. Though Starfleet is equipped with universal translators which make understanding even the far off races in the Delta and Gamma Quadrants easy, here the translators are no use. Initial attempts to communicate between the Federation and the Tamarians come to nothing. Although the Tamarians' words come over as being in English, the crew still cannot understand them, as they are comprised of epigrammatic statements which have no meaning to the Starfleet crew.

The Tamarians then take the extremely risky step (given their clearly inferior technology) of kidnapping Picard and sending him down to a nearby planet along with their captain, Dathon. While an angry Riker tries various means to recover him, Picard and Dathon are left together to battle against a shape-shifting electromagnetic 'beast'. When Picard and Dathon attempt to communicate, Dathon continually repeats the phrase 'Darmok and Jalad at Tenagra'. At first this puzzles Picard, until he finally comes to understand that the Tamarians communicate entirely through metaphor, and that their metaphors represent a number of archetypal situations from Tamarians mythology. Meanwhile, back on board the *Enterprise*, Data and Troi have finally come to the same conclusion, but explain that they still cannot understand the Tamarians, as they have no knowledge of Tamarian mythology. It is left to Picard, ever the master-diplomat, to 'learn' the

Tamarian means of communication and to find out how to communicate with them. One of the ways he does this is by relating the ancient Babylonian myth of Gilgamesh and Enkida, which has many parallels with the situation in which Picard and Dathon find themselves. Dathon understands the mythic parallel perfectly. But Dathon has already been injured by the 'beast' in a situation where, because Riker was unsuccessfully trying to beam him off the planet, Picard was unable to intervene. Dathon dies of his injuries and Riker finally succeeds in returning Picard to the *Enterprise*. The Tamarians appear ready for war, but Picard – who has now learned to communicate using their metaphors – diffuses the situation by presenting what happened as a heroic story whereby 'Picard and Dathon at El-Adrel' parallels 'Darmok and Jalad at Tenagra'. The Tamarians are now presented with a way of expression they can understand and conflict is averted. In the closing scenes, Picard is seen musing on a book of the Homeric hymns.

In many ways the story of *Darmok*, with its inbuilt mythic significance, symbolises what *Star Trek* has always set out to achieve. Although many new races or alien entities may appear to be hostile or 'evil', Roddenberry's creed insists that there are no intrinsically evil beings. Ultimately conflict within the universe is caused by a failure to communicate. In *Darmok* Picard marvels that the Tamarian captain was willing to pay the ultimate sacrifice – and that the Tamarians were willing to risk war – in order to achieve that communication. But here it is stressed that *real* communication is not just a matter of memorising a language but of attempting to learn and understand the cultural and mythical *logic* of any alien culture. *Darmok* is a story which combines psychological, political and social themes, and its resolution sums up the mythic essence of *Star Trek*. It reminds us that human culture, like that of the Tamarians, has a mythical basis and that storytelling itself has always played a major role in that culture. *Star Trek* thus defines itself as a system of modern mythology which focuses on fundamental human concerns, but always maintains an attitude of tolerance and open-mindedness. Above all, it offers a range of new perspectives on the present and a believable way of imagining a hopeful future in which human beings can avoid the mistakes of the past.

Appendix: *Star Trek* episodes and films

Star Trek (1966–9)

Writers

Pilot

The Cage	Gene Roddenberry

First season

The Man Trap	George Clayton Johnson
Charlie X	D. C. Fontana/Gene Roddenberry
Where No Man Has Gone Before	Samuel A. Peebles
The Naked Time	John D. F. Black
The Enemy Within	Richard Matheson
Mudd's Women	Stephen Kandel/Gene Roddenberry
What Are Little Girls Made Of?	Robert Bloch
Miri	Barry Trivers
Dagger of the Mind	S. Bar-David
The Corbomite Maneuver	Jerry Sohl
The Menagerie, Part 1	Gene Roddenberry
The Menagerie, Part 2	Gene Roddenberry
The Conscience of the King	Barry Trivers
Balance of Terror	Paul Schneider
Shore Leave	Theodore Sturgeon
The Galileo Seven	Oliver Crawford/S. Bar-David
The Squire of Gothos	Paul Schneider
Arena	Gene L. Coon
Tomorrow is Yesterday	Michael O'Herlihy/D. C. Fontana
Court Martial	Don M. Mankiewicz
The Return of the Archons	Boris Sobleman/Gene Roddenberry
Space Seed	Geen L.Coon/Carey Wilbur
A Taste of Armageddon	Robert Hamner/Gene L. Coon
This Side of Paradise	Nathan Butler/D. C. Fontana
The Devil in the Dark	Gene L. Coon
Errand of Mercy	Gene L. Coon
The Alternative Factor	Don Ingalls
City on the Edge of Forever	Harlan Ellison
Operation–Annihilate!	Stephen W. Carabatos

Second season

Amok Time	Theodore Sturgeon
Who Mourns for Adonais?	Gilbert Ralston
The Changeling	John Meredyth Lucas

Mirror, Mirror	Jerome Bixby
The Apple	Max Erlich
The Doomsday Machine	Norman Spinrad
Catspaw	Robert Bloch/D. C. Fontana
I, Mudd	Stephen Kandel
Metamorphosis	Gene L. Coon
Journey to Babel	D. C. Fontana
Friday's Child	D. C. Fontana
The Deadly Years	David P. Harmon
Obsession	Art Wallace
Wolf in the Fold	Robert Bloch
The Trouble with Tribbles	David Gerrold
The Gamesters of Triskelion	Margaret Armen
A Piece of the Action	David P. Harmon
The Immunity Syndrome	Robert Sabaroff
A Private Little War	Gene Roddenberry/Jud Crucis
Return to Tomorrow	John Kingsbridge
Patterns of Force	John Meredyth Lucas
By Any Other Name	D. C. Fontana/Jerome Bixby
The Omega Glory	Gene Roddenberry
The Ultimate Computer	D. C. Fontana/Laurence N. Wolfe
Bread and Circuses	Gene Roddenbery/Gene L. Coon
Assignment: Earth	Gene Roddenberry/Art Wallace

Third season

Spock's Brain	Gene L. Coon
The Enterprise Incident	D. C. Fontana
The Paradise Syndrome	Margaret Armen
And the Children Shall Lead	Edward J. Lasko
Is There In Truth No Beauty?	Jean Lisette Aroeste
Spectre of the Gun	Gene L. Coon
Day of the Dove	Jerome Bixby
For the World is Hollow and I Have Touched The Sky	Rik Vollaerts
The Tholian Web	Judy Burns/Chet Richards
Plato's Stepchildren	Meyer Dolinski
Wink of an Eye	Arthur Heinemann/Gene L. Coon
The Empath	Joyce Muskat
Elaan of Troyius	John Meredyth Lucas
Whom Gods Destroy	Lee Erwin/Jerry Sohl
Let That Be Your Last Battlefield	Gene L. Coon
The Mark of Gideon	George F. Slavin/Stanley Adams
That Which Survives	John Meredyth Lucas/ Michael Richards
The Lights of Zetar	Jeremy Tarcher/Shari Lewis
Requiem for Methuselah	Jerome Bixby
The Way to Eden	Michael Richards/Arthur Heinneman

The Cloud Minders	Margaret Armen/David Gerrold/
	Oliver Crawford
The Savage Curtain	Arthur Heinneman/
	Gene Roddenberry
All Our Yesterdays	Jean Lisette Aroeste
Turnabout Intruder	Gene Roddenberry

Star Trek – the animated series (1973)

More Tribbles, More Troubles	David Gerrold
The Infinite Vulcan	Walter Koenig
Yesteryear	D. C. Fontana
Beyond the Farthest Star	Samuel A. Peeples
The Survivor	James Schmerer
The Lorelei Signal	Margaret Armen
One of Our Planets is Missing	Marc Daniels
Mudd's Passion	Stephen Kandel
The Magicks Of Megas-Tu	Larry Brody
Time Trap	Joyce Perry
Slaver Weapon	Larry Niven
Jihad	Stephen Kandel
The Ambergris Element	Margaret Armen
Once Upon a Planet	Len Jensen/Chuck Menville
The Terratin Incident	Paul Schneider
The Eye of the Beholder	David P. Harmon
Bem	David Gerrold
Albatross	Dario Finelli
The Pirates of Orion	Howard Weinstein
Practical Joker	Chuck Menville
How Sharper Than a Serpent'sTooth	Russell Bates/David Wise
The Counter-Clock Incident	John Culver

Star Trek feature films (1979–96)

STAR TREK: THE MOTION PICTURE (1979)
Directed by Robert Wise
Produced by Gene Roddenberry
Screenplay: Harold Livingston from a story by Alan Dean Foster

STAR TREK: THE WRATH OF KHAN (1982)
Directed by Nicholas Meyer
Produced by Robert Sallin
Screenplay: Jack B. Sowards from a story by Harve Bennett and Jack B. Sowards

STAR TREK: THE SEARCH FOR SPOCK (1984)
Directed by Leonard Nimoy
Produced by Harve Bennett
Screenplay by Harve Bennett

STAR TREK: THE VOYAGE HOME (1986)
Directed by Leonard Nimoy
Produced by Harve Bennett
Screenplay: Steve Meerson, Peter Krikes, Harve Bennett and Nicholas Meyer
from a story by Leonard Nimoy and Harve Bennett

STAR TREK: THE FINAL FRONTIER (1989)
Directed by William Shatner
Produced by Harve Bennett
Screenplay: David Loughery from a story by William Shatner, Harve Bennett
and David Loughery

STAR TREK: THE UNDISCOVERED COUNTRY (1991)
Directed by Nicholas Meyer
Produced by Leonard Nimoy
Screenplay: Nicholas Meyer and Denny Martin Flynn from a story by Leonard
Nimoy, Lawrence Konner and Mark Rosenthal

STAR TREK: GENERATIONS (1994)
Directed by David Carson
Produced by Rick Berman
Screenplay: Ronald D. Moore and Brannon Braga

STAR TREK: FIRST CONTACT (1996)
Directed by Jonathan Frakes
Produced by Rick Berman
Screenplay: Ronald D. Moore and Brannon Braga

Star Trek: The Next Generation (1987–94)

Writers

Pilot

Encounter at Farpoint	D. C. Fontana/Gene Roddenberry

First season

The Naked Now	J. Michael Bingham/John D. Black
Code of Honor	Katharyn Powers/Michael Baron
The Last Outpost	Herbert Wright/Richard Krzemien
Where No One Has Gone Before	Diane Duane/Michael Reeeves
Lonely among Us	D. C. Fontana/Michael Halperin
Justice	Worley Thorne/Ralph Wills
The Battle	Herbert Wright/Larry Forester
Hide and Q	Gene Roddenberry/C. J. Holland
Haven	Tracy Torme/Lan O'Kun
The Big Goodbye	Tracy Torme/Joseph L. Scanlon
Datalore	Gene Roddenberry/Robert Lewin/ Maurice Hurley

Angel One   Patrick Barry
11001001   Maurice Hurley/Robert Lewin
Too Short a Season   D. C. Fontana/Michael Michaelian
When the Bough Breaks   Kim Manners/Hannah Louise Shearer
Home Soil   Robert Sabaroff/Karl Guers/Ralph
                                   Sanchez
Coming of Age   Sandy Fries
Heart of Glory   Maurice Hurley/Herbert Wright/
                                   D. C. Fontana
The Arsenal of Freedom   Richard Manning/Hans Beimler
Symbiosis   Richard Manning/Hans Beimler/
                                   Robert Lewin
Skin of Evil   Joseph Stefano/Hannah Louise
                                   Shearer
We'll Always Have Paris   Deborah Dean Davis/Hannah Louise
                                   Shearer
Conspiracy   Tracy Torme/Robert Sabaroff
The Neutral Zone   Maurice Hurley/Deborah McIntyre/
                                   Mona Glee

Second season
The Child   Jaron Summers/Jon Povill/
                                   Maurice Hurley
Where Silence Has Lease   Jack B. Sowards
Elementary, Dear Data   Brian Alan Lane
The Outrageous Okona   Burton Armus/Les Menchen/
                                   Lance Dickson/David Lansberg
Loud as a Whisper   Jacqueline Zambrano
The Schizoid Man   Tracy Torme/Hans Beimler/
                                   Richard Manning
Unnatural Selection   John Mason/Mike Gray
A Matter of Honor   Burton Armus/Wanda M. Haight/
                                   Gregory Armus
The Measure of a Man   Melinda M. Snodgrass
The Dauphin   Scott Rubenstein/Leonard Mlodinow
Contagion   Steve Gerber/Beth Woods
The Royale   Keith Mills
Time Squared   Maurice Hurley/Kurt Michael
                                   Bensmiller
The Icarus Factor   David Assael/Robert L. McCullough
Pen Pals   Melinda M. Snodgrass/Hannah
                                   Louise Shearer
Q Who?   Maurice Hurley
Samaritan Snare   Robert L. McCullough
Up the Long Ladder   Melinda M. Snodgrass
Manhunt   Terry Devereaux
The Emissary   Richard Manning/Hans Beimler
Peak Performance   David Kemper

Shades Of Gray	Maurice Hurley/Richard Manning/ Hans Beimler

Third season

Evolution	Michael Piller/Michael Wagner
The Ensigns of Command	Melinda M. Snodgrass
The Survivors	Michael Wagner
Who Watches the Watchers?	Richard Manning/Hans Beimler
The Bonding	Ronald D. Moore
Booby Trap	Ron Roman/Michael Piller/Richard Darius/Michael Wagner
The Enemy	Michael Piller/David Kemper
The Price	Hannah Louise Shearer
The Vengeance Factor	Sam Rolfe
The Defector	Ronald. D. Moore
The Hunted	Robin Bernheim
The High Ground	Melinda M. Snodgrass
Déjà Q	Richard Danus
A Matter of Perspective	Ed Zuckerman
Yesterday's Enterprise	Ira Steven Behr, Ronald D. Moore/ Richard Manning/Hans Beimler/ Trent Christopher Ganino/Eric A. Stillwell
The Offspring	Rene Echevarria
Sins of the Father	Ronald D. Moore/W. Reed Moran/ Drew Deigham
Allegiance	Richard Manning/Hans Beimler
Captain's Holiday	Ira Steven Behr
Tin Man	Dennis Putnam Bailey/ David Bischoff
Hollow Pursuits	Sally Caves
The Most Toys	Shari Goodhartz
Sarek	Peter S. Beagle/Mark Cushman/ Jake Jacobs
Ménage a Troi	Fred Bronson/Susan Sackett
Transfigurations	Rene Echevarria
The Best of Both Worlds, Part 1	Michael Piller

Fourth season

The Best of Both Worlds, Part 2	Michael Piller
Family	Ronald D. Moore
Brothers	Rick Berman
Suddenly Human	John Whelpley/Jeri Taylor/ Ralph Phillips
Remember Me	Lee Sheldon
Legacy	Joe Menosky
Reunion	Thomas Perry/Jo Perry/Ronald D. Moore/Brannon Braga/Drew Deigham

Future Imperfect	J. Larry Carroll/David Bennett Carren
Final Mission	Kacey Arnold-Ince/Jeri Taylor
Data's Day	Harold Apter/Ronald D. Moore
The Wounded	Jeri Taylor/Stuart Charno/
	Sara Charno/Cy Chermak
Devil's Due	Philip Lazenbik/William Douglas
Lansford	
Clues	Bruce D. Arthurs/Joe Menosky
First Contact	Dennis Russell Bailey/Joe Menosky/
	Ronald D. Moore/David Bischoff/
	Michael Piller/Marc Scott Zecree
Galaxy's Child	Maurice Hurley/Thomas Kartozian
Night Terrors	Pamela Douglas/Jeri Taylor/
	Shari Goodhartz
Identity Crisis	Brannon Braga/Timothy DeHaas
Nth Degree	Joe Menosky
Qpid	Ira Steven Behr/Randee Russell
The Drumhead	Jeri Taylor
Half a Life	Peter Allan Fields/Ted Roberts
The Host	Michael Horvat
The Mind's Eye	Rene Echevarria/Ken Schafer
In Theory	Joe Menosky/Ronald D. Moore
Redemption, Part 1	Ronald D. Moore

Fifth season

Redemption, Part 2	Ronald D. Moore
Darmok	Joe Menosky/Philip Lazenbik
Ensign Ro	Michael Piller/Rick Berman
Silicon Avatar	Jeri Taylor/Lawrence V. Conley
Disaster	Ronald D. Moore/Ron Jarvis/
	Philip A. Scorza
The Game	Brannon Braga/Susan Sackett/
	Fred Bronson
Unification. Part 1	Jeri Taylor/Rick Berman/
	Michael Piller
Unification, Part 2	Rick Berman/Michael Piller
A Matter of Time	Rick Berman
New Ground	Grant Rosenberg/Sara Charno
Hero Worship	Joe Menosky/Hilary J. Bader
Violations	Pamela Gray/Jeri Taylor/Shari
	Goodhartz/T. Michael Gray
The Masterpiece Society	Adam Belanoff/Michael Piller/
	James Kahn
Conundrum	Barry M. Schkolnick/Paul Schiffer
Power Play	Rene Balcer/Herbert J. Wright/
	Brannon Braga/Paul Ruben/
	Maurice Hurley
Ethics	Ronald D. Moore/Sara Charno/
	Stuart Charno

The Outcast	Jeri Taylor
Cause and Effect	Brannon Braga
The First Duty	Ronald D. Moore/Naren Shankar
Cost of Living	Peter Allan Fields
The Perfect Mate	Rene Echevarria/Michael Piller/ Gary Percante
Imaginary Friend	Edith Swensen/Brannon Braga/ Ronald Wilderson/Jean Louise Matthias/Richard Fliegel
I, Borg	Rene Echevarria
The Next Phase	Ronald D. Moore
The Inner Light	Peter Allan Fields/Morgan Gendel
Time's Arrow, Part 1	Joe Menosky/Michael Piller

Sixth season

Time's Arrow, Part 2	Joe Menosky/Jeri Taylor
Realm of Fear	Brannon Braga
Man of the People	Frank Abatemarco
Relics	Ronald D. Moore
Schisms	Brannon Braga/Jean Louise Matthias/ Ronald Wilkerson
True Q	Rene Echevarria/Matthew Corey
Rascals	Allison Hock/Diana Dru Botsford/ Michael Piller
A Fistful of Datas	Robert Hewitt Wolfe/Brannon Braga
The Quality of Life	Naren Shankar
Chain of Command, Part 1	Ronald D. Moore/Frank Abatemarco
Chain of Command, Part 2	Frank Abatemarco
Ship in a Bottle	Rene Echevarria
Aquiel	Brannon Braga/Ronald D. Moore
Face of the Enemy	Naren Shankar/Rene Echevarria
Tapestry	Ronald D. Moore
Birthright, Part 1	Brannon Braga
Birthright, Part 2	Rene Echevarria
Starship Mine	Morgan Gendel
Lessons	Ronald Wilkerson/Jean Louise Matthias
The Chase	Joe Menosky/Ronald D. Moore
Frame of Mind	Brannon Braga
Suspicions	Joe Menosky/Naren Shankar
Rightful Heir	Ronald D. Moore
Second Chances	Rene Echevarria/Michael A. Medlock
Timescape	Brannon Braga
Descent, Part 1	Ronald D. Moore/Jeri Taylor

Seventh season

Descent, Part 2	Rene Echevarria

Liaisons	Jeanne Carrigan Fauci/Lisa Rich/ Roger Eschbacher/Jaq Greenspoon
Interface	Joe Menosky
Gambit, Part 1	Naren Shankar/Christopher Halton
Gambit, Part 2	Ronald D. Moore/Naren Shankar
Phantasms	Brannon Braga
Dark Page	Hilary J. Bader
Attached	Nicholas Sagan
Force of Nature	Naren Shankar
Inheritance	Dan Koeppel/Rene Echevarria
Parallels	Brannon Braga
The Pegasus	Ronald D. Moore
Homeward	Naren Shankar/Spike Steingasser
Sub Rosa	Brannon Braga/Jeri Taylor
Lower Decks	Rene Echevarria/Ronald Wilkersdon/ Jean Louise Matthias
Thine Own Self	Ronald D. Moore/Christopher Halton
Masks	Joe Menosky
Eye of the Beholder	Rene Echevarria/Brannon Braga
Journey's End	Ronald D. Moore/Shawn Piller/ Antonio Napoli
Firstborn	Ronald D. Moore/Christopher Halton/Mark Kabfeld
Bloodlines	Nicholas Sagan
Emergence	Joe Menosky/Brannon Braga
Pre-Emptive Strike	Rene Echevarria/Naren Shankar
All Good Things ...	Ronald D. Moore/Brannon Braga

Star Trek: Deep Space Nine (from 1993)

Writers

Pilot

Emissary	Michael Piller, Rick Berman

First season

Past Prologue	Peter Allan Fields/Kathryn Powers
A Man Alone	Michael Piller/Gerald Sanford
Babel	Michael McGreevey/Naren Shankar
Captive Pursuit	Michael Piller/Jill Sherman Donner
Q-Less	Robert Hewitt Wolfe/Hannah Louise Shearer
Dax	D. C. Fontana/Peter Allan Fields
The Passenger	Morgan Gendel/Robert Hewitt Wolfe/Michael Piller
Move along Home	Frederick Rappaport/Lisa Rich/ Jeanne Carrigan-Fauci
The Nagus	Ira Steven Behr/David Livingston

Vortex	Sam Rolfe
Battle Lines	Richard Danus/Evan Carlos Somers/ Hilary Bader
The Storyteller	Kurt Michael Bensmiller/Ira Steven Behr
Progress	Peter Allan Fields
If Wishes were Horses	Nell McCue Crawford/William L. Crawford/Michael Piller
The Forsaken	Michael Piller/Don Carlos Dunaway
Dramatis Personae	Joe Menosky
Duet	Peter Allan Fields/Lisa Rich/ Jeanne Carrigan-Fauci
In the Hands of the Prophets	Robert Hewitt Wolfe

Second season

The Homecoming	Ira Steven Behr/Jeri Taylor
The Circle	Peter Allan Fields
The Siege	Michael Piller
Invasive Procedures	John Whelpley/Robert Hewitt Wolfe
Cardassians	Gene Wolande/John Wright
Melora	Evan Carlos Somers/Steven Baum/ Michael Piller/Hilary Bader
Rules of Acquisition	David Livingston/Ira Steven Behr/ Hilary Bader
Necessary Evil	Peter Allan Fields
Second Sight	Mark Gehred-O'Connell/Ira Steven Behr/Robert Hewitt Wolfe
Sanctuary	Frederick Rappaport, Gabe Escoe/ Kelley Miles
Rivals	Joe Menosky/Jim Trombetta/ Michael Piller
The Alternate	Bill Dial/Jim Trombetta
Armageddon Game	Morgan Gendel/Ira Steven Behr/ James Crocker
Whispers	Paul Coyle
Paradise	Jeff King/Richard Manning/ Hans Beimler/Jim Trombetta/ James Crocker
Shadowplay	Robert Hewitt Wolfe
Playing God	Jim Trombetta/Michael Piller
Profit and Loss	Flip Kobler/Candy Marcus
Blood Oath	Peter Allan Fields
The Maquis, Part 1	James Crocker/Rick Berman/Michael Piller/Jeri Taylor
The Maquis, Part 2	Ira Steven Behr/Rick Berman/ Michael Piller/Jeri Taylor
The Wire	Robert Hewitt Wolfe
Crossover	Peter Allan Fields/Michael Piller

The Collaborator   Gary Holland/Ira Steven Behr/
Robert Hewitt Wolfe
Tribunal   Bill Dial
The Jem' Hadar   Ira Steven Behr

Third season

The Search, Part 1   Ronald D. Moore/Ira Steven Behr/
Robert Hewitt Wolfe
The Search, Part 2   Ira Steven Behr/Robert Hewitt Wolfe
The House of Quark   Ronald D. Moore/Tom Benko
Equilibrium   Rene Echevarria/Christopher Teague
Second Skin   Robert Hewitt Wolfe
The Abandoned   D. Thomas Maio/Steve Warnek
Civil Defense   Mike Krohn
Meridian   Mark Gehred-O'Connell/Hilary
Bader/Evan Carlos Somers
Defiant   Ronald D. Moore
Fascination   Philip Lazebnik/Ira Steven Behr/
James Crocker
Past Tense, Part 1   Ira Steven Behr/Robert Hewitt Wolfe
Past Tense, Part 2   Ira Steven Behr/Rene Echevarria
Life Support   Ronald D. Moore/Christian Ford/
Roger Soffer
Heart of Stone   Ira Steven Behr/Robert Hewitt Wolfe
Destiny   David S. Cohen/Mark A. Winer
Prophet Motive   Ira Steven Behr/Robert Hewitt Wolfe
Visionary   John Shirley/Ethan H. Calk
Distant Voices   Ira Steven Behr/Robert Hewitt Wolfe
Through the Looking Glass   Ira Steven Behr/Robert Hewitt Wolfe
Improbable Cause   Rene Echevarria/Robert Lederman/
David R. Long
The Die is Cast   Ronald D. Moore
Explorers   Rene Echevarria/Hilary J. Bader
Family Business   Ira Steven Behr/Robert Hewitt Wolfe
Shakaar   Gordon Dawson
Facets   Rene Echevarria
The Adversary   Ira Steven Behr/Robert Hewitt Wolfe

Fourth season

The Way of the Warrior   Ira Steven Behr/Robert Hewitt Wolfe
The Visitor   Michael Taylor
Hippocratic Oath   Lisa Klink
Indiscretion   Nicholas Corea/Tony Marberry/
Jack Trevino
Rejoined   Ronald D. Moore/Rene Echevarria
Little Green Men   Ira Steven Behr/Robert Hewitt Wolfe
Starship Down   David Mack/John J. Ordover
The Sword of Kahless   Hans Beimler/Richard Danus

Our Man Bashir	Ronald D. Moore
Homefront	Ira Steven Behr/Robert Hewitt Wolfe
Paradise Lost	Ira Steven Behr/Robert Hewitt Wolfe/ Ronald D. Moore
Crossfire	Rene Echevarria
Return to Grace	Hans Beimler/Tom Benko
Sons of Mogh	Ronald D. Moore
Bar Association	Ira Steven Behr/Robert Hewitt Wolfe/ Barbara J. Lee/Jennifer A. Lee
Accession	Jane Espenson
Rules of Engagement	Ronald D. Moore/Bradley Thompson/ David Weddle
Hard Time	Robert Hewitt Wolfe/Daniel Keys Moran/Lynn Barker
Shattered Mirror	Ira Steven Behr/Hans Beimler
The Muse	Rene Echevarria/Majel Barrett
For the Cause	Ronald D. Moore/Mark Gehred-O'Connell
To the Death	Ira Steven Behr/Robert Hewitt Wolfe
The Quickening	Naren Shankar
Body Parts	Ira Steven Behr/Robert Hewitt Wolfe
Broken Link	Ira Steven Behr/Robert Hewitt Wolfe/ George A. Brozak

Fifth season

Apocalypse Rising	Ira Steven Behr/Robert Hewitt Wolfe
The Ship	Hand Beimler/Pam Wiggington/ Rick Cason
Looking for Par'mach in All the Wrong Places	Ronald D. Moore
Nor the Battle to the Strong	Rene Echevarria/Brice R. Parker
The Assignment	David Weddle/Bradley Thompson/ David R. Long/Robert Lederman
Trials and Tribble-ations	Ronald D. Moore/Rene Echevarria/ Ira Steven Behr/Robert Hewitt Wolfe
Let He Who is without Sin ...	Ira Steven Behr/Robert Hewitt Wolfe
Things Past	Michael Taylor
The Ascent	Ira Steven Behr/Robert Hewitt Wolfe
Rapture	Hans Beimler/L.J. Strom
The Darkness and the Light	Ronald D. Moore/Bryan Fuller
The Begotten	Rene Echevarria/Jesus Salvador Trevino
For the Uniform	Peter Allan Fields
In Purgatory's Shadow	Ira Steven Behr/Robert Hewitt Wolfe
By Inferno's Light	Ira Steven Behr/Robert Hewitt Wolfe
Doctor Bashir, I Presume	Ronald D.Moore/Jimmy Diggs
A Simple Investigation	Rene Echevarria

Business as Usual	Bradley Thompson/David Weddle
Ties of Blood and Water	Robert Hewitt Wolfe/Edmund Newton/Robbin L. Slocum
Ferengi Love Songs	Ira Steven Behr/Hans Beimler
Soldiers of the Empire	Ronald D. Moore
Children of Time	Rene Echevarria/Gary Holland/ Ethan H. Calk
Blaze of Glory	Ira Steven Behr/Robert Hewitt Wolfe
Empok Nor	Hans Beimler/Bryan Fuller
In the Cards	Ronald D. Moore/Truly Barr Clark/ Scott J. Neal
A Call to Arms	Ira Steven Behr/Robert Hewitt Wolfe

Star Trek: Voyager (from 1994)

Writers

Pilot

Caretaker	Michael Piller/Jeri Taylor/ Rick Berman

First season

Parallax	Brannon Braga/Jim Trombetta
Time and Again	Michael Piller/David Kemper
Phage	Brannon Braga/Skye Dent/ Timothy De Haas
The Cloud	Tom Szollosi/Michael Piller/ Brannon Braga
Eye of the Needle	Bill Dial/Jeri Taylor/Hilary Bader
Ex Post Facto	Evan Carlos Somers/Michael Piller
Emanations	Brannon Braga
Prime Factors	Michael Perricone/Greg Elliot/ Jeri Taylor/David R. George III/ Eric Stilwell
State of Flux	Chris Abbott/Paul Coyle
Heroes and Demons	Naren Shankar/John Sayers
Cathexis	Brannon Braga/Joe Menosky
Faces	Kenneth Biller/Jonathan Glassner
Jetrel	Jack Klein/Kenneth Biller/Karen Klein/James Thomton/Scott Nimerfro
Learning Curve	Ronald Wilkerson/Jean-Louise Matthias/Hilary Bader

Second season

The 37's	Jeri Taylor/Brannon Braga
Initiations	Kenneth Biller

Projections	Brannon Braga
Elogium	Kenneth Biller/Jeri Taylor/Jimmy Diggs/Steve J. Kay
Non Sequitur	Brannon Braga
Twisted	Kenneth Biller/Arnold Rudnick/Rick Hosek
Parturition	Tom Szollosi
Persistence of Vision	Jeri Taylor
Tattoo	Michael Piller/Larry Brody
Cold Fire	Brannon Braga/Anthony Williams
Maneuvers	Kenneth Biller
Resistance	Lisa Klink
Prototype	Nicholas Corea
Alliances	Jeri Taylor
Threshold	Brannon Braga/Michael De Luca
Meld	Michael Piller/Michael Sussman
Dreadnought	Gary Holland/Lisa Klink
Death Wish	Michael Piller/Shawn Piller
Lifesigns	Kenneth Biller
Investigations	Jeri Taylor/Jeff Schnaufer/Ed Bond
Deadlock	Brannon Braga
Innocence	Lisa Klink/Anthony Williams
The Thaw	Joe Menosky/Richard Gadas
Tuvix	Kenneth Biller/Andrew Price/Mark Gaberman
Resolutions	Jeff Taylor
Basics, Part 1	Michael Piller

Third season

Basics, Part 2	Michael Piller
Flashback	Brannon Braga
The Chute	Kenneth Biller/Clayvon L. Harris
The Swarm	Mike Sussman
False Profits	Joe Menosky/George A. Brozak
Remember	Lisa Klink/Brannon Braga/Joe Menosky
Sacred Ground	Geo Cameron/Lisa Klink
Future's End, Part 1	Brannon Braga/Joe Menosky
Future's End, Part 2	Brannon Braga/Joe Menosky
Warlord	Lisa Klink
The Q and the Grey	Kenneth Biller/Shawn Piller
Macrocosm	Brannon Braga
Fair Trade	Andre Bormanis/Ronald Wilkerson/Jean Louise Matthias
Alter Ego	Joe Menosky
Coda	Jeri Taylor
Blood Fever	Lisa Klink
Unity	Kenneth Biller

Darkling	Brannon Braga/Joe Menosky
Rise	Brannon Braga
Favorite Son	Lisa Klink
Before and After	Kenneth Biller
Real Life	Jeri Taylor
Distant Origin	Brannon Braga/Joe Menosky
Displaced	Lisa Klink
Worst Case Scenario	Kenneth Biller
Scorpion, Part 1	Brannon Braga/Joe Menosky

Bibliography

Books

Aldiss, Brian (1973) *The Billion-Year Spree: The History of Science Fiction* (London: Weidenfeld & Nicolson).

Alexander, David (1994) *Star Trek Creator: the Authorized Biography of Gene Roddenberry* (New York: Roc).

Allen, Robert C. (ed.) (1992) *Channels of Discourse Reassembled: Television and Contemporary Criticism* (2nd edn) (London: Routledge).

Ang, Ien (1985) *Watching Dallas: Soap Opera and the Melodramatic Imagination* (London: Methuen).

Ang, Ien (1991) *Desperately Seeking the Audience* (London: Routledge).

Asherman, Alan (1986) *The Star Trek Interview Book* (New York: Pocket).

Asherman, Alan (1989) *The Star Trek Compendium* (New York: Titan).

Asimov, Isaac (1952) *The Foundation Trilogy: Foundation, Foundation and Empire, Second Foundation* (New York: Gnome Press).

Bacon-Smith, Camille (1992) *Enterprising Women: Television Fandom and the Creation Of Popular Myth* (University of Pennsylvania Press).

Baggaley, Jon and Steve Duck (1976) *The Dynamics of Television* (Farnborough: Saxon House).

Barthes, Roland (1972) *Mythologies* (transl. Annette Lavers) (New York: Hill & Wang).

Barwise, Polrich and Antoine Ehrenberg (1988) *Television and its Audience* (London: Saga).

Bradley, Marion Zimmer (1982) *Mists of Avalon* (New York: Ballantine).

Bryant, Page (1991) *Awakening Arthur! His Return In Our Time* (London: Aquarian Press).

Caldwell, John Thornton (1995) *Televisuality: Style, Crisis and Authority In American TV* (New Brunswuck NJ: Rutgers University Press).

Campbell, Joseph (1949) *The Hero with a Thousand Faces* (New York: Pantheon).

Campbell, Joseph (1985) *The Inner Reaches Of Outer Space: Metaphor as Myth and as Religion* (New York: Vander).

Clifford, Gay (1974) *The Transformations of Allegory* (London and Boston: Routledge).

Collins, Richard (1990) *Television: Policy and Culture* (London: Unwin Hyman).

Connor, Steven (1989) *Postmodernist Culture: an Introduction to Theories of the Contemporary* (Oxford: Blackwell).

Cornell, Paul, Martin Day and Keith Topping (1995) *The New Trek Programme Guide* (London: Virgin).

Cousineau, Phil (ed.) (1990) *The Hero's Journey: Joseph Campbell On His Life And Work* (San Francisco: Harper & Row).

Deinst, Richard (1994) *Still Life in Real Time: Theory after Television* (Durham/London: Duke University Press).

Dillard, J. M. (1994) *Star Trek 'Where No One Has Gone Before': a History in Pictures* (New York: Pocket).

Doty, William G. (1986) *Mythography: The Study of Myths and Rituals* (Tuscaloosa/London: University of Alabama Press).

Dundes, Alan (ed.) (1984) *Sacred Narrative: Readings in the Theory of Myth* (Berkeley: University of California Press).

Dunnett, Peter (1990) *The World Television Industry: an Economic Analysis* (London: Routledge).

Eccleshall, Robert, Vincent Geoghegan, Richard Jay, Michael Kenny, Iain MacKenzie and Rick Wilford (1994) *Political Ideologies: An Introduction* (2nd edn) (London/New York: Routledge).

Eco, Umberto (1979) *The Role of the Reader: Explorations in the Semiotics of Texts* (Bloomington: Indiana University Press).

Eco, Umberto (1990) *The Limits of Interpretation* (Bloomington: Indiana University Press).

Eliade, Mircea (1961) *Images and Symbols* (Harmondsworth/London).

Ellis, John (1982) *Visible Fictions: Cinema, TV, Video* (London: Routledge).

Ember, Carol R. and Melvin (1981) *Anthropology* (Englewood Cliffs NJ: Prentice Hall).

Esslin, Martin (1982) *The Age Of Television* (San Francisco: W. H. Freeman).

Farrand, Phil (1993) *The Nitpicker's Guide for Next Generation Trekkers* (London: Titan).

Fiske, John and John Hartley (1978) *Reading Television* (London/New York: Methuen).

Fiske, John (1991) *Moments of Television: Neither the text nor the audience* in Seiter (1991).

Gallanter, Marc (1989) *Cults: Faith, Healing and Coercion* (New York: OUP).

Gibson, William (1984) *Neuromancer* (London: Victor Gollancz).

Gitling, Todd (ed.) (1968) *Watching Television* (New York: Pantheon).

Goethals, Gregor T. (1981) *The TV Ritual* (Boston: Beacon).

Graves, Robert (1955) *The Greek Myths* (Harmondsworth: Penguin).

Gregory, Chris (1997) *Be Seeing You: Decoding The Prisoner* (Luton: John Libbey Media).

Gross, Edward and Mark A. Altman (1993) *Captain's Logs: The Complete Trek Voyages* (London: Boxtree).

Gross, Edward and Mark A. Altman (1996) *Captain's Logs Supplemental: the Unauthorized Guide to the New Trek Voyages* (London: Little, Brown).

Hammond, J. R. (1979) *An H. G. Wells Companion* (London: Macmillan).

Hardy, Phil (1986) *The Encyclopedia of Science Fiction Movies* (London: Octopus).

Hartley, John (1992) *Tele-ology: Studies in Television* (London: Routledge).

Hawkes, Terence (1977) *Structuralism and Semiotics* (London: Methuen).

Homer (1950) *The Iliad* (transl. E. V. Rieu) (Harmondsworth: Penguin).

Hutcheon, Linda (1989) *Politics of Postmodernism* (London: Routledge).

Huxley, Aldous (1932) *Brave New World* (Harmondsworth: Penguin).

Irwin, Walter and G. B. Love (1988) *The Best of Trek No. 14* (New York: Signet).

Jenkins, Henry (1992) *Textual Poachers: Television Fans and Participatory Culture* (New York: Routledge).

Jewett and Lawrence (1977) *The American Monomyth* (New York: Dell).

Jung, Carl (1971) *The Portable Jung* (ed. Joseph Campbell) (Harmondsworth: Penguin).

Krauss, Lawrence M. (1996) *The Physics of Star Trek* (London: HarperCollins).

Leeming, David Adams (1990) *The World of Myth* (New York: OUP).

Levi-Strauss, Claude (1996) *The Savage Mind* (Chicago: University of Chicago Press).

Lewis, Justin (1991) *The Ideological Octopus: an Exploration of Television and its Audience* (New York/London: Routledge).

Livingstone, Sonia M. (1990) *Making Sense of Television: the Psychology of Audience Interpretation* (Oxford/New York: Pergamon).

Masterman, Len (ed.) (1984) *Television Mythologies: Stars, Shows and Signs* (London: Comedia).

McLuhan, Marshall (1964) *Understanding Media* (London/New York: Routledge and Kegan Paul); *Counterblast* (New York: Harcourt, Brace and World).

McLuhan, Marshall and Quentin Fiore (1967) *The Medium is the Massage* (New York: Bantam).

Mellencamp, Patricia (ed.) (1990) *Logics of Television* (Bloomington: Indiana University Press).

Muir, Ramsay (1934) *The Liberal Way: A Survey of Liberal Policy* (London: George Allen and Unwin).

Nemecek, Larry (1995) *Star Trek: The Next Generation Companion* (New York: Pocket).

Newcomb, Horace (1994) *TV: The Critical View* (New York: OUP).

Nichols, Nichelle (1995) *Beyond Uhura* (New York: Boxtree).

Nimoy, Leonard (1995) *I Am Spock* (London: Century).

Okuda, Michael and Denise (1993) *Star Trek Chronology: the History of the Future* (New York: Pocket).

Okuda, Michael and Denise and Debbie Mirek (1994) *The Star Trek Encyclopedia: a Reference Guide to the Future* (New York: Pocket).

Orwell, George (1949) *1984* (London: Secker & Warburg).

Ovid (1984 edn) *Metamorphosis* (London: Heinemann).

Parrinder, Geoffrey (1971) *Man and His Gods: Encyclopedia of the World's Religions* (London/Sydney/Toronto: Hamlyn).

Penley, Constance (1991) *Technoculture* (Minnesota: University of Minnesota Press).

Poe, Edgar Allan (1988 edn) *Collected Stories and Poems* (London: Octopus).

Radio Times Official Collectors' Edition: Star Trek, 30 Years (1996) (New York: Telemedia Communications).

Richards, Thomas (1997) *Star Trek in Myth and Legend* (London: Orion).

Rose, Brian G. (1985) *T.V. Genres: a Handbook and Reference Guide* (Westport Connecticut: Greenwood).

Samuels, Raphael and Paul Thompson (1990) *The Myths We Live By* (London: Routledge).

Segal, Robert A (1987) *Joseph Campbell: An Introduction* (New York/London: Mentor/Penguin).

Seiter, Ellen *et al.* (eds) (1991) *Remote Control: Television, Audiences and Cultural Power* (London: Routledge).

Shatner, William and Chris Kreshi (1993) *Star Trek Memories* (New York: HarperCollins).

Shatner, William and Chris Kreshi (1994) *Star Trek Movie Memories* (New York: HarperCollins).

Silverstone, Roger (1981) *The Message of Television: Myth and Narrative In*

Contemporary Culture (London: Heinemann).
Smith, Anthony (ed.) (1995) *Television: an International History* (Oxford: OUP).
Solow, Herbert F. and Robert H. Justman (1996) *Inside Star Trek* (New York: Pocket).
Sorensen, Theodore C. (1965) *Kennedy* (London: Hodder and Stoughton).
Stapledon, Olaf (1930) *Last And First Men* (London: Methuen).
Storey, John (1997) *Cultural Theory and Popular Culture – A Reader* (2nd edn) (London: Prentice Hall).
Taylor, Rogan (1985) *The Death and Resurrection Show* (London: Blond).
Toolan, Michael J. (1988) *Narrative, a Critical Linguistic Introduction* (London: Routledge).
Tulloch, John (1990) *Television Drama: Agency, Audience and Myth* (London/ New York: Routledge).
Tulloch, John and Manuel Alvarado (1983) *Doctor Who: the Unfolding Text* (London and Basingstoke: Macmillan).
Tulloch, John and Henry Jenkins (1995) *Science Fiction Audiences: Watching Doctor Who and Star Trek* (London: Routledge).
Van Hise, James (1995) *The Unauthorized History of Trek* (London: HarperCollins).
Van Hise, James (1997) *The Unauthorized Trekker's Guide to the Next Generation and Deep Space Nine* (London: HarperCollins).
Vonnegut, Kurt (1970) *Slaughterhouse-5* (London: Cape).
White, T. H. (1958) *The Once and Future King* (London: Flamingo, Fontana Paperbacks).
Whitfield, Stephen E. and Gene Roddenbery (1968) *The Making of Star Trek* (London: Titan).
Williams, Raymond (1974) *Television: Technology and Cultural Form* (London: Fontana/Collins).
Willis, Roy (1993) *World Mythology: The Illustrated Guide* (London/New York: BCA).
Wilson, Robert Anton (1977) *The Cosmic Trigger* (New York: Dell).
Wilson, Tony (1993) *Watching Television: Hermeneutics, Reception and Popular Culture* (Cambridge: Polity Press).
Wyver, John (1989) *The Moving Image: an International History of Film and Television* (Oxford/New York: Basil Blackwell/B.F.I. Publishing).
Zolla, Elemire (1981) *Archetypes* (London: George Allen & Unwin).

Articles

Berger, John, 'A Step Towards A Small Theory of the Visible', in *Tate* (Spring 1977).
Dardel, Eric, 'The Mythic', *Diogenes*, 7: pp. 33–51.
Fiske, John, 'Dr. Who: Ideology and the Reading of a Popular Narrative Text', *Australian Journal of Screen Theory*, nos. 13–14.
Gaster, Theodore, 'Myth or Story', *Numen 1* (1954).

Internet sites

Purple Haze KAG Newsletter (October to November 1995).

CD Roms

Star Trek Omnipedia
Star Trek: Captain's Chair
Star Trek: Klingon
(All Simon & Schuster Interactive)

Grolier Encyclopedia 1995
Microsoft Encarta Encyclopedia 1995

Star Trek Index

General Index